RANALD MACDONALD

Pacific Rim
Adventurer

R A N A L D   M A C D O N A L D

Pacific Rim Adventurer

JO ANN ROE

WSU
PRESS

Washington State University Press
Pullman, Washington

Washington State University Press
PO Box 645910
Pullman, Washington 99164-5910
Phone: 800-354-7360   Fax: 509-335-8568
©1997 by the Board of Regents of Washington State University
All rights reserved
First printing 1997

Library of Congress Cataloging-in-Publication Data

Roe, Jo Ann, 1926-
    Ranald MacDonald : Pacific Rim adventurer / by Jo Ann Roe.
      p.   cm.
    Includes bibliographical references and index.
    ISBN 0-87422-147-1 (hdb : alk. paper). —ISBN 0-87422-146-3 (pbk : alk. paper)
    1. MacDonald, Ranald, 1824-1894. 2. Pioneers—Columbia River Valley—Biography.
3. Adventure and adventurers—Pacific Area—Biography. 4. Frontier and pioneer life—Columbia River Valley. 5. Columbia River Valley—Description and travel. 6. Northwest, Pacific—Description and travel. 7. Hudson's Bay Company. 8. Japan—Description and travel. 9. Americans—Japan—History—19th century. I. Title.
F853.R65   1997   97-2019
979.7—dc21   CIP

Contents

Foreword

It is fitting that a man from the Pacific Northwest played a role in the earliest trade maneuverings among the United States, Canada, and Japan, since in 1995 American-Japanese trade totaled 187.8 billion dollars, with a significant percentage of that emanating from Washington State. In 1995, total trade between Canada and Japan was about 24 billion dollars. However, it was curiosity and a genuine desire to share knowledge that propelled this man to enter forbidden Japan, not any idea of gaining commercial or political advantage.

Ranald MacDonald was the first son of Hudson's Bay Company clerk Archibald McDonald and his wife Koale' zoa. Also dubbed Princess Raven, she was the daughter of King Comcomly, leader of the Chinook nation, who resided near the mouth of the Columbia River. With the proud blood of the Scottish MacDonalds, Highland warriors, and the intelligent Chinook leader in his veins, Ranald was a handsome, stalwart youth. His Scottish father groomed him to take his place in the fur trading world, but the restless blood of his forefathers led him, instead, to run off to sea from a bank apprentice's stool in St. Thomas, Ontario.

After several years of high adventure, he left his whaling ship with the permission of the captain. MacDonald feigned shipwreck off the coast of Japan, hoping to gain entry to the nation then closed to foreigners. The months he spent confined to Japanese jails enabled him to satisfy his curiosity about the mysterious Japanese. More important, he became the English teacher for fourteen Japanese interpreters, who as precursors of international statesmen would figure in negotiations with Commodore Perry and Townsend Harris and in the earliest delegations sent from Japan to Washington, D.C.

After his release to the *Preble*, captained by Commodore Glynn, MacDonald resumed his wanderings to the gold fields of Ballarat, Australia, to Europe, eastern Canada, and finally to the Pacific Northwest. There he continued to press for developing trade routes to Japan from British Columbia and the State of Washington. He led exploring expeditions little recognized in history and worked on the supply routes for the famous gold fields of Barkerville, British Columbia.

His adventures spanned the world—a roistering tale of verve and courage. His important contributions to intercourse with Japan have been recognized only faintly and are particularly interesting to review as we close the twentieth century vigorously conducting trade with Asia. From 1853 to his death in 1894, MacDonald intermittently made notes as to his experiences. In 1853, he first related his adventures in Japan to the family barrister and later political writer, Canadian pioneer Malcolm McLeod.

As early as 1857, McLeod prepared MacDonald's story for publication. The manuscript, amplified considerably by McLeod's own observations about Asia and other matters, was shelved after a publisher's rejection letter. In the late 1880's, McLeod renewed his efforts. Having lost track of Ranald MacDonald, he pursued the matter under his own authorship as *A Canadian in Japan*. By 1889, the two men made contact again and worked together in the ongoing publishing effort. However, Ranald died without realizing his fervent desire to share his startling experiences with the world. In 1923, respected historians William S. Lewis and Naojiro Murakami published MacDonald's notes with commentaries of their own, a valuable piece of research, for the Eastern Washington State Historical Society.

MacDonald was a friend or acquaintance of such historically important persons as James Douglas, the Provincial Governor of British Columbia; David Douglas, the famous botanist; Sir George Simpson of the Hudson's Bay Company; traders Francis and Edward Ermatinger; Dr. John McLoughlin of Fort Vancouver; and countless travelers, explorers, and other Hudson's Bay Company officers. Yet Ranald was a humble man, working at ordinary tasks for most of his life, even as his contacts with Japan and his explorations in British Columbia for roads and railways went unsung. He lived his life through a time of change, including the ending of the Hudson's Bay Company's fur empire, the beginning of settlement of western Canada and its developing ties with the United States, the expanding whaling industry of New England that figured closely in developing contacts with Japan as a trading partner, and the turbulent gold rushes of the nineteenth-century that transformed Australia and western Canada. To present MacDonald's adventures in context, I have drawn on numerous historical documents and sources. I also have traveled and conducted research in Hawaii, Australia, Japan, and Canada. In this way, we can vicariously relive the sweeping true adventures of one of the most colorful men of the nineteenth-century Pacific Northwest.

NOTE: Ranald and his siblings used the surname "MacDonald," the traditional spelling of the family name. Their father Archibald, however, used the spelling "McDonald."

I

Columbia River Beginnings

On June 27, 1848, the whaling ship, *Plymouth*, captained by Lawrence B. Edwards, Master, hove to off the Rishiri Islands that punctuate the northwest coast of Hokkaido, Japan. Even from the deck her masts disappeared into the fog, while ghostly figures launched a small sailboat on the formless sea below. As a stocky sailor clambered over the side into the bobbing craft, his compatriots hung over the side of the *Plymouth* to grasp his hand repeatedly and bid him farewell, some of them weeping unashamedly, for they were convinced that Ranald MacDonald was sailing off to certain death.

"God bless you, Mac!" came the universal cry as MacDonald cut the line that bound him to the ship (since his shipmates refused to do so, thinking him mad to leave) and slowly rowed away from the ship, his sails flapping uselessly.

A light breeze intermittently blew away small wisps of fog shrouding the ship like a spider web. Captain Edwards ran up the Stars and Stripes, causing MacDonald to suppress a sob as he feebly waved a small white flag. Soon the ship vanished and MacDonald was alone on the sea, wrapped in a soft cocoon of dampness, navigating toward a nearby island listed on the *Plymouth*'s maps as Timoshee (thought to be Reibun Island). Hours passed as Ranald reflected with misgivings on the events that brought him to this perilous adventure. His intention was to land on the Japanese shore as a defector from his whaler, pretend that his boat had been shipwrecked, and hope that he could penetrate the veil that Japan had drawn around herself from contacts with the western world. He fully realized the dangers ahead, that he might be summarily executed or worse. But the hazards were outweighed by his overwhelming curiosity, an obsession with Japan that began in his childhood . . .

Ranald MacDonald was born at Fort George, today's Astoria, Oregon, on February 3, 1824, to Archibald McDonald, clerk of the Hudson's Bay post, and his wife, Koale' zoa, Princess Raven, also called Princess Sunday by the

British. She was a favorite daughter of Comcomly, king of the Chinook nation. The royal household was across the Columbia River from Fort George at a point near today's Scarboro Hill in Washington. MacDonald said in his later notes that the birth "would seem without loss of time," since the marriage had taken place on September 12, 1823.

Although no record is given of the preliminaries to McDonald's marriage, *The Chinook Indians*, a book by Robert H. Ruby and John A. Brown, describes a slightly earlier marriage of another Hudson's Bay employee, Duncan McDougall, to a daughter of Comcomly:

> Aware of Chinook protocol in matrimonial matters, McDougall sent two clerks to Comcomly to ask for his daughter's hand in marriage. In Chinook marriages it was customary for a young man's parents, other relatives, or third parties to handle preliminaries, among which was the dowering of a man's intended bride and the return of gifts by her people to equal or surpass those of his. With time, these dowries had become more elaborate. In addition to dentalia [the Chinook currency] and slaves, there were now added, thanks to coastal traders, axes, beads, kettles, brass and copper bracelets, and many other things. Finally, there followed a ceremonious journey by the bride and groom to her home, accompanied by a few old women, to begin a married life.

> . . . the soon-to-be father-in-law was arrayed in a bright blue blanket, always a favorite of Pacific Northwest natives, and a red breechclout, with extra paint and feathers.

No doubt, similar preliminaries took place before McDonald's alliance with Koale' zoa.

The marriage ceremony at the bride's residence was as opulent as befitted a king. Comcomly's home was a very large cedar longhouse with a gabled roof and carved doors. The front may have been decorated. The nearby homes of the king's attendants, almost five hundred of them, and the general villagers comprised a large settlement.

From the water's edge to Comcomly's longhouse, a distance of about three hundred yards, the marriage path was carpeted with sea otter and beaver furs. While Comcomly and his daughter awaited the arrival of the bridegroom, two hundred slaves formed an honor guard along the luxuriant fur path. Accompanied by friends and company compatriots, who jovially tried to ease his nervousness, McDonald stepped out of his canoe and came to meet his bride.

With little ceremony the king gently directed his daughter to clasp McDonald's hand, and the deed was done. There were cakes and ale for the guests, and the wealthy Comcomly made potlatch for all—both traders and Indians—as a token of celebration. When the bridal couple returned to the canoe, the furs were gathered up and presented to them as a wedding gift. (Unfortunately, Hudson's Bay Company rules forbade any of its employees to accept furs as gifts, so the generous dowry of Comcomly went into Hudson's Bay coffers).

Since only an occasional religious man happened into distant frontier settlements, marriages between frontiersmen and natives often began without clergy but were just as real and lasting as those hallowed in a church. Unfortunately, McDonald's union was doomed; soon after Ranald's birth, his wife died. Ranald was given to the care of his aunt Car-cum-cum for about a year and a half.

Years later Ranald said that he remembered an older woman that he believed to be this aunt and that he felt she really did not like him. But, cheerful baby that he was, old King Comcomly lavished his love on the boy. The nickname his grandfather gave him, "Tool," a Chinook word for bird (as he was the son of Princess Raven), stuck with him throughout his youth. In letters to friends his father Archibald referred to Ranald as "Toole."

While his father lived in bachelor's quarters across the river, later working to build Fort Vancouver upriver, Ranald was passed from hand to hand in the longhouse, cherished by his extended family. As head of the Chinook nation Comcomly lived well by native standards. Food was plentiful with little of the intermittent poverty and starvation that plagued inland Indians. Bounty from the sea included shellfish, salmon, giant sturgeon from the depths of the Columbia River, lush berries, wapato roots and other bulbs, ducks and geese. Life was so easy that chasing deer and bear was not a priority for food. Women wove watertight baskets from grasses and reeds to cook salmon by dropping heated stones into water.

Extended families lived in cedar longhouses, often decorated outside with elaborate carvings, although not as grand as those of their far northern coastal neighbors, the Haidas. The practical Chinooks were more interested in functional efficiency than display.

Serving multiple purposes for the households of wealthier natives were legions of slaves obtained through raids or by trading with other tribes. Usually Chinooks kidnapped women and children, because adult males were too difficult to control and keep. If a Chinook master fathered a child by a slave, the offspring was also a slave. These poor creatures were treated abominably, barely clothed and fed, forced to live lives of drudgery and danger. If a chief wanted someone eliminated, the slaves usually were dispatched to take care of the deed. When the slave fell ill and required undue care, his master often killed him to escape the bother of nursing him back to health.

Chinook natives flattened the heads of infants, binding on the malleable skulls a board that gradually formed the frontal lobe into a wedge shape. White explorers found this appearance hideous, but Chinooks had their own interpretations of beauty. Slaves were not permitted to flatten the heads of their babies; the appearance was reserved for genuine Chinook tribal members. Apparently Archibald McDonald prevailed upon his wife's family, because Ranald's head remained untouched.

Native clothing was originally made from cedar bark or animal furs with conical rain hats fashioned of reeds or grasses. Women wore skirts and modest clothing, but both sexes went barefoot in all weather. Even after the introduction of western clothing the males often wore the tops of suits or jackets but preferred to leave off the trousers, as inhibiting to free movement. Men and women enjoyed intricate jewelry, necklaces made from shells, copper obtained from the northern tribes, and beadwork imported from the interior tribes.

The Chinooks were the original middlemen, canny traders long before the advent of foreigners. Until diseases brought by the intruders decimated them, the Chinooks firmly controlled trading activities along the lower Columbia River. At designated times the Chinooks traveled upriver to the eastern slopes of the Cascades Mountains, to the rapids we know as the Dalles, to meet interior tribes for a gigantic "trade fair." From their rich coastal lands they brought dried salmon, shellfish, dentalia (a sort of shell currency), birds and feathers, and the treasures gleaned from ancient shipwrecks that washed up on Pacific beaches—metals and other oddities from the flotsam of many lands. From northern tribes the Chinook traders obtained copper and often slaves, bringing these items of property to exchange with the Cayuse, Yakima, Okanogan, and other landlocked tribes.

From the interior Indians and their Clatsop neighbors on the Columbia's south shore the Chinooks purchased items of sheephorn, pelts, jade from the Fraser River, and clamons. The latter was a hide shirt that repelled arrows and—to some extent—bullets, after guns came into the natives' possession. The Chinooks then traded the clamons to the warlike northern tribes, who prized them highly.

After white traders began to appear at the mouth of the Columbia just before 1800, Comcomly welcomed them as sources of new and innovative trade goods that he could bring to natives of the interior. To consolidate his position as the intermediary Comcomly spread rumors that it was dangerous for the interior tribes to come to the coast, that white men took captives to trade as slaves to the fierce northern tribes, and that some white men were cannibals. If fright tactics did not suffice, Comcomly, his well-armed slaves and freemen were perfectly willing to resort to war.

At Fort George, across the river from Comcomly's stronghold, a site originally founded by John Jacob Astor's American fur traders and later sold to the British, the Hudson's Bay traders realized how dependent they were on Comcomly and pondered how to deal with the situation.

II

At Fort Vancouver

In 1824, at distant York Factory near Hudson's Bay, the situation on the Columbia was under scrutiny by the top managers. Three years earlier, after a merger with the North West Company, the Hudson's Bay Company appointed a powerful and energetic administrator, George Simpson, as Governor-in-chief of Northern Operations—a vast fiefdom that included the shores of Hudson's Bay itself west to the Pacific and south to the Columbia River's east/west reaches.

With little delay, accompanied by John McLoughlin, a man who would figure heavily in the Pacific Northwest's future, Simpson set out on an inspection tour of the fur trading posts, arriving at Fort George without warning to confront a somewhat embarrassed McDonald and Chief Factor Alexander Kennedy enjoying a leisurely sail on the Columbia.

While Simpson commended Archibald McDonald on his record keeping (for his main task had been to inventory the trading post), he briskly set out to "clean house." He noticed that the post was taking the easy way of supplying itself—importing food from England and purchasing horses from the Indians for meat, or hiring the natives to hunt for wild game. Simpson's aim was for each fort to become more self-sufficient, to raise its own livestock and produce or utilize local foods. Furthermore, he found that much merchandise intended for trade was being diverted to the workmen's families; and, since the extended families of the men's Chinook wives could number in the dozens, the drain on trade goods was substantial. Under Simpson's stern direction these practices were to cease.

After receiving full reports on the trade stranglehold held by Comcomly, reports of which had been considered at the Hudson's Bay Company's annual council at York Factory, a large distribution center on the Hayes River about five miles from Hudson's Bay, Simpson set about looking for a new site for a fort upriver beyond the close control of the Chinooks. On the north side of the Columbia River across from its junction with the Willamette he surveyed a pleasant bluff called Belle Vue and decided to locate Fort Vancouver there, about eighty miles upstream from the mouth of the river and out of Comcomly's clutches. It was roughly equidistant from the Dalles and the Pacific Coast, and on a natural travel route from Puget Sound to the southern Oregon valleys.

When Comcomly learned in March, 1824, that the fort was to be moved, he actually cried—whether it was from genuine dismay that his old friends were moving away or frustration at the threat to his trading empire, no one knew.

The projected move had other political overtones. Increasingly hemmed in by Russian holdings and restrictions on the north and the growing American influence on the east and south, a besieged Great Britain hoped to hold the international line at the Columbia River. A stronger and more centrally located fort in that area would bolster England's case.

Ranald did not see much of his father during his first year because McDonald and Kennedy were assigned to supervise the building of Fort Vancouver. McLoughlin, too, aided in the planning as he was to be the new fort's chief factor. In the prime of his life at age thirty-nine McLoughlin was impressive, both in his manner and in physical stature. He was six feet four inches tall with a shock of prematurely white hair above a ruddy, dignified countenance, a kindly person who managed to make his will followed without antagonizing his staff. He would befriend thin, haggard American explorers like Jedediah Smith (who fled northward from hostile Umpqua Indians), and even the American settlers who thronged increasingly westward to settle in the Oregon valleys across the river. He would tangle, though, with Sir George Simpson and eventually quit the Hudson's Bay Company in frustration, becoming an American.

By March, 1825, the rudimentary layout of Fort Vancouver was completed on the bluff. Then, in 1829, the fort was moved to the plain near the Columbia River where a replica now stands. Exact descriptions of the earliest fort are sketchy and confusing but it seems likely that a stockade of pickets thirteen feet high surrounded it, not so much to defend the traders from hostile natives as to prevent thievery of goods. The 1829 fort measured 734 feet by 318 feet and included more than twenty buildings— barracks for single employees, homes for married ones, vast warehouses and mess halls, blacksmith shop, woodworking shop, and shelters for some of the horses. The chief factor's new home of 1838 was the most impressive structure west of the Mississippi, it was said. A low picket fence surrounded the white wooden house that had a broad veranda where men and women gathered on warm summer evenings for conversation.

Even the original factor's home must have enjoyed some distinction, as accounts tell of a splendid table being set in considerable style. Polished silver and oiled mahogany furniture, fine Spode china and gracious manners marked the factor's home (when it was finally furnished properly from supply ships). McLoughlin entertained local Indian chiefs like Casseno, as well as visiting Hudson's Bay dignitaries or transient adventurers.

The formal christening of the fort occurred at sunrise on March 19, 1825, just before Governor Simpson and Alexander Kennedy were to depart on their return trip to York Factory. The noted historian, David Lavender, described those attending the dedication:

> People: A mixed crowd numbering 40 or more persons. Among them were short, bandy-legged French Canadian voyageurs in red stocking caps; shivering, dark-skinned laborers from the Sandwich (Hawaiian) Islands; and a sprinkling of Chinook Indians whose foreheads had been "flattened" during childhood so that the skulls sloped upward to a curious peak. [The group may well have included Chief Comcomly, Ranald MacDonald's maternal grandfather, as he was a frequent visitor to the fort.] A step or two removed from those onlookers were the half dozen or so Scottish and English gentlemen, clad in frock coats and tall beaver hats, who oversaw the varied operations of the post. Towering above the assembly was the post's chief factor, John McLoughlin. Although he was only 40 years old, his hair, which fell almost to his shoulders, was snow white. Beside the massively built McLoughlin stood a smaller, pudgier man of about the same age. He was George Simpson, at that time the governor of the vast Northern Department of the Hudson's Bay Company, the most extensive monopoly, as far as land area is concerned, that the world has ever known.

Archibald McDonald continued to work at refining the systems at Fort Vancouver, including the record keeping, and in dismantling old Fort George, where he could visit his happy little toddler at every opportunity. He wondered where he would fit into the Hudson's Bay scheme, since McLoughlin had been brought to head operations in the Columbia. His fate was revealed in a letter from Governor Simpson to John McLoughlin dated July 11, 1825. McDonald was to be promoted to chief trader at Thompson's River, today's Kamloops, British Columbia. Simpson said:

"This young gentleman has not had much experience as an Indian trader, but from his manner and address I think he would very soon gain popularity, he knows the value of property and I have every reason to believe would turn it out to the best account; he appears thoughtful, steady and discreet and I am satisfied he will spare no pains or exertion to put things on a proper footing and give satisfaction & we may depend on his following instructions implicitly."

First, though, McDonald had to wait for his successor to arrive from the north so he could train the man, Edward Ermatinger. While he waited, Archibald managed a trip to the Jasper post in the northern Rocky Mountain country to bring back a new bride, Jane Klyne, daughter of Michel

Klyne, a Hudson's Bay postmaster. It is not clear just when he had met her or conceived the idea of wooing her as his new mate.

After returning to Fort Vancouver on September 1, 1825, he shortly retrieved his toddler son Ranald, now a year and a half old, from Chief Comcomly. With a generous and loving heart Jane welcomed the sunny little boy and always thereafter treated him exactly as if he were her own true son. It was with a heavy heart, though, that the old chief saw his grandson leave his longhouse. He would seldom see the boy again. Comcomly died of the virulent plague that swept the lower Columbia in 1830-1.

Edward Ermatinger finally arrived and learned the accounting, freeing Archibald to leave on January 7, 1826, for Thompson's River. Despite winter weather on the eastern side of the Cascades Mountains it was a happy family that paddled upriver to Fort Okanogan, bound for the northern post. Since facilities were still crude at the post, McDonald decided to leave Ranald and Jane in the care of the traders at Fort Okanogan until he could get things ready for them.

Taking over the post at Thompson's River from John McLeod, his first responsibilities included winning the confidence of the local Indian chiefs of the area: Nicola, the Okanagan chief, and Tranquille of the Shuswaps. Both seemed friendly enough, although troublesome in the past, and McDonald turned his attention to the operations of the fort, very different from that of Fort George and Fort Vancouver. Thompson's River was a sort of crossroads between the east/west and north/south trails, a refitting station for overland parties. The post maintained a large herd of horses, pasturing and doctoring them as replacements for brigade pack trains and general mounts. Horse brigades could number as many as two hundred fifty animals, quite a sight to see. The site was well chosen on a fertile plain at the head of the Okanagan Valley, overlooking the broad Thompson River, near huge Shuswap Lake, almost an inland sea. Hemmed in on the east and west by mountains, the Okanagan valley was a natural waterway, too, boasting a series of deep lakes connected by the Okanagan River to the Columbia. The fort was compact and well palisaded, with corrals or stockades a short distance away, large enough to hold three or four hundred horses.

Within two months of his arrival McDonald was asked to resupply horses for a fur brigade stranded at Fort Alexandria, nearly two hundred miles northwest of Thompson's River, when most of the horses died of some mysterious disease. Since insufficient numbers of horses were on hand, Archibald sent all that he had and hastened south to Fort Vancouver in

April (stopping for a brief visit at Fort Okanogan with his pregnant wife and Ranald, now an active two-year-old getting into every part of the small fort with his mischief). After delivering a limited amount of goods from Thompson's River by boat—baled dried salmon and furs stored there—to McLoughlin, McDonald set out for the Nez Perce horse fair in what is now eastern Oregon. Accompanying him on this adventure were James Douglas, later the first governor of British Columbia province; Francis Annance; John Work; and an old acquaintance from Fort Vancouver days, botanist David Douglas, who was on assignment from the Horticultural Society of London to bring home specimens of flora and fauna to England. No doubt, the colorful horse fair was an exciting and unexpected treat for the wanderer. With some minor disagreements and lively bargaining the horse purchases were completed, seventy horses were sent north immediately, and several more were driven back to Thompson's River by McDonald and the rest of his crew. He arrived at Fort Okanogan to find his wife had given birth to a son, Angus, on August 1st, only a few days earlier.

After resting with his family at Fort Okanogan for four weeks, Archibald, Jane, Ranald and Angus traveled on to Thompson's River with eight men and fifty horses. Jane carried the baby on horseback, while a delighted Ranald rode with his father, keeping his father entertained with his comical baby talk. Years later when Ranald wrote his diary, he remembered his many trips with his father:

"Again with my father, after my babyhood in the palace, I remained with him, his constant companion, save when out on expeditions of special danger—from trade post to trade post throughout the Columbia, and northward in the region now known as British Columbia."

In 1827, Archibald reported that the peak of fur production in that area had passed, that the area had been over-trapped. He reported that the climate was agreeable, but that the soil was not suitable to gardens or farming. He reported that Fort Okanogan, then managed by Francis Ermatinger with his wife, was decreasing in importance as well, a small post facilitating transfer from Columbia River canoes to horse brigades on the trail between Fort Vancouver and Thompson's River or Kamloops. McDonald mentioned that dried salmon was the chief sustenance for the fort, with three one-pound dried salmon allotted for each man daily, two for each woman and one for a child. Other foods included venison, berries, horse meat (a special delicacy, as were beaver tails), swans, geese, ducks, badger, rabbits, fresh trout, bear, etc.

Darlings of the new post, Ranald and Angus, cheerful little fellows, could do no wrong. Separated from their own families, the men, many of them French voyageurs, Iroquois trappers and boatmen, were willing targets for childish pranks and prattle. Francis Ermatinger at Thompson's River was remembered fondly by Ranald MacDonald, who said of "kindly Frank Ermatinger" that he gave the children cakes, a rare treat, for the allowance of flour was two sacks brought from London by way of Cape Horn, then transported to the interior with tea and sugar. "And I must not forget to us children that great luxury—a few cakes of gingerbread—and how Frank Ermatinger would say, 'I won't tell.'" In February, 1828, another brother, Archibald, Jr., joined their ranks, just before Archie Sr. was sent to the Hudson's Bay Council Meeting at York Factory. Jane and the growing brood of McDonalds went to Fort Vancouver during this period, giving Ranald a chance to visit his grandfather and numerous relatives on the Columbia. The toddler of less than two years old returned a stocky lad of four.

Arriving at York Factory, Archibald felt particularly honored to be invited to attend the Northern Council in the first year of his appointment as a chief trader. Perhaps his illustrious Scottish pedigree dating back to Glencoe of Argyllshire gave the needed status, or his yeoman service at the Selkirk settlement of the Red River.

Governor Simpson presided over the meeting, and following the conference he selected Archibald to ride with him in his own canoe en route to the Pacific Coast. Accompanied by a lively group of eighteen French voyageurs to paddle the two large canoes, plus a few other men, the party made its way 3,126 miles down to Fort Langley in sixty-five days by a route different from that usually traveled by the Express. On this occasion Governor Simpson requested McDonald to keep a diary, a work published much later as *Peace River. A Canoe Voyage from Hudson's Bay to Pacific by the Late Sir George Simpson, (Governor, Hon. Hudson's Bay Company.) in 1828. Journal of the Late Chief Factor, Archibald McDonald, (Hon. Hudson's Bay Company), Who Accompanied Him* (1872).

In general, the route went north on the Athabasca River, then south on the Peace to the Fraser River, with difficult portages intermittently required between waterways or to skirt impassable stretches of river. At Fort Alexandria (between today's Prince George and Quesnel on the upper Fraser River), Simpson, McDonald and some of the men went by horseback to Thompson's River (Kamloops), while fourteen men under James Yale went ahead to build boats for the attempted descent of the lower Fraser River from its junction with the Thompson River. After a stopover at the Thompson's River post, Simpson's party descended the Thompson to meet Yale's group. Near its junction with the Fraser at today's Lytton, the

Thompson rolls through sandstone canyons in white-teethed rapids that hurled the canoes from side to side, whirling them through eddies and shooting them like arrows down rock-strewn reaches. As frightening as this trip was, Simpson was encouraged that the party did come through intact and determined to descend the Fraser, probably against the best advice of his cohorts, a feat attempted only once before by Simon Fraser.

Awed and almost overwhelmed by the massive mountains that rose abruptly from the Fraser River to seven thousand feet, the party floated down with an ever-quickening current. The water grew swift and wild, caroming off the rocky walls of the waterway like a logging flume, forming great whirlpools that spun the craft madly before releasing them. Miraculously all canoes made it through the area known today as Hell's Gate without losing a man, fighting their way downstream into canyons where the current was so swift that the middle of the river was actually higher than the water at the sides. This was the first known voyage by any explorer through the mighty Fraser River Canyon, for Fraser had taken to the shore in a few places.

A white-knuckled Simpson emerged from the Fraser Gorge into the broad, placid channels that wend westward to the sea, and exclaimed fervently that the Thompson and Fraser rivers as a water route for hauling furs and supplies were totally impractical. At newly built Fort Langley on the north shore of the Fraser, about thirty miles from the Gulf of Georgia, Chief Trader James McMillan heard the bagpipes of the arriving party with amazement and came down to the water to greet the unexpected visitors.

While McDonald had been north with Simpson, Dr. John McLoughlin of Fort Vancouver had dispatched James McMillan in 1827 to supervise the construction of the new Fort Langley. It had been Simpson's own idea back in 1825, when he was at Fort Vancouver, that this fort should be built on the Fraser to take advantage of trade with the natives of the northwest mainland and Puget Sound. Puget Sound was only twenty miles south overland, or boats could traverse the Fraser to its mouth, coast down a pleasant shore interspersed with literally hundreds of islands to the lower end of Puget Sound at Nisqually (west of today's Tacoma, Washington), also scheduled to be a fort.

Even though Archibald was assigned to take over Fort Langley immediately as chief trader, releasing McMillan to go east on furlough, quarters were not completed for his family until July, 1829. An impatient Archibald greeted his family then, setting out in a small boat to meet them when they entered the river on the Hudson's Bay ship *Cadborn*. According to Jean Murray Cole in her book, *Exile in the Wilderness*:

"The chief trader's wife and children quickly became the focal point of family life at Fort Langley. The fair skinned, dark-eyed youngsters were favorites with the French-Canadian voyageurs and the gentle Owyhees (Sandwich Islanders) alike. They lived with a variety of languages: French, their mother's native tongue (although Jane is said to have been part Cree Indian); English, the language of all Hudson's Bay Company posts; as well as the Gaelic which, John McLeod asserted, was closer to North American native dialects than any other. The friendly little boys had the run of the fort and their natural curiosity and rather quaint courtesy made them welcome companions to the men of the establishment as they went about their daily tasks."

The boys watched with keen interest as Hudson's Bay men packed salmon in barrels formed in the fort's cooperage . . . dodged chips when a man shaped planks with a broadaxe for shipment to Fort Vancouver and beyond . . . gazed in awe at the forge glowing red while the smithy shaped horseshoes, pack supports, and tools. The McDonald home boasted finery, linens, silver and fine dishes for entertaining Hudson's Bay visitors or important Indian people. Even the daily family dining was in a surprisingly gracious atmosphere for the remote post.

Life was not all play for the oldest son Ranald. Concerned about the limited opportunities in the West for his well-born sons, slated for lives as gentlemen, Archibald was determined to start their education as early as possible. Ranald was assigned to regular hours of study in writing, reading and arithmetic under his father's tutelage, a class that was joined by his mother Jane, and Angus and Archie Jr., as they grew older. Jane recognized that, eventually, she and Archibald would be sent East to administrative posts in the more sophisticated cities, where she would have to hold her own with ladies of different backgrounds. She worked assiduously to learn the skills she might need to remedy her shortcomings as a gentleman's wife.

Despite the classes Ranald had plenty of time to play games around the fort and often accompanied his father on short inspection trips and the annual or semiannual treks to Fort Vancouver. He delighted in the comradeship of his cheerful father and was spellbound by his tales of Scottish ancestors. The skirl of bagpipes and swirl of kilts were heady imaginings for the boy, who dreamed of adventures, tales of derring-do where he was the boy hero. At the fort he listened intently to the tales of the voyageurs and fur trappers, whose arrivals in colorful bateaux from far places were special events. Dark-eyed French paddlers and rough Hudson's Bay trappers clustered around the fires of the fort, swapping exaggerated stories of rogue rivers, strange Indian encounters, and narrow escapes from death. Indians came and went, the friendly ones retreating to the fort's environs when pressed by the warlike Yucaltas that swept down in huge war canoes from the northern mainland coast.

When Ranald was just past nine years old, Archibald received word from Doctor McLoughlin that he should travel to Fort Vancouver to discuss new assignments. Since Archibald was scheduled for a furlough or vacation in 1834, planning to travel to his ancestral Scottish home, he hoped nothing would interfere with that plan.

During the turmoil of the change of assignments and what promised to be an extended trip to Fort Vancouver, McDonald sent his family—all except Ranald—to Jane's father, Michel Klyne, at Jasper House. He planned to rejoin them in 1834 en route to the Red River settlement (Winnipeg). He said to Edward Ermatinger in a letter that "it was high time for me to get my little boys into school," and hoped to enroll the older ones in 1834 at Red River Academy, to which most young Hudson's Bay employees' children went for higher education.

But before Ranald went to Red River Academy, his father thought he would need some further training to be accepted, even though Ranald had become quite adept at arithmetic and reading. For the winter Ranald would be enrolled at school in Fort Vancouver.

With a lump in his throat vying with the excitement of going off to new experiences among boys of his own age, Ranald set out with Archibald for Fort Vancouver to enroll in John Ball's new school and stay until the family went to Red River.

John Ball was a young man who had graduated from Dartmouth, later had been admitted to the bar in New York, then was smitten with wanderlust, traveling west with the Nathaniel Wyeth party. After arriving at Fort Vancouver in October, 1832, Ball confessed to Doctor McLoughlin that he was destitute and did not merit the hospitality extended to him. He asked for some kind of work.

McLoughlin shrugged off Ball's protests. As Ball related in a letter to friends:

"He repeatedly answered me that I was a guest and not expected to work. But after much urging, he said if I was willing he would like me to teach his own and the other boys in the fort, of whom there were a dozen. Of course I gladly accepted the offer."

Thus Ball became the teacher of Oregon's first school, starting his instruction on November 17, 1832, after a swift trip to see the ocean eighty miles distant. In the letter to his friend, Ball continued:

"All were half-breeds, as there was not a white woman in Oregon. The doctor's wife was a 'Chippewa' from Lake Superior, and the lightest woman was Mrs. Douglas, a half-breed from Hudson Bay. I found the boys docile and attentive, and they made good progress. The doctor often came into the school, and was well satisfied and pleased. One day he said: 'Ball, anyway you will have the reputation of teaching the *first* school in Oregon.' So I passed the winter of 1832 and 1833."

Ranald joined the ranks of the schoolboys on arrival at Fort Vancouver in March, 1833, saying good-bye to his father who was assigned to assist in the establishment of Fort Nisqually that spring.

Of course, Ranald was no stranger to the fort and, since his father was a particular friend of Doctor McLoughlin, his life was not unpleasant.

In Ball's school only a few boys, including Ranald and David McLoughlin, spoke English fluently. Many of the children were more fluent in French or the various Indian languages of their mothers. An observer said that, of Ball's original twenty-four pupils (which included grown men and women) some spoke Klickitat, Nez Perce, Chinook and Cree.

With few books the educational curriculum was rather basic but one key text was Murray's Grammar, which students were required to memorize. The students learned English vocabulary by rote and learned to cipher.

III

Exciting Travels for Ranald

At Ball's school in late January, 1834, an event took place that was pivotal in Ranald MacDonald's life. In his notes written several years after his Japan adventure Ranald does not directly mention his fascination with the tale of Japanese castaways. However, historians surmise that his profound curiosity in Japan began at this time.

On January 29, 1834, an Indian arrived at Fort Nisqually with the unpleasant news that a vessel had been wrecked at Cape Flattery near the mouth of the Strait of Juan de Fuca. All hands except two were said to be drowned. The following day a man named Ouvre set out to determine the truth of the report, returning to say that the shipwreck story was a fabrication, according to Indians at the Chlallum village at New Dungeness.

But he was wrong. When a British trading ship called at the Makah Indian post to barter for furs, the captain noticed the Oriental features of two captives. When the Indians told him the story of a shipwreck and showed him a piece of the ship with Oriental characters upon it, the captain felt sure the craft had drifted from Asia. The desperate captives managed to smuggle a piece of rice paper to the captain, on which they had written their names, drawn a picture of a shipwreck, and a sketch of three— not two of them—bound as slaves. When the captain gave the message to Dr. McLoughlin, he sent Thomas McKay and a party of men to check on the situation, but the party was unable to work around Point Grenville on the Washington coast and returned to the fort. Thereafter Captain McNeill sailed the brig *Llama* to the village of Ozette, where he determined that a third castaway had been sent inland to another village. Promising to return and pick up all three foreigners, McNeill went on to Fort Langley. Upon his later return, rowdy Makah Indians boarded the ship and were seized by the ship's crew. An indignant Captain McNeill held the Indians hostage until they surrendered the survivors of the wreck, three Japanese sailors, frightened and dirty, and returned them to Fort Vancouver in May, 1834.

As the three sailors were scarcely older than schoolboys, McLoughlin placed them in John Ball's school to learn English. Otokichi was fourteen years old, Kyukichi was fifteen, and Iwakichi was twenty-eight. As they quickly learned English, their harrowing story was told:

The sailors were the three youngest of the crew on a coastal freighter, *Hōjun Maru,* based in Toba, Japan, on the eastern coast. With a cargo of rice and porcelain dishes of a pretty willow pattern intended for the Shogun in Edo (Tokyo), the ship left Toba on October 11, 1832, en route north along a turbulent shore. A storm washed away the ship's mast and rudder, leaving it to drift helplessly.

By catching fish and rainwater and with rice as a cargo the hapless sailors survived more storms and calms, but several of them died of varying causes, their bodies stacked in barrels aboard ship.

After more than fourteen months of drifting with the Kuroshio or Japanese Current, the disabled craft washed up on the rocks south of Cape Flattery. (Pieces of the Shogun's pottery washed up on ocean beaches for months afterward.) Hostile Makah Indians promptly stormed aboard and vandalized the ship, enslaving the three survivors. As indicated in Chapter I, slaves of coastal Indians lived a miserable life, indeed, so the three were fortunate to be rescued by Hudson's Bay men.

Young Ranald had already left Fort Vancouver in March to rejoin his father at Fort Colvile and proceed to the Red River settlement. Unquestionably, though, through the Hudson's Bay channels, he was fascinated to learn about these foreigners and hear about the conditions that caused them to be shipwrecked.

In these times Japan was an entirely closed country. It desired no contact with the outside world, only trading annually with a few Dutchmen at Deshima Island in Nagasaki Bay at the southern end of Kyushu Island. Ships such as the *Hōjun Maru* were restricted to a design that was not seaworthy enough to sail to foreign lands—just so that mariners would not be tempted to explore beyond Japan. If any person contacted western civilization, and shipwreck was no exception, he was not allowed to return home to Japan.

Ranald wondered what kind of a country this was, that would not help its own citizens. And what of the differing manners and ways of life described by Hudson's Bay Company travelers who had met them? (It is possible that, much later in his wanderings, Ranald could have met Otokichi, who eventually lived in Macao, a stopping place for whalers.)

The young sailors continued in school until 1835, about a year after Ranald had left Fort Vancouver. McLoughlin then sent the three men to

London on a Hudson's Bay ship. In letters to his London offices he out-lined his suggestions that the three men should see the superiority of England's way of life and her friendliness, and take home to Japan good impressions that might lead to opening of trade with that isolated nation. The men, the first Japanese to visit England, were sent on to the Orient later and transferred to the United States ship *Morrison* for repatriation.

Unfortunately, when the *Morrison* entered Edo Bay on July 30, 1837, Japanese shore batteries fired on the unarmed vessel. The ship's captain sailed south and tried to enter the bay of Nagasaki, where the Dutch trad-ers had limited rights. He was unable to persuade local emissaries who came by boat to intercept the ship that he merely wanted put ashore the three refugees washed up in North America, plus four others he had picked up in Macao, survivors of shipwreck in the Philippine Islands.

Angered by their country's behavior Otokichi and his two friends retreated to Macao and vowed never to return to Japan, no matter if their countrymen invited them back.

Meanwhile, Ranald MacDonald left Vancouver in March, 1834, with Duncan Finlayson and the spring Hudson's Bay express that left Fort Vancouver on March 20th each year. The express was bound for Norway House and the Red River settlement with some of the chief traders attend-ing the annual general council meeting at York Factory. No doubt, Ranald's spirit must have soared at the prospect of seeing his father again—and shaking off the chains of the schoolroom. After a brief visit in Fort Colvile, where he delighted in the beauties of his father's new post located near Kettle Falls on the Columbia River (a site under the waters of Lake Roosevelt behind Grand Coulee Dam today), he and his father continued north with the express to Jasper House, arriving about May 5th.

Not long after leaving Fort Colvile, ascending the Columbia River where it widened into a series of lakes, the canoes pulled near shore for the night. Enjoying the scenery, Ranald noticed far up on the cliffs what ap-peared to be a cache of arrows in a crevice of the rock. Obligingly a voyageur succeeded in knocking down one or two of the arrows, and all speculated as to the reasons for the deposit . . . was it an offering to the gods by an unknown Indian . . . was it a hiding place for spare supplies to be retrieved later? Who could know. But thereafter these lakes were known as Arrow Lakes.

At Jasper House the family was reunited and baby Mary Anne was warmly welcomed into the clan by her father Archibald and brother Ranald.

Before long the entire McDonald family moved on to the Red River settlement, now about five thousand population, where Jane and the children would stay with the Reverend William Cochrane while Archibald went on to England and Scotland on furlough. He left from York Factory after the annual council meeting in July, boarding the ship *Prince George* on September 12. During her husband's absence Jane acknowledged Episcopalian beliefs and Reverend Cochrane baptized her and the six children—Ranald, Angus, Archibald Jr., Alexander, Allan and Mary Anne—on November 2, 1834.

Archibald came home from Britain in time to attend the meeting of the Northern Council in June, 1835, after which he made the difficult decision of leaving the four oldest boys behind at Red River Academy, when he, his wife, and two youngest tots returned to Fort Colvile. It was possible that he might not see the four boys again for five years, but his agonized decision was based on the necessity for education of his sons, if they were to take their place in the world.

Archibald McDonald was hoping secretly that the separation would not be that long, but he needed to return to his duties as a chief trader if he was to gain the coveted chief factor status, a designation assuring him of a comfortable pension for seven years after his retirement. Tears flowed copiously as the little boys, Ranald the oldest at age eleven, watched their parents disappear from sight in the canoes of the westbound party. As far as we know, this was the last time Ranald ever saw his father, although there are puzzling comments in Ranald's notes that might indicate he had returned to Fort Colvile for a visit during his years at Red River Academy.

IV

Red River Settlement

Situated around the junction of the Red and Assiniboine rivers, straggling north and south, the Red River settlement numbered about five thousand people, certainly a metropolis to the MacDonald boys from the wilderness. Four groups made up the community. About two hundred yards from the rivers' junction, on the banks of the Assiniboine, the Hudson's Bay Company was centered at Upper Fort Garry, a square stone building with round bastions pierced for cannon at the corners, the red H.B.Co. flag snapping above it in the prairie winds. Before this structure, the first fort had been founded as Gibralter by John McDonald of Garth.

Within the fort were quarters for employees and military personnel, offices, warehouses and stores. The fort was the center of social life; at parties and important meetings the ladies wore their best gowns and men their beaver hats. Red River had a reputation for rollicking good times. The fort was the scene of business negotiations, too, where settlers brought their produce and exchanged it for supplies. Local hunters, metis (halfbreeds, usually with French fathers) and Indians, brought furs for sale or barter.

At the north fringe of the settlement lived the French-Canadians, in the middle the Scots, and to the south the Indians. These diverse groups lived together harmoniously, with the Scots most industrious at farming, the French and Indians adept at buffalo hunting. The latter was of critical importance to the settlers' survival, since supplies sent from England occasionally did not arrive due to storms, untimely ice jams or other catastrophes.

Many of the Scots settlers were remnants of the partly unsuccessful colonization attempt of 1812—Scotsmen led by Lord Selkirk and his adjutant, Archibald McDonald. Facing the river for several miles were their homes, often situated among the trees that formed a narrow belt along the water. The farmlands extended as much as two miles inland from the river's edge. Barley was grown as feed for stock, but wheat was the chief cereal crop. Farmers commonly kept pigs and chickens and tapped the maple trees for sugar each spring.

Driven from the lower Mississippi River area in 1822 and 1823, cattle had increased to sizable herds, sharing prairie grass with buffalo and deer. Robert Campbell was sent by the Hudson's Bay Company to Kentucky in 1832 for the purpose of buying sheep for Red River. He only managed to save 250 out of 3,000 sheep in the long drive from Kentucky, and the remainder never prospered.

This polyglot population needed churches and schools. Two miles downriver from the forks, John West of the Church of England, chaplain to the Hudson's Bay Company, founded the Church of St. John on the west bank of the Red River in 1820 and 1821. A school, forerunner of the later Red River Academy, formed part of the missionary establishment, serving both Indian children as boarders and local children as day pupils. West laid out a farm and hired a manager to run it with help from boarding students, as the means of feeding the staff and children.

By 1822, West had wrested funds and labor from settlers and the Hudson's Bay Company to build apartments for the schoolmaster (William Harbidge), simple quarters for the growing flock of boarders, and classrooms.

While the Hudson's Bay administrators appreciated West's zeal in educating the children, they were less than enthusiastic when he encouraged the halfbreeds and Indians to leave their nomadic ways to become farmers. If this occurred, reasoned the company, where would they obtain the stalwart boatsmen needed for the supply boats, or the reckless hunters who chased buffalo across the prairie?

Amid growing uneasiness about West's evangelism, plus the ineptness of his schoolmaster Harbidge, who proved to be barely educated himself, the Church Missionary Society recalled West and replaced him with Reverend David Jones as chaplain. Jones took on an assistant, Reverend William Cochrane, and engaged William Garrioch to teach school.

Increasing numbers of boys and girls attended the school, with Mrs. Cochrane and later Mrs. Jones teaching the segregated girls' school. However, with imperfect chaperonage, one of the female boarders became pregnant by a male student. Buildings were crowded, and missionaries' homes bulged with the overflow of students. Clearly some improvements in management were needed.

In 1828, after returning from England with a new bride, Reverend Jones received permission from Governor George Simpson to build a substantial seminary for the "moral improvement, religious instruction and general education of boys; the sons of gentlemen belonging to the fur trade." Fees of 20 pounds a year were charged to the parents for board, washing, and education, or 30 pounds if a uniform was furnished.

Simpson requested that a similar school be founded for the girls, encouraging Jones to request a tutor/governess from the Church Missionary Society. He suggested that such a woman should not be interested in marriage but, while the first governess, Mary Lowman, was single when she came in 1833, she married a retired chief factor, James Curtis Bird, in 1835.

The Red River Academy or Seminary was an entirely new educational institution. The original school building was moved downriver to St. Andrews (where subsequently a church was built that still stands in Winnipeg), a community of retired Hudson's Bay employees, their Indian wives and halfbreed children.

A tutor, John Macallum, age twenty-eight and with a Master of Arts degree from King's College in Aberdeen, Scotland, arrived in the fall of 1833, serving the Red River Academy until his death from acute jaundice in 1849.

When Archibald McDonald left his four sons at Red River on June 9, 1835, the school was operating vigorously. There were twenty-three boys and twenty-four girls, plus the teacher and fifteen servants, at the school. Despite losing money, with food the largest expense, the Hudson's Bay Company considered that the school served a need for its far-flung employees.

According to letters from Archibald McDonald to his friend, Edward Ermatinger of St. Thomas, Ontario, three of his sons lived with the Cochranes, the fourth with his grandparents, the Michel Klynes, who had moved to the Red River settlement. At first, all of them attended a preparatory school taught by Richard Pritchard. In the summer of 1835, within days of his arrival, Ranald was transferred to the high school at Red River, soon followed by Angus and Archie Jr.

The brothers found their studies demanding and Macallum a stern taskmaster. In an article in *The Beaver* magazine, winter 1974, Thomas F. Bredin wrote that Macallum was a stern, red-wigged, snuff-taking man who kept by his desk a finger-sized native brown willow stick, about three and a half feet long, to mete out punishment to dullards. With his bright mind and good grounding in arithmetic and reading from his parents' teachings, John Ball's school and Pritchard's school, perhaps Ranald escaped the worst of Macallum's discipline.

For all the good it would ever do them on the frontier, the students learned Latin, Greek, Euclid, English literature, and geography. Ranald's religious upbringing was intense. There was family worship morning and evening, usually with the Reverend reading the Bible and all singing hymns. On Sunday the family would gather to read the Bible out loud, each person taking turns, including the children.

No one in the community labored on Sunday. Even at hay cutting time, when most men and older boys in a festival atmosphere rode out of town to live in tents on the prairie, everyone would return home on Saturday night or Sunday to be with their families.

Any outbreak of serious illness among the children was especially worrisome for teachers and guardians, since many parents of Red River Academy students, such as the McDonalds, were unreachable for months at a time. In December, 1834, several children died of whooping cough that was followed by a severe intestinal disorder. Ten years later, long after Ranald had left Red River, a dysentery epidemic swept through the settlement, leaving dead in almost every home. Nevertheless, the perils probably were no greater at the settlement than elsewhere on the frontier.

In 1838, thirty-four boys and fourteen girls were attending the Red River Academy. Macallum wrote to a friend: "we are all as happy in this here place as the day is long. The schools are well supported, & supply us with as much work as we can all execute . . . all is well with regard to my immediate charges. Their progress is pleasing, their deportment correct, and their docility, attention, & application, highly commendable."

When not in school, life at the Red River settlement must have been engrossing for the growing McDonald sons. Always a provisions depot for the Hudson's Bay Company since its establishment, Fort Garry, as well as York Factory on Hudson's Bay, and Norway House on Lake Winnipeg, had warehouses and accounting offices. Upper Fort Garry's very existence was devoted to storing supplies and the dispatch of boat brigades, spring and fall, to the northern and western posts. As soon as the ice left the rivers and lakes, the spring brigade departed from Fort Garry for the Athabasca and Mackenzie River districts. Ranald watched them leave with longing, understandably lonesome for his distant parents.

A brigade consisted of four to six boats in charge of an experienced guide. For a big York freight boat there was a bowsman, a steersman, and six oarsmen, often called "tripmen" because they signed on for a "trip." Usually they were of French-Canadian, halfbreed or Indian descent. The York boats that replaced canoes after 1821 averaged 34 feet overall, with a 9-foot beam amidships. They were propelled by oars in quiet water or a stable current; to negotiate rapids they were managed by poles or tracked through by line. If the wind was astern on a lake or large river, sometimes the brigademen raised a square sail, a welcome time of rest from the grueling work.

Brigades returned to Fort Garry by way of York and Norway House, picking up or distributing goods; others in fall carried Red River furs to York and returned with supplies.

Brigademen were laughing, colorful fellows, who usually approached a destination only after stopping to deck themselves in their best finery. They arrived at a port singing and cheering. As a student at Ball's school in Vancouver, Ranald had watched similar supply brigades arriving—the other end of a vast supply network.

Despite the relative prosperity of the colony, at times (such as in 1837) the supplies did not arrive from York Factory and England, or heavy snows reduced food supplied by hunters. One correspondent said that Macallum at Red River Academy provided only dry bread and milk for breakfasts and might withhold meals from a child who misbehaved, as well as flog them. Ranald himself wrote that the students often had only pemmican for lunch. Even in freezing weather, students were required to take walks outside in the snow but the girls, forbidden to wear Indian leggings, sometimes suffered from the cold.

Mrs. Duncan Finlayson, whose husband was a Hudson's Bay official, voiced a different view. She wrote to a friend that one would be amazed at the wealth of foods in residents' icehouses—beef, mutton, pork, hams, tongues, fowls, turkeys, rabbits, sturgeon, white fish and frozen vegetables.

Certainly any frontier menu was largely devoid of fruits, except for berries picked in the summer. Almost the only sweets a child enjoyed was browned flour with molasses. Families were self-sufficient, making most of their own clothes and even shoes from buffalo hide.

By no means did Ranald's father forget him and his brothers, but thousands of miles separated the family members. Writing to his friend, Edward Ermatinger of St. Thomas, Archibald philosophized that, despite his employment at Fort Colvile so that he could provide for his children, no amount of money could make "a good parson, a shining lawyer or an able physician," if one were left to his own ends as a youth. He wrote further to Ermatinger in 1836 about his plans to send Ranald to become an apprentice in Ermatinger's bank.

Archibald McDonald received intermittent reports of his sons' progress, with the Reverend Cochrane writing in the fall of 1838 that he had seen Ranald and his brothers recently. He added that Ranald had certain qualities that probably would make him the best adapted to the outside world. Possibly these qualities were his intelligence, his deep curiosity about the world beyond his immediate circle, and his easy-going demeanor, because he made friends easily.

To ensure that Ranald would have a means of livelihood, no matter what his schooling might produce, his father directed Reverend Jones that he be taught carpentry skills.

Seemingly, Macallum found Ranald to meet his strict standards, because he gave him a good recommendation in March, 1839, when his father requested that Ranald be sent on to Edward Ermatinger. In a letter carried by Ranald, Archibald asked Ermatinger to report back to him within a year, indicating whether or not Ranald should follow the gentlemanly business path or be assigned to a trade for his life's work.

It is doubtful whether or not Ranald was consulted in the matter. However, he was delighted to leave school that spring of 1839, traveling east in the custody of Roderick McLeod with a brigade from Red River as far as Fort William on Lake Superior, then across to Fort Bradley. Fort William originally was the principal factory of the North West Company. In his notes Ranald described sightseeing at the fort, of seeing his first Negro and his first American soldier. The "first" that thrilled him most was passage on a steamboat, the *Governor Marcy*, from Fort Bradley to Mackinac, the city on the strait joining Lake Michigan and Lake Huron. There he transferred to a steamer bound for Detroit, alone for the trip. He enjoyed a degree of fame, when fellow passengers were impressed by his birth in the far away Columbia River country.

Alerted to Ranald's arrival through a letter from the Hudson's Bay Company, Mr. Abbott, agent of the American Fur Company, met Ranald in Detroit, showed him around the city, and put him on the stage for St. Thomas, Ontario.

After Ermatinger showed Ranald around the small town of St. Thomas, Ranald was assigned to the bank as an apprentice clerk, one notch above a mere apprentice because of his education, laboring on a high accountant's stool. The reality of the working world had begun for Ranald, a very long way from the crash of the Pacific Ocean, the half wild days in Hudson's Bay posts, or the Red River settlement at the edge of the wilderness. For the restless youth it seemed like a prison.

V

Rebellion

Ranald complied with the requirements of his job, dull though he found it, and soon found that his leisure time was far more exciting.

St. Thomas, a town of almost 1,000 people, had been named in 1817, after Thomas Talbot, private secretary to John Simcoe, first lieutenant governor of the Province of Upper Canada. Traveling with Simcoe through the southern Ontario region in 1793, Talbot was charmed by the rolling farmland, pleasant woods and frequent lakes. Lake Erie lay a few miles south, a part of the ocean-like Great Lakes that were used for shipping and transportation by early settlers and explorers moving west.

Somehow Thomas Talbot wrangled a 5,000 acre land grant bordering Lake Erie in 1802. By 1824, Talbot's land grant encompassed 540,443 acres, a huge fiefdom where he was the squire and the new settlers to whom he sold land his informal subjects. He vigorously developed the lands, building a road from Port Stanley to London and another from Fort Erie to Sandwich, then north to Sarnia. Indeed, Talbot's road was the only decent thoroughfare between Toronto and Windsor.

The fledgling town of St. Thomas, about fifteen miles north of Lake Erie, was actively settled in 1819, mostly by Argyllshire Highlanders, men of the same Scottish district as MacDonald's forebears. Others came from the Red River settlement, some retired Hudson's Bay employees on pension. Later Yankee settlers moved northward across the rather informal border to settle among their British neighbors and consider themselves Canadians—a term yet to be totally respectable, for most residents of Ontario considered themselves loyal Britishers.

Although Talbot lived at Port Talbot on Lake Erie, he considered St. Thomas his business stronghold. Like most early settlements, downtown St. Thomas consisted of a somewhat dreary business center with a few shops, a bank, a hotel or inn, post office, eventually a town hall and library. However, the residential streets were places of more dignity and beauty. Prospering businessmen soon built Victorian houses with spreading lawns, flower beds, lilacs and shrubs. The streets were lined with maples, elms and oaks. Red curtains, anticamassars and what-nots, domestic servants and hammocks, carriages pulled by fine horses, were part of daily life before mid-century. Edward Ermatinger lived as a respected upperclass business-man with his wife and small child, but did not build the fine mansion still standing today in St. Thomas until the late 1840's.

As a member of Ermatinger's household, living virtually as a son of the manor, Ranald found himself swept up in a genteel society that be-dazzled him, but was not beyond his graces. Despite his frontier past, Ranald had been taught social behavior by his parents and the spartan but intellec-tual Cochranes, in whose home good manners were demanded of all. Ranald's demeanor reflected the pride he felt in his well-born ancestors, the Argyllshire Scots, complacent about the native blood he carried from his mother Jane (he did not know yet he was not her true son). He was a fairly good looking youth, above average in height, well built and sturdy, his dark hair and eyes not uncommon among even full-blooded Scotsmen. Ranald became a popular member of the youths whose parents formed the "upper crust" of St. Thomas.

His fun was tempered by Edward Ermatinger's solemn manner and religious bent. Furthermore, Edward and his wife Achsah, daughter of the Honorable Zaccheus Burnham of Coburg, an upper echelon social family, experienced considerable marital friction. Ermatinger had started his St. Thomas business life by opening a store, and in 1833, he became agent in St. Thomas for the Bank of Upper Canada. When this bank moved to London, Ontario, he was associated agent for the Commercial Bank for a short time, and then opened an agency for the Bank of Montreal, manag-ing it for fourteen years. It was this institution which employed Ranald. (In the 1850's he started the Bank of Elgin, which failed, but Ermatinger paid back all his investors.)

Ermatinger was a staunch Tory, writing letters to newspapers and jour-nals and actively engaged in politics for thirty years or more as a British Canadian. In 1857 he wrote numerous letters to different newspapers re-garding the inadvisability of Canada trying to annex the Red River area and Saskatchewan, because it was impossible to put a road from Red River east to Toronto, that there were seventy portages just from Red River to Lake Superior. He likened the acquisition to buying an elephant at a raffle—what do you do with it when you get it? His letters also hotly defended the Hudson's Bay Company when the Liverpool Financial Reform Association published a pamphlet (republished in the Toronto Press), attacking the company as a monopoly and saying that the resources would have been developed a half-century earlier, had it not been for its monopoly. Ermatinger said the company was not a swindler but had legitimate leases from England, and he resented the way the Hudson's Bay Company was depicted in the Toronto newspapers.

As a part of this public family, then, Ranald participated in such fashionable activities as football, cricket, skating, and horse racing. During winter snows a favorite sport of the young people was galloping around the countryside in a light sleigh called a carriole. There was horse racing on the ice, with wagering a part of the sport, no doubt disapproved of by Edward Ermatinger, an active member of the local church. With his Christian upbringing, Ranald participated in the youth activities of the local church, as well—basket socials, community sings, and bible readings.

Between 1838 and 1841, in parts of the province there was active rebellion against British rule by loosely organized units of those who called themselves Canadians instead of British. Since all men from 16 to 65 were in the Upper Canadian Militia, Ranald probably participated, but apparently these armed units did not clash with the rebels. However, the militia parades, held on the King's or Queen's birthdays, were splendidly formal affairs with much pomp and ceremony. Often part of the celebrations included mock battles between 300 to 400 men that tended to get out of hand, especially when fueled by drink.

Apparently Ranald was not immune to the drinking problem, even as a protege of the somewhat stern Ermatinger. His father expressed concern in a letter to Edward that his son not fall victim to drink saying, "I fear from what you say of his thoughtless and indolent disposition that Mr. John Clair's store has too many tempting cordials in it to be a fit nursery for the young gents of the far west." And worry he should, because in those days a moderate drinker was deemed to be one who did not exceed four glasses of liquor daily.

Still Ranald was a long way from being in serious trouble over drink; he was too steadfast for that. But he decidedly did not like banking or accounting. Decades later when he was an old man, Ranald told an acquaintance that at the time dealing with money in any way was distasteful to him, that "give us our daily bread," was prayer enough. He expressed the pain of knowing that his father and his family were far beyond the "terrible" mountains of the West, that in spite of the steadfast hospitality of the Ermatingers, he lived in a home which still was not his home. Knowing that it was time, however, for him to cease being a financial burden to his distant father—who had many other sons to educate and feed—he resolved to seek his own fortune. Edward Ermatinger had communicated

Ranald's apparent inattention to business to his brother Francis, still in the Northwest, for Francis' response to Edward was "Why do you trouble yourself about Ranald? If he will not do any good, write to his father to take him back, and while you await the opportunity, put him out to board and make the father pay for it."

A possible military career appealed to Ranald, as he sat daydreaming on his bank accountant's stool. His first choice was further higher education, but there was no college except in Toronto which, at that, had rather sketchy facilities. His father could not afford to send him to England for schooling, but Ranald discussed with Ermatinger the possibility of obtaining a commission in the British Army and going to London, England.

By letter Archibald snorted at this idea, particularly since commissions, too, cost precious money. In his reply to Edward's queries, he said "I fear much the stupid fellow takes no right view of his situation. He is now approaching the age of manhood, and he must be given to understand that I cannot afford to make a gentleman of him, nay, to put him even in the way of gaining a decent livelihood for himself, without the proper exertion on his own part. What in the universe could have put the army in the head of the baby—does he forsooth think I am going to buy a commission for him? Please have the goodness to tell him I am exceedingly displeased at his notions and that the sooner he drops them the better."

Before the spring brigades left Fort Colvile for York Factory, Archibald added to his same letter that he was going to bring Ranald back to Indian country, if he could. He said he had already written Ranald and Governor Simpson, asking the governor about finding suitable employment for Ranald within the Hudson's Bay Company in the West. Until arrangements could be made, Ranald's father admonished Ermatinger to keep an eye upon the youngster.

Governor Simpson did write to the Hudson's Bay Company offices in London. In case Simpson's intercessory letter did not arrive, Archibald sent a similar plea directly to London on a vessel bound for England via Cape Horn.

Before his father's frantic and concerned maneuverings bore fruit, Ranald had taken matters into his own hands. Discouraged by his prospects of obtaining an Army commission, bored with the career chosen for him, and disappointed by an unrequited love for a St. Thomas girl, Ranald conceived the idea of going to faraway Japan to become a teacher. He remembered the stories told him of the castaways at Fort Vancouver, and experienced renewed interest and curiosity about the mysterious land of the Orient, where no Westerner was allowed to enter. He vowed to discover a way to get into the forbidden country. There, he reasoned, he might become a teacher.

Reminiscing years later, Ranald said about his dream of entering Japan, "It was foolish, no doubt! a mad scheme! as the world, in its smug common prudence, gauges such action. Be it so, or not! I did it: Did it—not for, or from any vainglory to myself that might arise from it, but merely that some good to my fellowmen in general might be the result. As to self, for self, in all truth I can sincerely say it was not there: no more so than in the case of many thousands of our race, who in thousands of ways, in peace, as in war, voluntarily breast danger for something good in itself and without hope of reward other than the consciousness of having done well: merit being, in such case, 'its own best reward.' . . . there was no thought of self in the matter. Standing now on the verge of my grave I solemnly say so."

Resolving to move toward his objective, one day in 1842, without advising anyone, Ranald put together a small package of clothing and favorite books and walked away from St. Thomas.

Due to the slow communications by Hudson's Bay Company brigades with Fort Colvile, his distraught father did not learn of Ranald's actions until the fall of 1842 or early in 1843. In a shocked letter to Ermatinger dated March, 1843, he indicated that Ranald had written him from London (believed by some to be London, England, but probably from London, Ontario). He told Ermatinger that "the case of the unfortunate Ranald gave me great pain."

Ranald somehow reached St. Paul, Minnesota, possibly by lake packet or a series of travels from London, Ontario, to Lake Erie or Lake Huron, or overland through Sault Ste. Marie—where Ermatinger had relatives, but this is pure conjecture. At any rate, Ranald later said he shipped onto a "palace" boat at St. Paul bound for New Orleans.

"Palace boat" or "floating palace" was a term often given to the packets that plied the Mississippi and Ohio rivers, sidewheelers that mostly carried passengers. The golden age of steamboats was said to be between the 1840's and 1850's, since the rivers carried almost all the cargo and passengers of the time. In the 1840's steamboat tonnage on the Mississippi alone, exclusive of traffic at New Orleans, was greater than that of all the Atlantic ports combined. Even though the average age of a prime packet between 1823 and 1863 was about five years, due to accidents and explosions, they were splendid vessels for their time.

Many immigrants and young pioneers like Ranald got their first jobs as deckhands on such boats. A "palace" boat had scrollwork on the cornices, brass balls on the cross braces between the stacks, and garish paint on the boxes that protected the paddlewheel. In the main salon a long dining table bisected the area, a stove at each end warming the passengers. Stateroom doors were decorated tastefully with carvings or paintings. The captain presided from a grand pilothouse, using brass-knobbed levers to signal the stokers, and twirling a huge wheel of inlaid wood. Riverboat captains or pilots were legendary, well-paid and colorful figures who virtually had mental blueprints of every nuance of the river's channels. To ease his concentration a steward's helper furnished the pilot, upon command, with coffee, cookies or tarts, served smartly with silver service in the pilothouse heated by a polished stove.

Another kind of palace boat plied the rivers between 1831 and the 1860's—the entertainment boats. Floating theaters or floating circus palaces, they brought live productions to the isolated settlements along the river in a continuous series of one-night stands.

After working his way to New Orleans, Ranald left the palace boat and made his way to New York, where he hoped to sign on with a ship bound for the Orient and thus further his goal of entering Japan. Meantime, a year or so later, Duncan Finlayson and Archibald, still upset by Ranald's precipitate departure the previous year, went to New York to search fruitlessly for him on the busy waterfront.

Not only did Archibald hope to retrieve his wayward son and return him safely to a post with the Hudson's Bay Company in the frontier West, but also he hoped to establish that Ranald was the proper heir (through his mother) to the lands of Comcomly, as the United States and England were negotiating about ownership of Oregon and Washington lands. It was many years later that Ranald learned of this attempt and the possibility of an inheritance from his Indian grandfather, and by then it was too late to make the claim. By the time he returned to Canada in 1853, his father had abandoned the idea long before, believing Ranald to be dead. Newspaper reports published in the Honolulu newspaper, the *Seaman's Gazette*, reported Ranald lost at sea, that the rudder of his small boat had been found, but no trace of Ranald—who was, of course, in Japanese prisons after his feigned shipwreck off Hokkaido.

VI

MacDonald Sails the Seven Seas

Meanwhile, Ranald had reached New York to search for a ship that would hire him, a totally inexperienced sailor. Thinking an unusual appearance might cause a captain to give him an interview, he presented a bizarre figure, dressed in flamboyant rough clothing, a buckskin shirt trimmed with fringe, heavy wool trousers tucked into his fur-trimmed leggings, and a fur cap with an animal tail hanging from it—a veritable Daniel Boone in appearance. Whether it was his unusual garb, or just his stalwart frame, a captain did sign him onto a ship called the *Tuskeny*, bound for London, England.

For about two years Ranald roamed the world as an ordinary seaman, his stints on diverse ships including trips to Calcutta and Africa. Not all ships plying the seven seas dealt in legal cargo, but in those times a seaman did what he was told and asked few questions. Ranald recounted a sailing from Calcutta to Liverpool, England, where the cargo included several kegs of coins. As various foreign ports were visited and cargo discharged, crew members were dismissed and left at several of the same ports, until there were only a few essential men remaining on board. The ship's officers then sailed this ship (the name was not disclosed) toward the California coast to a lonely mooring point where the crew transported the kegs of coins ashore. After the coins and everything of value had been stripped off and taken ashore, the ship was taken to deep water, scuttled and sunk. The officers gave the crew members, including Ranald, their pay and a small bonus, admonishing them to say nothing of this incident or the officers would find them eventually and silence them permanently. The crewmen were directed to find their way from that lonely beach to some California port, where they could find another ship. MacDonald went to San Francisco, readily finding a new berth aboard an outbound ship.

On another occasion, on what appeared to be a standard cargo-carrying voyage, MacDonald found his ship off the coast of Africa, taking on a cargo of African men and women bound for slavery in the United States. Slave ships were somewhat uncommon by mid-century, but the nefarious trade had not entirely ceased. Despite his revulsion at the traffic in human lives, MacDonald was himself a "captive" aboard ship, powerless to affect the outcome of the smuggling. Worse yet, when the ship was chased by a suspicious British man-of-war, the unfeeling captain disposed of his human cargo by putting them overboard. When boarded by the British, the ship showed no evidence of its true intent.

Rejecting such unsavory adventures, Ranald searched out a more reputable ship, sailing in December, 1845, on the *Plymouth*, a whaler out of Sag Harbor, New York, commanded by Captain Lawrence B. Edwards. Life aboard a whaler would be grueling, but it was at least an honest profession. Furthermore, Ranald knew that whalers usually put in at Hawaii, from which he hoped to sign onto some ship bound for whaling in the waters near Japan. He had never relinquished his dream of entering that country and eagerly sought all news about current Japanese conditions.

In 1845, whaling was at its zenith with hundreds of ships in the trade. It was one of the earliest pursuits of New Englanders and, earlier than they, the Indians frequently hunted whales or dragged ashore stranded ones. According to Edouard A. Stackpole in his excellent book on whaling, *The Sea-Hunters,* Captain George Waymouth, an English navigator, said of the Indians in 1605, "they go in company of their king with a multitude of their boats; and strike him with a bone made in fashion of a harping iron fastened to a rope; which they make great and strong of bark of trees, which they veer out after him; then all their boats come about him as he riseth above water, with their arrows they shoot him to death; when they have killed him and dragged him to shore, they call all their chief lords together and sing a song of joy."

Sparking the growth of whaling was the demand for whale oil as a lamp fluid. Initially, Boston dominated the trade, but when settlers moved to Nantucket, a small island eighteen miles south of Cape Cod, it became the chief whaling center for nearly two centuries. (The island belonged to the province of New York from 1660 to 1692, before becoming part of Massachusetts.) At first most whalers plied the waters just offshore, towing captured whales to the beach for butchering and "trying out" or boiling the blubber for oil. As time went by, larger ships were built, crews became more skillful, and, because whales became scarcer offshore, whaling expeditions ranged farther and farther to sea. By the 1700's whaling boats searched the seas up to fifty miles off the coast, and a century later New England whalemen cruised from Arctic waters to the Falkland Islands off Argentina, with a few venturesome captains soon weathering the Cape Horn storms and frightening seas to sail into the South Pacific. Usually these early ships clung to the western shores of South America, going no farther than off the Peruvian coast, a popular whaling ground.

The teeming whale oil industry was caught up in the Revolutionary War, with England endeavoring to cut off and capture rebellious American ships bound for Europe to sell their oil. Indeed, England attempted to re-equip some captured ships under loyal Tory captains to continue to supply English merchants with whale oil. After a turbulent two decades, when American whaling was throttled by wartime conditions, New England ports regained their domination of the world whaling trade. Among them were New Bedford with thirteen whaling vessels, Nantucket with twenty-two, and Sag Harbor with two. By 1809, Nantucket had thirty-nine ships in the whale industry, New Bedford seven, and Sag Harbor six. Within two decades hundreds went a-whaling.

By 1800, in addition to whale oil, far-ranging New England captains were killing seals and sea-elephants, mostly in the extreme southerly lati-tudes, and beginning to trade extensively with China, vying with British ships for that lucrative business. Ships returned to New York and Massa-chusetts with cargos of tea, chinaware, silks, muslins, nankeens, and gin-seng, an herb with many purported medicinal qualities. Inevitably the captains happened upon attractive South Pacific islands, where supplies could be obtained from friendly natives and men could rest ashore from months on a rolling deck.

Again conflict, the War of 1812, disrupted seagoing commerce. Know-ing nothing of any war, ship captains homeward bound into the Atlantic were hailed and boarded by the British, their enemies once more. How-ever, by 1815, it was business as usual.

Eventually about seven hundred vessels sailed from the eastern coast of the United States in search of whales, with sealing and the Chinese trade as a profitable sideline.

By the time Ranald MacDonald was born in 1824, in his remote Columbia River village, whalemen already had explored northward into the Pacific as far as the Hawaiian or Sandwich Islands. Two American ships are credited with being the first whalers to Hawaii: the *Equator*, out of Nantucket under Captain Elisha Folger, and the *Balaena*, out of New Bedford under Captain Edmund Gardner, who met at Honolulu, Oahu Island, on September 29, 1819. During 1819-20, another Nantucket ship, *Maro*, under Captain Joseph Allen, was the first American to enter the whaling grounds "on Japan," as the whalemen termed it. In those waters at the same approximate time, although the two ships did not meet, was the *Syren* out of London, England, but captained by a Nantucket man, Frederick

Coffin. Before long other ships followed, until the Loo-Choo Islands (as sailors called the Ryukyu Islands at the southern tip of Japan) were familiar sights. From there they surged northward along the coasts of Japan into Arctic waters and ranged off today's Alaska and British Columbia, sometimes circling back south along the American coasts.

More typically the route for a whaler was around Cape Horn, then up the coast to Peru and California, from which the navigator set a course for the South Pacific islands, later the Hawaiian or Sandwich Islands, then veering northward, later to return the same way. Part of the routing was governed by the spacing of ports of call where the ships could take on water and supplies before heading off into the broad Pacific. Also the whalers, generally speaking, were following the ocean currents like their prey, the whales.

It was this booming whale oil market, well before the intrusion and destruction of that market by the discovery of electricity or petroleum for lighting, that made it easy for Ranald MacDonald to sign on as a crew member in Sag Harbor. So eager were some ships for crews that they stooped to shanghaiing or kidnapping them from dockside saloons; men would awaken from a drunken stupor or a deep sleep induced by a knockout powder placed in their grog, to find themselves far out to sea.

Ranald's life would be adventurous, but dangerous and often lonely, aboard a whaling vessel. Typical voyages lasted two to three years from time of embarkation in New England. Ranald did not leave a diary of his experiences at sea, and we can only conjecture as to the specifics. However, when twenty-year-old whaleman James F. Munger left New Bedford on the whaler *St. George* in September, 1850, about five years later than Ranald sailed, he kept a remarkably detailed journal of his daily life. From this journal and other writings, we can imagine life aboard the whaling ship *Plymouth*.

The typical whaling ship fitted for a Pacific voyage carried forty barrels of salt beef and pork, three and a half tons of bread, thirty bushels of peas and beans, one thousand pounds of rice, twenty-four barrels of flour, forty gallons of molasses and four hundred barrels of iron hooped casks plus fourteen hundred wooden-hooped casks. About seventeen sailors were aboard, plus the captain, making it possible to put overboard three whale boats to chase down the whales, each carrying five men. Two men were left aboard to care for the mother ship. The ship, with clean bottom, started out making about eight knots; later, with barnacles and sea growths, this speed was reduced to barely six knots. The deck of the whaler had a raised quarterdeck from which the captain and his appointed officers or crewmen ruled and guided the ship. The captain could be a benign dictator (for dictator aboardship he must be) or a tyrant. He was responsible for the welfare of his crew, medically if they were injured or sick, and morally. Since New England captains often came from strong religious backgrounds, some handed out Bibles to their crews and insisted that everyone attend Sunday services on deck.

Infractions of the ship's rules or moral infractions such as theft bore grave repercussions. For theft one captain flogged a young sailor eighteen lashes on his bare back, while he was tied to the rigging by his thumbs. Munger says in his journal, "The captain of a ship has more power than the grand segnior of Turkey, if possible. His word is law in all cases. Many are the poor devils that have been seized up and flogged, or put in irons to subsist on bread and water, for the slightest offences, perhaps a single misspoken word. I would not have you think that this is the character of our officers. Fortunately I have got into a good ship, and with good officers. But there are ships in this harbor [Lahaina] that have treated their crews in a manner that no christian would treat a dog. Numbers are deserting here every day." In fact, tyrannical ship captains permitted their crewmen ashore only under guard, lest they desert.

On a typical ship the tryworks or boilers were set into a brick and mortar support, complete with fireplace and flues. Between the decks aft were the quarters of captain and officers, amidships, the boat-steerers and cooper, and the forecastle or fo'c'sle, the ordinary crewmen. There was nothing luxurious about the accommodations for sailors; each slept below decks with little space to call his own. Crude bunks were arranged in two rows, the area ventilated through a small hatch which usually was closed. Below decks in winter it was frigid and in summer sweltering. The basic diet was salt pork or beef, hard tack and coffee; on some ships the sailors habitually floated their hard tack in the coffee until the maggots climbed out. Vegetables and fruits were obtained at South Seas islands, and turtles taken from the Galapagos Islands to be stored upside down, where they would live for a year or more without food or water. Having sailed on other ships, Ranald had become accustomed to the confinement, a radical change for one raised in the limitless spaces of the wild Pacific Northwest and broad prairies of the Red River settlement. The forecastle seldom was more than twelve feet square, where sixteen or seventeen whalemen had their sleeping space and sea chests. Sitting elbow to elbow during times they were not on watch, in foul weather and fair, these doughty men dreamed of women and fortunes, exotic foods to enliven their dull daily diets, or of wives and children left behind in New England or elsewhere.

There were Negro sailors on New England ships, freemen since the early 1770's. Nantucket whaling families were predominantly Quakers at the time and felt slavery to be unjust. On board the whaleships of Nantucket and New Bedford early in the nineteenth century, Negroes started as ordinary seamen and advanced through the ranks to become officers and masters, like their Caucasian counterparts.

The weather off the eastern coast soon seasoned the new sailors aboard the *Plymouth*, with frequent gales and heaving swells making their watches miserable. Even below, the ship seemed perpetually damp as they sailed southward, watching for whales as they went.

On favorable days the cooper and carpenter were busy on deck plying their trades and, when possible, green sailors practiced reefing and furling. If the seas were calm, boats were lowered for practice at pulling or rowing. Those not on duty might do scrimshaw on whale's tooth or baleen, whalebone, or on shells, wood or walrus tusks.

Not long after leaving port, blackfish were sighted and boats lowered to chase them down. Although they varied considerably, whaleboats tended to be shaped like a pair of opposing parenthesis, some over twenty feet long and about five feet wide. Usually there was a crew of five or six crammed into the boat with harpoons, lances, a lantern, and a keg of emergency gear. Mounted on the prow often was a Greener's gun (developed in Birmingham in the 1840's), a 75-pound gun loaded with a 4-1/2 foot harpoon with a range of 84 yards. It was a muzzle loader fired with double percussion caps struck by a massive hammer. The rowers sat amidships to port and starboard, plus another single oarsman in the bow. In the stern was the officer, manning a long, heavy steering oar. When whales or blackfish were captured, the crew dragged the hulks aboard the ship or lashed them alongside to "try" out the oil and pack it away.

Even at a mere eight knots per hour, the ship sighted the Canary Islands about forty days after leaving New Bedford, putting in at one of the smaller islands for supplies, especially oranges, bananas and coconuts. Sparrows and butterflies hovered about. From time to time the *Plymouth*'s crew sighted other sails and occasionally "spoke." "Speaking" might consist of coming close enough to shout between ships, or, if the weather was calm enough, the two ships tied together and "gam'd" or traded news, broke out a bit of grog, or shared meals together.

Near the equator water spouts sometimes were seen and carefully avoided as they could do damage to a ship (although usually not as vicious as their land cousin, the tornado). Ranald escaped the hijinks attending the crossing of the equator, since he had made that voyage before.

Experienced crew members delighted in dreaming up pranks to play on the newcomers to pacify King Neptune for invading his domains. Among the pranks played on the uninitiated might be that a first-timer was asked to look "through a telescope" at the equator, whereupon he was painted with coal tar, then plunged, face down, into a vat of cold water.

Munger's journal told of Christmas Day off the coast of South America, appearing "more like that of July 4th at home than that of Christmas, and on the whole it reminds me much more of a quiet sabbath upon the shore of our little lake 'Oneida.'" Three days later Munger said: "a large school of sperm whales was descried at a short distance from the ship. The boats were immediately lowered, and the starboard and larboard boats soon fast to two large sperm whales, and fortunate enough to capture both . . . Smyth was knocked out of the boat by the flukes of the whale hitting his oar, and slightly injured." On December 30th, a strong wind arose, threatening to tear away the whale tied alongside, but Munger said: "were about to abandon it, when luckily the ship came up and succeeded in securing the prize. Our boat's crew were completely chilled through, having been constantly wet . . . we were obliged to keep almost continually at work bailing the boat, on account of the heavy sea which occasionally came over the side." There was no rest for Munger and his fellow crewmen, for two days later he said they were "in the blubber up to our chins . . . I must say that this is not the most agreeable part of whaling."

According to Georges Blond in his book *The Great Story of Whales*, as soon as a whale was fought to its death, the carcass was fastened alongside for towing back to the mother ship. There a hole was bored in its tough, compact, fatty surface, to which a block and tackle was secured to lift the carcass and fasten it to one of the masts. Then a kind of wooden balcony was fashioned to jut out beyond the ship's railing about nine feet. A few men then stood on this platform to butcher the animal with long-handled knives, passing the flesh and blubber into furnaces for melting down into oil. Blond said, "the weary men flounder about barefooted in fat and blood, with that sickening reek in their nostrils."

In a later note diarist Munger reported that the larboard boat took a whale that produced 120 barrels of oil. However, "he gave us a little trouble . . . He came up under the boat, and at one time had his jaw on one side of the boat, and 'junk' on the other. If he had closed his jaw, the boat would never have been seen again, except in splinters."

Ranald and his fellow crewmen undoubtedly had similar adventures, as they took whales on their southward voyage toward the Falklands and Cape Horn. Lying three hundred miles east of Argentina, the Falklands had become a favorite resupplying station and safe harbor for whalers, since John Davis first put in there in 1592. Port Egmont on Saunders, a small island off West Falkland, was the most favored anchorage. After an abortive attempt at colonization by the French in 1764, these islands had come into the possession of Spain in 1766. In 1771, England took over the Falklands through a convention agreement with Spain, but the whalers and sealers had used the remote islands for reprovisioning long before any settlers came.

The Strait of Magellan, a more benign but complex passage into the South Pacific Ocean, was less known than the rugged waters of Cape Horn, at South America's land's end. Winds, giant swells and storms often marked the turbulent passage from Atlantic to Pacific. Accounts by sailors tell of being beaten back for days, even weeks, on the westbound reaches especially.

Once attained, the Pacific proved to be a fruitful hunting ground for whales. The Society Islands or Marquesas and, farther north, the Sandwich Islands became popular provisioning and socializing points. The chief ports were Lahaina on Maui, Honolulu on Oahu, Kealakekua Bay (where Captain Cook was killed) on the west side of Hawaii, and Hilo town on the east. After the arrival of missionaries in Hilo, it was not as popular a port with seamen because of the lack of liquor and women, but the *captains* liked it for the same reason and sometimes would live ashore with reverends Titus and Coan, the fervent Hilo missionaries. Between 1852 and 1857, an average of sixty-five whaling vessels a year came to Hilo, a boon for the economy in supplying the ships, but not so much for the expenditures on recreation.

After a brisk passage from the Peruvian coast to Hawaii, taking advantage of the northeast trade winds and taking any whales that appeared, the *Plymouth* hove to in Lahaina harbor, Maui, early in 1848. There Ranald left the ship, having fulfilled his contract to sail only that distance.

Ranald said, "The place was of special interest to me, as during my life in the Columbia our [Hudson's Bay Company] trade relations with the Islands were very intimate, and many of the men in the Hudson's Bay Company's service, as boatmen (and excellent they were) were from there."

Indeed, this was true. Ever since whaling and trading ships had called at the Sandwich Islands, Kanakas (as native Hawaiians were termed then) signed on as crew members, making two- and three-year voyages before returning to their homes—just as New England seamen made similar round trips. According to Archibald Campbell, in *A Voyage around The World*, King Kamehameha encouraged his subjects to make voyages in the ships that touched Hawaiian shores. Since they were, by nature, seafaring men, they adapted to western ways and became excellent sailors. During Archibald McDonald's management of Fort Langley, British Columbia, where Ranald had lived as a small boy, tons of dried salmon were shipped to the residents of the Sandwich or Hawaiian Islands. Inevitably Hawaiian sailors left their ships in British Columbia and other ports to explore new lands. In the Pacific Northwest it was not uncommon for Hawaiians to work at diverse shoreside jobs, some marrying the daughters of Indians or settlers. During the early settlement of the American Northwest, there were large numbers of Hawaiians working as sheepherders on San Juan Island.

As Ranald related in his memoirs, Hawaiian crewmen also appeared on the decks of the earliest ships to enter the Columbia River and trade at Astoria or Fort Vancouver. In Oregon, Owyhee County, Owyhee River, and the Owyhee Mountains commemorate those Hawaiians who became Hudson's Bay brigade members.

Of course, there is no way of knowing whether Ranald actually encountered any ex-employee of the Hudson's Bay Company or his relatives in the port of Lahaina, but he did feel the bond of kinship, remembering the young men he met as a son of the Hudson's Bay factor Archibald McDonald.

VII

Whaling on Japan

After a few days of shore leave in Lahaina, Ranald made a short cruise through the various islands on another ship. Uppermost in his mind was finding a ship bound for the whaling grounds "on Japan." Ranald believed his old ship, the *Plymouth*, had departed for other ports but, to his surprise and pleasure, found the ship back in Lahaina for repairs. Sustaining some damages, it had limped into Kealakekua Bay on the southwestern shore of Hawaii Island, and on into Lahaina. Learning that the *Plymouth* now planned to whale "on Japan" after repairs were completed, Ranald appealed to Edwards for a berth aboard on the condition that he could leave the ship off the coast of Japan. As a further condition, he requested instruction from Captain Edwards in use of Hadley's quadrant and the nautical almanac in determining longitude and latitude. Although Edwards privately thought Ranald's dream of no substance, he badly needed another crewman and agreed to MacDonald's conditions of employment.

In company with another Nantucket whaler, *David Paddock*, the *Plymouth* set sail for Hong Kong. The course would take the ship through the Ladrones Islands, later called the Mariannas, of which Guam is a part. En route there, the ship narrowly escaped destruction near a previously unknown shoal, the French or Frigate Shoals. A screaming gale arose, blowing out the *Plymouth's* mainsail and several of the fore and aft sails, and, before new sails could be bent, the ship drifted perilously close to the shoals. At Guam (which Ranald called Gregan Island) MacDonald was chosen to go ashore with the captain to search for wood and fresh water. It was believed that the island was uninhabited, but Ranald said:

"The Island was fringed with cocoa nut trees near the beach. On landing we discovered—Robinson Crusoe like—human foot prints on the sand . . . On ascending the beach we saw a naked man dodging from tree to tree. By following him we came to a clearing, with a yard, and three or four thatched cottages, and eight other men, with several women, and a few children. Before arriving at the place, we were met by the mysterious dodger; but now in full dress, wearing a shirt—just a shirt—nothing more! He introduced himself as 'Liverpool Jack.' He told us that there was another white man, living about a mile north of him, named by him 'Spider Jack,' living with a sickly wife. He gave me to understand that they had a falling out about a child they both claimed."

It was not unusual for deserters or those lost from shipwrecked whalers and trading ships to settle on remote islands, e. g., the famous tale of the mutineers from the ship *Bounty*. As the two white fugitives on Guam were questioned, their strange and sordid stories emerged. Spider Jack had been on the island almost twenty years, and Liverpool Jack five years less. Liverpool Jack's background was unclear, but apparently Spider Jack had been deposited on the island by a whaler, *Peruvian*, out of New London, Connecticut, after the whale ship had plucked Jack and twenty other survivors of an undisclosed disaster from a large canoe. They were put ashore on the island of Guam, together with pigs and chickens to sustain them. The two Jacks told of intra-colony strife, murders and mistrust, and of the colony being much larger in the past. Edwards and his crew viewed the wild-looking castaways as unsavory at best and possibly dangerous, maintaining considerable caution around them.

Spider Jack persuaded one crew member to visit his hut, where he freely showed the man a horde of silver dollars, explaining that at one time, during a South American revolution, a party of wealthy people placed money and valuables aboard a ship and fled the country. At some point in the Pacific a group of pirates took them over and set course for the Mariannas or Ladrones, where they buried this treasure, intending to return later for it.

In time, all the thieves vanished or were murdered and the one remaining man came ashore at Manila in the Philippine Islands, telling the story of buried treasure to the authorities. The "Jacks" said that the Philippine government sent a warship to investigate but, just when they were disembarking, the one man who knew the location of the treasure was killed, accidentally falling between the shore boat and ship, leaving the location of the treasure forever a mystery. Jack was vague about exactly where he had found the cache of coins.

After provisioning, leaving the enigma to history, the ship sailed westward to the groups of islands that sprawl, almost continuously, from the Philippine Islands to Japan. They landed on the Batan Islands, a small group separating the China Sea from the Pacific, for supplies. Thereafter they successfully hunted sperm whales north of the islands, even though heavy gales lashed the ship. Eventually the ship veered west for Hong Kong, staying in port for a month, refitting and supplying for the cruise "on Japan."

The picturesque, capacious port was a combination of the old and new, a well-established Chinese culture amid a frontier-like British architecture. The settlement had a long history. Five thousand years ago, Hong Kong's earliest visitors left graffiti still visible on rocks in Big Wave Bay on Hong Kong Island. People from the Han, Tang and Sung dynasties all left their influences on the small collection of islands, known today as Hong Kong. Until 1757, the Chinese restricted all foreigners to Macau, a small peninsula (five and a half kilometers square) claimed by Portugal, forty miles across the muddy Pearl River from Hong Kong, and bordered on the north by China. There along narrow, twisting streets of cobblestones brought from Portugal as ballast for early Portuguese ships, the traders built warehouses and factories and missionaries tried to convert the natives to Catholicism. Since the Ming dynasty forbade Chinese citizens to trade directly with Japan at the time, Macau and the Portuguese became middlemen for a lucrative trade between the two. This was before the rule of the Shogunate and the expulsion of overzealous missionaries from Japan.

Ambitious Dutch and British traders quickly stepped into the vacuum—"taipans" who established huge enterprises for the Orient trade. Such traders (but not their families) were permitted to live for eight months of each year outside Canton, China, and in a highly restricted small zone of Hong Kong. All commerce was handled through a monopoly of government-authorized merchants called the *Co-hong*.

Chinese ports and Portuguese Macau soon developed a roaring business with Europeans, chiefly the British, trading opium for goods. When the imperial Chinese government tried to end the trafficking, Britain and China went to war over the right to trade in opium, although other factors were involved—chiefly the objection by foreigners to be held accountable to Chinese judges for infractions of Chinese law. After two years, hostilities with the Chinese ceased. In 1841, through the Treaty of Chuenpi, reconfirmed by the Treaty of Nanking in 1842, China ceded Hong Kong Island to the British. Traders lost no time in moving from Macau to select sites for homes and warehouses. By midsummer, 1841, temporary European homes, often covered with mere palm leaves, were in place as well as rough warehouses called "go-downs." Military men installed gun emplacements and camps at strategic points.

Therefore, when MacDonald came to Hong Kong on the *Plymouth*, the British had controlled the island for seven years. There were three main land masses: Victoria Island, Kowloon, and the somewhat rural New Territories. Most of the British lived in increasingly substantial homes on Victoria Island, a mountainous land standing between the harbor and the

South China Sea, its soaring peaks forming a bulwark that created calm waters for the inlets and harbors between Victoria and Kowloon.

It was an exciting place: the cries of Chinese hawking their wares and pulling rickshaws, or man-drawn carts—the junks of all sizes and descriptions crowding the harbors and sailing up and down—the ships from many foreign nations anchored in the harbor, as few docks were available. Lighters scurried back and forth to load or unload the ships. Chinese women with babies strapped to their backs cooked aboard the junks, permanent homes to thousands of Chinese families. Coastal junks carried opium, cotton shirtings, woolen goods, spices and nuts, rattan for furniture, etc. From the cavernous mouths of some shops or taverns the cloying odor of opium wafted into the street. Sailors of many nations and colors weaved out of dockside bistros after quenching their thirsts—mighty thirsts from months at sea—or made their arrangements with women of easy virtue. The homes of wealthy Chinese merchants and government officials decorated the hillsides of the rugged island domain, their distinctive roof lines and archways harmonizing with Buddhist pagodas, impressive structures often, and temples diligently frequented by the Chinese believers. The British had erected hospitals and private club buildings, adding a few carriage roads around the settlements. Schools had been organized, even the Anglo-Chinese College of the London Mission and St. Paul's College.

Crewmen hated to leave the lively port, but the *Plymouth* finally weighed anchor and sailed out to sea, heading easterly until the lovely peaks of Victoria Island disappeared over the horizon. As the ship left Hong Kong, an extra watch was posted on the ship, because pirates infested the coastal waters—mostly Asian, but often joined by lawless European sailors in search of quick booty. The British Colony of Hong Kong had to maintain a gunboat to patrol the outer reaches of the shipping lanes into the China Sea around Hong Kong, Macau and Canton.

After several days the ship put in at Batan once more to obtain fresh vegetables for the voyage north, but it was too early in spring. Instead, the captain gave the natives some seed potatoes, beans and Indian corn, the latter of a larger variety than the local one, hoping that future voyages could be supplied.

Continuing north, the ship wound its way through the Ryukyu Islands that string out southward from the coast of Japan like a green necklace. For a week or more the *Plymouth* sought whales near Quelpert Island, about sixty miles off Korea, but did not land. Whaling was good but about March 1, Captain Edwards decided to move north into the Japan Sea, capturing whales successfully for the next three months. The whales were so numerous that seldom was it necessary to chase down the whale pod with the big ship; instead, the crew had only to lower skiffs to harpoon an individual, bringing it alongside the ship for processing. In June off the northwest coast of Hokkaido, Ranald sighted twenty-five to thirty whaling ships at work.

The ship was almost full of stored oil; the captain talked of returning to Sag Harbor. Ranald's time for departure was at hand. The captain, who really had not believed that Ranald would leave, made good his bargain and provided the requested boat and supplies—a box of books and stationery, a few clothes, a quadrant for navigation, two pistols, two small kegs of water, a barrel of bread, anchor, 35 fathoms of tow line, oars and miscellaneous items. In turn, Ranald assigned to the captain his share of the whaling venture, estimated to be about six hundred dollars, a considerable sum that Ranald would never recover in later years. Ranald also gave to Captain Edwards a letter to his father Archibald, which apparently never reached him.

The obsession with Japan that had begun as a child's curiosity about events that had occurred at Fort Vancouver, Washington, was about to lead Ranald into an adventure affecting the world's international relationships. But he could not know that. All he knew was that he must satisfy his intense curiosity about this land. He had read extensively about the secrecy surrounding the Japanese empire, about the unwillingness of the nation to permit its very own citizens to return home if they contacted Western civilizations through shipwreck—in fact, he had read everything he was able to find about Japan during the past few years. In a letter given to Captain Edwards to be mailed to his father, Ranald wrote, "He has tried to pursuade me to give up the adventure, but I am going." He set sail that fateful day into a very dangerous world.

For more than two hundred years Japan had been under the rule of powerful and ruthless Shoguns, members of the Tokugawa family, a rule that commenced with the holders of lands around Matsudaira. Since the early 1400's the family of Ieyasu Tokugawa, who came to the head of his family in 1566, had aggressively accumulated lands nearby until Ieyasu was able to seek successfully the title of Shogun in the early seventeenth century. He exerted the domination of his family and its vassals over a large part of Japan, the three great islands of Honshu, Kyushu and Shikoku, as well as smaller land areas.

The imperial court under an Emperor originally had traditional authority over all Japan, with practical control seized by military lords in the 11th and 12th centuries. As E. H. Norman stated in his *Origins of the Modern Japanese State*, political domination of the Emperor's court by some great family was not new, but the Shogunate implied a distinctly separate seat of government, with the Emperor and his court shorn of all actual power. Yoritomo Minamoto in 1192 was the first to be appointed by the Emperor *seii taishōgun* or "barbarian-subduing generalissimo," the highest possible military title. Interim political rulers had not sought the prestigious title, but Ieyasu coveted it and consolidated the title's immense powers.

With considerable diplomacy he assigned lands to the Emperor and aristocratic followers, giving them a newfound wealth (since the Emperor did not necessarily enjoy great land ownership). Cleverly Ieyasu ingratiated himself with the Emperor, while effectively immobilizing the Emperor's authority over anything but religious and ceremonial affairs.

Those lords who sided with Ieyasu from the beginning were the *fudai daimyo,* often related to the Tokugawa family, enjoying special favors in the pretentious court at Edo or Tokyo. Many were given large estates and homes in Edo. It is said that there were 176 liege vassals. Eighty-six *tozama* or outside daimyo, owners of their own lands, were more or less loyal to the Tokugawas out of necessity but did not operate directly under the Shogunate at Edo.

The Tokugawas now proceeded to set up possibly the tightest control over a people ever witnessed in the world. All society was frozen into a rigid mold. Every social class and sub-class had special regulations pertaining to clothing, ceremonies, and behavior. For example, lowest on the social scale (of lower status than peasants, who were considered little better than horses or cattle) were the merchants or *chonin,* regarded as unproductive and shifty. Merchants could not live in the samurai district, and their style of clothing, foot gear, umbrellas and other tiniest details were prescribed by law.

To reduce the possibility of outside daimyos cooperating in any scheme to overthrow the regime, these lords were not allowed to retain large police forces or armies, their travels were restricted and reported upon, and the eight great highways of Japan were watched closely. Daimyo were forbidden to have foreign contacts, with two exceptions: the Sō daimyo of Tsushima were allowed to trade with Korea, and the Shimazu, lords in southern Kyushu, were permitted to carry on limited trade with the Chinese in the Ryukyu Islands. Edo even had to be consulted in marriage plans and castle construction. Finally, the daimyo were required to spend alternate years in Edo, leaving their families in the city while they returned to manage their own lands, a tacit hostage system.

Secrecy was paramount in all things. For a time translations of foreign books were banned, but the Shogun Yoshimune (1716-1744) removed this restriction for limited numbers of scholars and politicians, since the

Bakufu (Shogunate council) needed to monitor happenings in the outside world affecting Japan. When important men or groups passed through the countryside, the common people were supposed to stay inside. Curtains to cover windows of homes along city streets were draped like colorful banners to insure secrecy. (However, one may well imagine that the people found cracks or holes to survey the outside curiosities.) Preoccupation with closing out the foreign world deepened.

Like a flower that bloomed, then faded into obscurity, Japan became a mysterious place. During the time of Nobunaga Oda and Hideyoshi Toyotomi's power, even earlier than Tokugawa, foreign powers had "found" Japan, at first quite by accident.

It all began, really, with Marco Polo, who returned with vivid if inaccurate accounts of the palaces of gold in Japan, spurring others to search for "El Dorado." Vasco da Gama's voyage around the Cape of Good Hope into the Indian Ocean in 1497 further encouraged interest until the Portuguese were trading in Java, Borneo, Malacca and elsewhere from 1541 to 1641 and afterward. In 1493, the Pope had issued a Bull of Demarcation dividing the entire world into two spheres, the Spanish and Portuguese. Balboa, Magellan, Cortez in Mexico, Pizarro in Peru, and permanent settlers in the Philippines followed.

Meanwhile, the Portuguese, after the accession of Pope John III in 1521, started a systematic missionary movement to the Far East, including inquisitions in countries that clung to their own idols. In 1540, the Society of Jesus was formed and, in 1549, Jesuit Francis Xavier arrived in Japan, well received by the local daimyo, who saw the new religion as a bulwark against the troublesome power of the entrenched Buddhists. After only thirty years there were fifty Jesuit missionaries, two hundred churches, and 150,000 Christian converts, chiefly in southern Japan. An unnamed Kyushu daimyo sent a good will mission to the Pope, the first embassy ever sent by the Japanese to the Occident, even though it was not a political but a religious one.

On the military level, shipwrecked sailors washed ashore on the island of Tanegashima in 1542 were welcomed cordially by the residents. From these sailors the local daimyo received firearms and were instructed in the art of manufacturing guns and gunpowder. By 1555, the Japanese had successfully manufactured many guns, but niter, a component of gunpowder, had to be imported as it did not exist in Japan; nor did lead, an element of cannon balls. Therefore, trade in these and other items began.

Hideyoshi began to have second thoughts about the Portuguese combination of trade and religion, however, when Portuguese merchants forced the local daimyo to pledge the revenues of the city of Nagasaki as security for a loan they made to him. The merchants also began to make arrogant statements about administering the city; if denied a voice in government, they said, they would cease trading.

Complicating matters were the Spanish Franciscan fathers, who came in 1592. The Japanese became confused as to divisions in this religion of the Kirishitans. Furthermore, while the Jesuits tended to work among the ruling classes, the Franciscans tended to work among the lower classes. This displeased the lords.

Then in 1596, when Japanese officials confiscated the cargo of a Spanish galleon, *San Felipe*, a crew member boasted that Spain would soon "get even," that Spain sent out missionaries and traders to new lands followed by troops, who then conquered the countries. Although the chance mouthings of an underling, these thoughts had already occurred to Hideyoshi. He brooded.

Still more pressures arose. In 1600, the Dutch ship *de Liefde* blew off course and anchored off the coast of Bungo in northeast Kyushu, where Dutch sailors, many sick to the point of death, came ashore. The Japanese were distraught at the "invasion" but treated them kindly, although six men died anyway. Among the crew was Will Adams, the English pilot sailing on a Dutch ship. Learning of Adams and eager for knowledge about navigation, the Shogun himself sent for Adams, eventually retaining him as his own servant. Adams' grave is a revered place today on Hirado Island.

The Dutch returned in 1609 to ask about trade, setting up a trading factory or settlement on Hirado Island at the southeast corner of Kyushu, the ancient domain of the Matsuura daimyo. Two years later the English came to set up trade, too, as the English East India Company. However, intense competition and preoccupation with other world affairs led the English to abandon their trade by 1624.

Throughout this tumultuous ingress by Europeans into a country previously unfamiliar with the western world, Hideyoshi groped for a way to control these Kirishitans, the Portuguese. In 1587, he issued a decree prohibiting dissemination of Christianity but did not enforce it too strongly.

Following Hideyoshi to power, Ieyasu bided his time about Christianity, welcoming foreign trade at first, even with Mexico via Manila, a stronghold for the Spanish. Beginning in 1603, Spanish ships called at Uraga (on Edo Bay) each year, and Ieyasu sent a personal envoy to Philip III of Spain in 1610. The Spanish became too bold. In 1611, Sebastian Viscaino, an envoy from the viceroy of New Spain came to Japan, securing permission from the Shogunate to survey the northeastern islands of Japan.

His real purpose was to search for the fabled "El Dorado" of silver. When the Shogun's spy system revealed this, the Spaniard was sent home in 1613.

Worrying now about the possibility of the Portuguese and southern daimyo (particularly the influential Satsumas) mounting a challenge to Tokugawa rule, in 1609 the Bakufu, or Edo government, placed a ban on possession of any large ships by daimyo and ordered the destruction of large ships they already possessed. In 1611, the Dutch (whom the Shogun tended to trust because they seemed to have no ties with the Kirishitans, the Catholics) told the Shogun that there was, indeed, a plot among the powerful southern daimyo to overthrow him. Ieyasu promptly responded by issuing a decree banning Christianity in 1612, ordering converts to renounce their faith under pain of death. By 1639, all Europeans except the Dutch, who did not press their Protestant faith, had been expelled from Japan. The Dutch were moved to the islet of Deshima in Nagasaki Harbor, where they continued to trade on a strictly regulated basis for the next 214 years.

In 1616 foreign vessels were barred from trading in ports of the *tozama*, the outside daimyo, but enterprising traders merely leased Chinese ships, leading to further oppression by Edo. By 1635, the seclusion system of Tokugawa Japan was nearly complete; in 1636, the Portuguese were ordered to move operations onto Deshima Island, Nagasaki Bay. As indicated above, even that was insufficient for Edo—and they were expelled, one and all, in 1639.

As the long years of seclusion ensued, the Bakufu was able to invent new ways of closeting its subjects from the outside world. Authorities perfected the *gonin-gumi* system, a group of five people. This basic administrative unit was responsible for its individual members, for tax collection, and reporting on unusual movements. Misdeeds of any one of them meant punishment for all five. It kept the people in a state of mutual suspicion, rendering impractical any joint action against authorities. Peasants were ruthlessly exploited and thought to be unable to even comprehend normal human emotions.

The feudal rulers deliberately sowed hatred and fear of the West in order to make the lower classes forget their miseries and to more easily control the populace through such fear. Among a collection of Tokugawa edicts and prohibitions is written: "We must make our people hate the foreigner and the foreigner hate us." Western "barbarians" were painted in the most lurid terms as fearsome beings. Yet the people were warned about the treachery of barbarians, "Foreigners are by nature clever at winning over the people." During the latter part of the Tokugawa regime contempt for all things foreign and superiority of all things Japanese permeated every facet of life.

Despite these chilling attitudes, the authorities continued to learn about the outside world through the Dutch, who were required to make at least one trip a year to Edo to report to the Shogunate. The trade goods and armaments handled by the Dutch were essential, as well, so the Dutch were tolerated at their prison-like but profitable enterprise at Deshima. The Chinese, also, were afforded very limited space and trading privileges in Nagasaki, the window to the world.

Ignoring the official sowings of discord and hate, some Japanese did not appear to believe the Bakufu and were not at all unfriendly to foreigners. Influencing some thoughtful and courageous Japanese to speak out publicly were the experiences of fishermen rescued at sea by American whalers near the turn of the nineteenth century. These waifs were treated kindly, not at all what they expected of the barbarians. Chishin Matsuura (1770-1841) of Hirado, known for his liberal views and sympathy for the hated Christianity, wrote in a book, *Kasshi Yawa*, according to the writings of E. H. Norman, "Foreign sealers treat Japanese mariners well and without meanness. They most kindly received us who had suffered from wind and rain on the high seas or who had endured cruel cold and excessive heat or were ill and without medicine so that both strength and spirit were failing. These foreign sailors in no way hurt our fishing as they are only interested in hunting. For what reason does our government treat foreigners as enemies?"

Other Japanese scholars of Dutch learning, the only Western learning available, stubbornly persisted, sometimes paying with their lives for their desire for knowledge of the outside world. Among these vocal scholars were Shozan Sakuma, Kazan Watanabe, Choei Takano, and Shoin Yoshida, who wanted to apply Western knowledge to solve desperate Japanese problems.

After more than a century and a half of seclusion, European ships began to appear off Japan's shores, alarming the Bakufu once more. Off Yezo (Hokkaido) and the Straits of Soya, Russian ships, including that of Golownin in 1811, appeared on explorations and surveys. In 1791, six whalers, five from Nantucket and one from New Bedford, skirted Cape Horn and went into the Pacific, with penetration of Japanese waters not far behind. Two British ships, *Charlotte* and *Maria*, sailed into Nagasaki harbor in 1813, but left again; possibly they came to survey their chances of replacing the Dutch as traders with the Japanese.

Inevitably whalers attempted to put into shore for supplies or were shipwrecked. On May 28, 1824, two whalers came ashore at Mito, northeast of

Edo, to obtain vegetables and fruits, since crewmen were suffering from scurvy. Local police promptly arrested them, holding them until a representative from the Bakufu could advise what to do. Upon learning of their purpose, the whalers were given provisions and released.

Two months later an English whaler landed on Tokara Island in the Ryukyus to barter for oxen and vegetables. When frightened villagers refused, the sailors took the oxen by force, leaving behind a dead sailor, shot by a villager. The man was pickled in salt and delivered to the authorities at Nagasaki.

Feeling the pressures of so many foreign intrusions, the Bakufu issued on February 15, 1825, its exclusion edict, or *Uchi-harai-Rei*:

> As to the mode of proceeding on the arrival of foreign vessels many proclamations have formerly been issued, and one was expressly issued in 1806 with respect to Russian ships. Also several years ago an English vessel committed outrages at Nagasaki (the *Phaeton*, in 1808) and in later years the English have visited the various ports in boats, demanding fire-wood, water and provisions. In the past year, they landed forcibly, and seized rice and grain in the junks and cattle on the islands. The continuation of such insolent proceedings, as also the intention of introducing the Christian religion having come to our knowledge, it is impossible to look on with indifference. Not only England, but also the Southern Barbarians and Western Countries are of the Christian religion which is prohibited among us. Therefore, if in future foreign vessels should come near any port whatsoever, the local inhabitants shall conjointly drive them away; but should they go away (peaceably) it is not necessary to pursue them. Should any foreigners land anywhere, they must be arrested or killed, and if the ship approaches the shore it must be destroyed. (From Murdoch's *History of Japan*)

Thereafter the Bakufu launched the most violent anti-foreign agitation. Four years after the edict, an English ship filled with mutineers, convicts bound for Australia who had taken over the ship, approached Japan and was greeted by shell fire.

But the despotic Tokugawa rule was beginning to fracture under the frantic demands of maintaining seclusion from outside forces, and from the ravages of unprecedented natural disasters from 1833 to 1837—earthquakes, floods, and fire, all followed inevitably by famines of gargantuan proportions. In 1837, hundreds of corpses lay unburied in the streets of Nagoya. The peasants revolted out of hunger in the rice riots of *uchi-kowashi*, often led by lower-class samurai, themselves with few rights, who gradually were aligning with forces bent on overthrowing the Shogunate. In Osaka unrest during 1837 was associated with Heihachiro Oshio, who felt that more individualistic and democratic policies might help to cure the desperate poverty of his fellow Japanese. Although his coup was smashed, other uprisings in the name of "Oshio's disciples" occurred in other cities. Highwaymen infested the roads, so that travelers hired bodyguards. The merchants, always without rights under Tokugawa, conspired with the great *tozama* daimyo, the families of Satsuma, Choshu, Tosa and Hizen, who were tempted by the possibility of overthrowing the Tokugawa. Not that these factions favored foreigners, either; rather the political schism seemed to be over how to deal with the foreign threat. Many now felt the Tokugawa Shogunate was failing its responsibilities.

Abroad the move was westward, ever westward, in the United States— all the way to the Pacific Coast, to the Northwest, to California and beyond. When Caleb Cushing successfully negotiated a treaty with China in 1844, American missionaries and merchants working there urged a treaty attempt with Japan. After much deliberation, Secretary of State John C. Calhoun, in consultation with President Polk, sent word to Cushing that he should proceed—but Cushing was already en route home from China.

Through its Dutch traders Japan learned of the Opium War, the defeat of China by the British, and the cession of Hong Kong in 1841. Bakufu officials also were influenced by the moderate leanings of their own philosopher, Chōei Takano, who urged modest foreign cooperation. The Bakufu began to wonder if total antagonism toward England and America was really wise. In 1842, the following decree, modifying the 1825 edict, was distributed:

> In accordance with the ordinance of 1825, all foreign vessels must be driven away. But now that the administration has reverted to the principles of the Kyōhō-Kwansei periods, it is the Shogun's gracious will that all measures should be taken in a humane spirit.
>
> It is not thought fitting to drive away all foreign ships irrespective of their condition, in spite of their lack of supplies, or of their having stranded, or their suffering from stress of weather. In accordance with the ordinance of 1806, after investigating the circumstances of each case, you should, when necessary, supply them with food and fuel and advise them to return, but on no account allow foreigners to land.
>
> This does not mean that less attention is to be paid to coast defence. Still greater care must be taken than before, both as regards armament and men. Even in case vessels sail along the coast to observe the situation, you must still act in accordance with the gracious principles of humanity, not being unreasonably disturbed by their proceedings. If, however, after receiving supplies and instructions they do not withdraw, you will, of course, drive them away, adopting such measures as are necessary.
>
> As regards coast defence, other instructions will be issued. (From Murdoch's *History of Japan*)

The following year, because of concern over expansion by the English, the Netherlands sent an envoy to meet with the Bakufu officially, assuming that, because of the Deshima relationship, they would be received. They were not; only a minor officer received the official envoy at

Nagasaki. Meanwhile, the Bakufu had extended its censorship upon Dutch books, scholars and communications—to no avail.

The Americans were at work. Alexander H. Everett, the first appointed commissioner to China after the Cushing Treaty, left for China in June, 1845, with orders to attempt a treaty negotiation with Japan; but he became ill and returned to the USA, rescheduling his voyage to China in October, 1846. Earlier, in July, 1846, Commodore James Biddle, at the request of Everett, arrived at Uraga with two of the feared "black ships," the *Columbus* and *Vincennes*. The Japanese would not speak with him until he dismantled the guns and weapons aboard, which Biddle refused to do. Biddle's efforts to talk with even minor officials were repulsed rudely, so Biddle had no choice but to depart.

In June, 1848, eighteen deserters (including six Hawaiians) from the whaler *Lagoda* landed near Matsumae on Yezo Island (Hokkaido), only to be imprisoned promptly by the Japanese and held for several months— indeed, until April 26, 1849, when survivors were surrendered for repatriation to the *Preble*. By then at least one had died of natural causes, and a despondent Hawaiian committed suicide.

THIS was the world Ranald MacDonald faced as he cast loose his little boat on the waters off Yezo. He had asserted earlier that he knew of the risks he was taking, but intended to take with equanimity whatever fate dealt him.

VIII
Ainu Capture MacDonald

Adrift on the Japan Sea Ranald found tears streaming down his face as he watched the *Plymouth* disappear from sight. He remarked later, "A sailor's feelings are ever warm and true. The companionship of peril forges a masonic bond stronger than the tinsel chain of mere worldly interest. Life for life is the motto of his comrade heart. 'Happy to meet; sorry to part,' is ever truth with him. I sorrowed for their sorrow, expected not to meet them again!"

The captain had given Ranald a bearing for the nearest island, about five miles northeast. On a map compiled from MacDonald's rough sketch later in the century, the island was just south of Yageshiri Island. When it loomed up out of the fog, Ranald was alarmed by the heavy, breaking surf on the rough shore, so he set sail for Yageshiri Island, putting in safely at a small bay. He theorized that he should let the *Plymouth* get well away from the Japan shore if he were to make good his story about deserting and shipwreck; hence he spent three days on Yageshiri, sleeping in the decked-over portion of his skiff at night, exploring by day. The island was home to countless roaring sea lions, about twelve feet in length and weighing as much as a half ton. Climbing a hill, he found the island to be about five miles in circumference and was able to make out another island to the north, one with a snowcapped mountain rising from the center of the land, a volcanic cone. That would be his destination—Rishiri Island off the northwestern shore of Yezo.

On the last day before his departure from Yageshiri, Ranald unloaded his boat and took it into the bay to practice capsizing and righting. During this exercise, he managed to lose the rudder. Within a few days the ship *Uncas* out of Massachusetts picked up the rudder, somehow identifying it as that of MacDonald. From this evidence the Honolulu newspaper, *Seaman's Friend*, wrote an article conjecturing that MacDonald was undoubtedly dead, victim of a real shipwreck in the Japan Sea. The account was related to Archibald McDonald, who mourned his son unnecessarily.

For Ranald was very much alive. On July 1, 1848, Ranald set off for Rishiri Island. During the day he accidentally fell overboard, and his presumed death almost became a reality, as the sails were set and the boat kept moving. With great difficulty Ranald caught his sailboat and clambered aboard, but his chest, pitched out by a wave during this incident, was floating. Carelessly Ranald had not locked it, and his compass was lost to the sea and the other materials dampened. Rishiri Island loomed larger but, with night coming on, Ranald stood offshore until morning, fearing that he could crash onto the rocky shore. He saw flocks of birds flying offshore, some as far as his skiff. At dawn on July 2, Ranald saw smoke on the island and men launching a rather large skiff.

As soon as Ranald determined that the islanders really were coming his way, he partly pulled the drain plug on his small boat, replacing it when the boat was half-filled, thus hoping to substantiate his planned story, and to elicit the islanders' sympathies for his plight. Waving mightily, Ranald hailed the oncoming rescuers.

About a hundred yards away the rowers hove to and saluted Ranald in a peculiar manner, rubbing their hands together, drawing back first one and then the other so the points of the fingers gently touched the palm of each hand. Then each of the four stalwart, hairy men bowed and stroked his luxuriant beard while making a rumbling sound in his throat. Not knowing this was a proper Ainu greeting, Ranald shouted cheerfully, "How do you do?" and saluted with his right arm. The men seemed satisfied.

They were a frightening lot, brawny men of moderate stature, perhaps five feet two to five feet four, rather fair-skinned, with unkempt masses of hair and beard, but their actions were friendly. They approached Ranald's boat somewhat hesitantly, seeming more amazed than hostile. When they came alongside, Ranald jumped into the Ainus' boat without challenge and, using sign language, indicated that his boat needed bailing. The Ainu sailors obliged and lashed Ranald's boat to their own. The men looked to their leader for the next move. Ranald indicated to the puzzled group that he wanted to go ashore, and the crew complied.

On the beach about a hundred villagers of all ages sat cross-legged, waiting to see what manner of creature their sailors were escorting. The crowd did not appear unfriendly, just intensely curious, and, as Ranald alighted from the boat, the men greeted him in the same unusual way as had the sailors, rubbing their hands together, stroking their beards and making guttural noises. A short way above the beach stood the village of Notsuka, little more than a haphazard collection of small homes and one large building.

The Ainu gestured that Ranald was to go with them to the building over a rough trail through the brush and coarse grass, first putting sandals on Ranald's bare feet. Unaccustomed to wearing sandals, Ranald stumbled about and was unable to maintain the brisk pace of his captors but, when he showed his displeasure, they slowed to accommodate themselves to Ranald's awkward gait.

Ranald and the party of Ainus were met by a man of apparent authority. Since he was clad in a loose gown resembling a clerical robe, Ranald conjectured that he might be a priest. His orders, issued in an unintelligible language to the men, were obeyed promptly and, from the smartness with which the men complied, Ranald concluded he was the headman or chief.

Like the other men of the village, the headman's hair was shaved back an inch or so from his forehead and at the neck the hair was shaved upward in a quarter moon. The balance hung freely and profusely to the shoulders, thick and matted, ragged in appearance. His earlobes were rather long, his round eyes a warm brown beneath curling eyelashes and a somewhat protruding or "beetling" brow. Another of the men escorting Ranald had wavy brown hair that cascaded to his shoulders, blending into his beard so the man resembled an upright bear.

Dismissing the gawking crowd that had followed Ranald, the headman beckoned Ranald into his house (the large building), still conducted by a small guard. The house was of one story with glazed paper windows letting in soft light; inside was a dirt courtyard at the end of which were two steps leading to a room about twenty feet long, beyond which— another foot higher—a second room. The headman gestured that Ranald should remove his sandals and place them in a particular place, and led him into a bedroom, where he offered Ranald a gown to replace his wet clothes and left him to change.

Ranald was astonished to find that there were books in the room, including an almanac written in the Japanese language. At the front of the book was a drawing of a mariner's compass with twelve points of the zodiac, but with the needle pointing South instead of North as western compasses did. Before Ranald could absorb this baffling depiction, the host brought food, silently joining Ranald in a meal of broiled fish, rice, ginger, preserved shell fish and pickles. The headman washed all this down with liberal sips of a bottled liquor, which Ranald recognized as sake, a rice wine. The headman offered it to Ranald as "grog-yes?" Later Ranald learned that earlier castaways had offered up samples of their liquor, saying "grog? yes?" Ranald declined the drink; although he had indulged as a youth, at this time he was a total abstainer from spirits, a "temperance man."

The headman touched the gown Ranald wore, saying *"attushi,"* an all-purpose gown made from thick cloth woven of the inner fibrous bark of elm trees and embroidered with Japanese cotton thread. The Ainu also made attractive, white cloth from hemp nettles. For festivals they sometimes adopted a Japanese kimono of colored cotton cloth with curved appliques of white cloth forming a design. In winter they wore deerskin robes, the women adding cloth trim, especially of blue color.

After the two had dined, the headman left, indicating Ranald was free to stroll out of doors, attended discreetly by guards and ogled from a suitable distance by the villagers. He found most homes had log supports with walls and roofs of thatch, woven from pampas grass, and were about fifteen to twenty feet long by around twelve feet wide. Gesturing to a curious resident that he would like to enter his hut, Ranald was admitted with much bowing and waving of arms. Each hut appeared to consist of one large room, carpeted by grass matting held down tight with woven reed bands. In addition to the living area, a small porch or storeroom held nets formed from twine made of birch bark, and other gear; the dogs also lived in this room, out of bad weather.

When his eyes adjusted to the meager light cast through a sort of paper window, Ranald noticed that bulrush mats were scattered throughout the living area for reclining. Above a hearth were displayed a few lacquer-ware vessels and old Japanese swords. The host pulled down a lacquer vessel and poured sake, offering it ceremoniously to Ranald, who again refused the drink as politely as possible. Among the displayed treasures were clusters of wooden whittled wands, sacred pendants dedicated to household gods. Outside of the hut more whittled wands were fastened to a pole several yards long, and about three feet high. Several of these clusters were implanted in a row and, in order to support them further, poles had been fastened crosswise in two rows, appearing like a fence. Through the exchange of sign language Ranald concluded this display was religious and sacred to the resident. Near each hut was a storehouse raised eight or ten feet off the ground on poles, no doubt to protect stores from marauding animals. Log canoes ranging in size to twenty-five feet long were scattered about near water.

Returning to the headman's dwelling, Ranald found a bed and mosquito netting had been provided. The bed clothes consisted solely of a roomy cotton gown padded thickly. The Ainu also had brought Ranald's sail, anchor, kegs and chest to the house and, at his request, his soggy sailor's clothes were washed and dried. As night fell, Ranald felt quite secure in the belief that no harm would come to him from these friendly people and went to sleep comfortably in the warm cocoon of his bedding.

The Japanese Isles—based on a map from *National Geographic* LXIX (January-June 1936). When held by the Japanese in 1848-49, MacDonald was transported the full length of the country, from Soya Strait in the north to Nagasaki in the south.

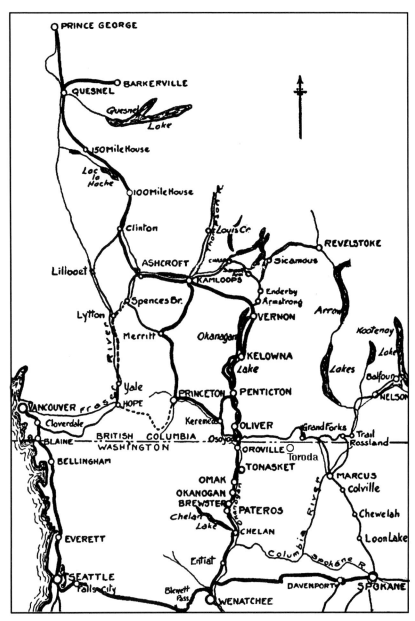

Central British Columbia and northern Washington—based on a map compiled and drawn for the Okanogan-Cariboo Trail Association, 1922. (William Compton Brown Collection, MASC, Washington State University Libraries)

The astute interpreter Einosuke Moriyama (left), "went on to instruct Ranald in proper etiquette, saying that, when the governor entered, he must not look at him but must bow low, to which Ranald angrily responded that he would not" (p. 82). (Perry and Hawks, *Narrative of the Expedition of an American Squadron*, 1856)

Jane Klyne McDonald, second wife of Archibald McDonald, in Montreal about 1865. When Ranald suddenly turned up in 1853 at his stepmother's home in eastern Canada, "he gave her a considerable fright since Ranald was supposed to be long dead, drowned in the Japan Sea" (p. 115). (Cage 196, 9-45, MASC, Washington State University Libraries)

Street scene in the port city of Hakodate, located east of the Matsumae Peninsula in southern Hokkaido (Yeso). (Perry and Hawks, *Narrative of the Expedition of an American Squadron*, 1856)

Commodore Matthew G. Perry in conference with Japanese officials at Hakodate, May–June 1854. Perry arrived "to the consternation of local officials—who had not been notified about the treaty and were understandably agitated" (p. 138). A half-decade earlier, MacDonald had been interrogated in similar settings by Japanese officials. (Perry and Hawks, *Narrative of the Expedition of an American Squadron*, 1856)

Christina MacDonald as she appeared in the mid 1870's when about 23 years old. A trader, entrepreneur, and interpreter with a lively intellect, Christina along with her cousin Ranald were "cut from the same cloth . . . [and] a lively pair in the Cariboo and at the Kamloops post" (p. 218). (Cage 196, 9-45, MASC, Washington State University Libraries)

Ranald MacDonald: February 3, 1824 - August 5, 1894. This portrait was taken July 5, 1891. "I realized how imposing a figure he really was. He wore a light-blue, army overcoat, made with capes and brass buttons . . . it certainly added to his size and dignity" (p. 234). (Cage 196, 13-121, MASC, Washington State University Libraries)

After about 1882, Ranald spent the rest of his life with his cousin Donald's active family at old Fort Colvile, by then abandoned by the Hudson's Bay Company. In this 1901 view, visitors and relatives stand in front of Donald's ranch house. Though Ranald had a cabin nearby, "he spent most of his time with Donald's family" (p. 219). (Cage 196, 9-45, MASC, Washington State University Libraries)

A view of Ranald MacDonald's grave at Toroda in north central Washington, probably taken early in the 20th century. Today, Ranald's grave is a Washington State Parks heritage site. (William Compton Brown Collection, MASC, Washington State University Libraries)

The following morning two major chiefs of the island, Kechinza and Kemon, visited MacDonald and examined everything in his chest, seeming especially intrigued by his books and letters. Upon opening his keg of provisions, the men recoiled at the sight of the salt beef and pork, refusing to touch it and poking it with a stick. Ranald thought perhaps they were vegetarians on religious grounds; however, Ainu usually subsisted on deer, bear, and marine animals such as seals and sea-otters and salmon, so they may not have identified the salted meats as such. Excitedly talking among themselves but completely mystifying Ranald, the two chiefs left after presenting a gift of preserved ginger.

With no further word or indication of interest from the headman, Ranald tentatively went outside to wander about the village, his guard padding behind. On the third day of Ranald's adventure, Kechinza returned with several men and made Ranald understand that he was going to Soya, the nearest military station, to report Ranald's presence to the authorities. Soya was on the mainland of the bigger island, Yezo, or today's Hokkaido, at the tip of a cape nearest Siberian Sakhalin or Sagalien.

For the ensuing ten days Ranald remained under minimal guard, with a Japanese man, not Ainu, assigned to be his constant companion. Tangorō and Ranald developed a keen friendship, each bent on learning the other's language, pointing to objects and saying the term for it. Ranald intrigued the villagers by writing such Ainu words on a slate from his chest. Whittling a pen from a crow's quill, he progressed to writing words and notes about his experiences on crude paper, although the villagers seemed apprehensive about whether or not he should be recording anything.

Tangorō wrote with a brush, Japanese fashion, no doubt making his own notes about how English words sounded and his impressions of Ranald from their close association. Gradually, using a mixture of newly learned words, sign language, and body language, Ranald grasped more information about his hosts, the Ainu.

Even in the twentieth century the origin of the Ainu is one of the world's anthropological mysteries. Well-known scientists offer divergent theories: (1) a mixture of Polynesian and Mongoloid races, (2) a branch of the Aryan family moved east from central Asia, or (3) stone age aboriginals who developed their own unique qualities over eons. Certainly the pure Ainu resembles an Aryan more than an Asian. Elements of Ainu legends and culture closely parallel ancient biblical stories and those of the South Pacific, as well. In *Ainu Life and Legends*, Kindaiti states that Dr. Erwin Baelz (1849-1913) reasoned that the Ainu resembled the Indo-Atlantic race; and that A. C. Haddon, a noted British anthropologist, said they were the relics of an ancient group of white persons who left no other representatives in Asia, although they resembled the Russian *mujik* strongly. Dr. Huruhata Tanemoto from Tokyo Imperial University believed the Ainu to be a racial solitary island.

According to researcher Fred Peng, the first known encounter between Japanese and Ainu was in 654, with bitter battles of a localized nature developing as the Ainu chieftains retreated to Yezo from northern Honshu Island. In 720, it took the soldiers of nine Japanese provinces to beat them back when they made raids on northern Honshu. A civil war so decimated the numbers of the Ainu in 855 that the Japanese were able to gain clear supremacy over them by the end of the ninth century. Over the next centuries there was considerable intermarriage and adoption of unwanted Japanese children into Ainu clans, blurring the ethnicity of the Ainu as a distinct race. In 1604, the Matsumae daimyos were given authority over Yezo, and brisk trade developed between that island and Japanese farther south, principally fish, bear and deer hides in exchange for swords and lacquered boxes. Recognizing the advantage of their position, the Matsumaes were ruthless in their dealings and suppression of the advancement of the Ainu and carefully sought to deceive their Japanese overlords, as well, about the resources of Yezo. At that time the Ainu were not considered Japanese citizens and assimilation was not encouraged.

However, the Bakufu or Japanese government began to mistrust the Matsumaes' activities, removing their authority over Yezo in the late 1700's. Reversing its policies, the government encouraged total acculturation of the Ainu into Japanese society, although not encouraging assimilation through intermarriage. Paying lip service to these edicts, the Ainu adopted many Japanese customs but rebelled at becoming submerged totally as a culture, so much so that the Japanese relaxed their edicts for another century and a half. At the beginning of the Meiji era in 1868, the government decided to totally assimilate the Ainu, forcing them to abandon their ancient customs such as tattooing a pattern around the women's mouths. The Ainu were to learn Japanese, adopt a Japanese name, attend school, etc. As the twentieth century draws to a close, only a handful of Ainu of any blood purity remain.

Ranald found that the Ainu language had certain similarities to English. The Ainu had the same five vowels, fourteen consonants and at least five double-letter combinations of consonants. Verbs had different "persons," three to be exact, as English does. There were suffixes and prefixes of constant nature, such as "pet" for river, making "so-pet" a "waterfall-river," and a "mo-pet" a "small-river." However, it was a spoken, not a written language; Tangorō's writings were from the Japanese schooling.

Ranald was not tempted by the Ainu women, finding distasteful their custom of tattooing themselves. Little girls had a small patch on the upper lip, with additional tattooing as they matured; at the time of marriage the final marking was a sharp point on the cheek, so that the appearance was that of a turned-up moustache. Women also had tattooed rings from wrist to elbow. The females wore a long cloth dress with a three- or four-inch sash, and both men and women wore large earrings. Although the women traditionally performed the daily work, except for hunting, with a lower status than man, some were credited with a kind of shamanism or witchery, wielding great power in the village and often marrying a major chief. The shamanic woman wore a leather belt for ceremonial occasions, from which pieces of metal clanked pleasantly together.

As far as Ranald could determine, the Ainu villages each had a Japanese headman, appointed by a governmental body. The headman, his host, might have been the Ainu chief or the village authority appointed by the Japanese with Tangorō, his aide, a Japanese person.

The secretive behavior that dominated Japanese society of the time was emphasized when, one day while Kechinza was gone to Soya, Tangorō drew Ranald off into a field of high grass to question him privately about conditions outside Japan. Squatting down into the grass so as to be hidden, Tangorō produced a good map of Japan, with distances marked on it in terms of "one day's journey," which Ranald computed to be about twenty-five miles. He asked Ranald to point out where his ship was last seen, asked whether he knew anything of southern Japan, and showed deep curiosity about his own nation, yet apprehension about being discovered *asking* such questions.

Even as his future was extremely uncertain and hazardous, Ranald delighted in experiencing the life of a virtually unknown people. He reflected that some aspects of the Ainu customs resembled those of the North American coast, especially the native peoples around Bella Coola. He also noticed the vague similarities between his own appearance and that of the Ainu and Japanese people—except for the hairiness, for he was clean-shaven.

Ten days after Kechinza left for Soya, Ranald looked up from his scratchings to see two junks crossing Notsuka Cove to drop anchor offshore at the nearby village of Pontomari. Later that evening the officers of the junks came to visit Ranald at Notsuka, brought him a gift of sweet meats, and departed after questioning Tangorō.

The next morning Tangorō and the headman told Ranald to remain in his room and Tangorō covered the windows with mats. Soon the honored officers from the junks reappeared, accompanied by several soldiers.

The officers were seated on the highest floor, it being a custom to place the honored persons on the highest level. Ranald sat on a stool before this impromptu "court" to be questioned through Tangorō, who spoke now bits of English, and sign language. Ranald made the officials know that he had left the ship because he had differed with the captain, that his small boat had been shipwrecked, and reviewed the reasons for his surprising appearance on Rishiri Island. The group examined every item of his equipment, expressing interest in his quadrant, anchor and kegs. They even measured Ranald's height. Ranald towered over his hosts; at five feet eight inches, he was a tall man for the mid-1800's.

Apparently satisfied by Ranald's story, the officer in charge indicated that Ranald was to accompany them. Flanked by two officers from the junks and two lines of Ainu soldiers or subjects, Ranald was escorted the four miles to Pontomari on foot. Though the Ainu chief himself was dressed in an ordinary silk gown, Ranald felt conspicuously shabby in a flapping cotton gown, too short for his height, and the unaccustomed sandals. The escort was not unkind, stopping to rest part way and inquiring if Ranald was tired.

Near Pontomari the party was met by more Ainus. As the growing escort entered the village, all doffed their hats except the two officers. Curtains of striped, varicolor cotton—black, red and blue, according to the insignia of the different feudal families—covered the windows along their line of march, an attempt to conceal Ranald from the view of ordinary citizens, who were not worthy to see this important sight.

In the village Ranald was led into the principal house and placed in a room about twelve feet square, with a grating of wooden bars about four inches thick and four inches apart. The accommodations were clean enough, and Ranald was supplied with food and bedding, even tea and tobacco. After a day or two, the officers departed in their junks, leaving a foot samurai, Shonosuke Miyajima, about twenty-two years of age, and Tangorō to guard Ranald. Under house arrest, Ranald remained thus confined for thirty days, leaving his prison only three times to bathe.

In early August his captors prepared to send Ranald on board a larger junk for parts unknown. On a bright, sunny day, Ranald gladly emerged from his confinement, bidding goodbye to the chief Kemon; Tangorō was assigned to accompany Ranald. Most of the villagers turned out, this time without the shielding curtains, to wave goodbye. Chiefs Kechinza and Kemon led the procession, next a soldier, then Ranald with two attendants behind him, then the rest of the soldiers, with the officers bringing up the rear. Ranald and his attendants were relegated to a junk having a small covering; the other carried his baggage including his skiff, which was taken aboard the junk. While the junks were outbound from the cove, Ranald was required to remain in the cramped covered section, where he could barely sit upright, even crosslegged. The crew consisted of a chief from Soya who acted as captain, a distinguished headman dressed in a faded silk gown trimmed with gold, and nineteen men.

Ranald's junk was propelled by twelve men, using oars with a dipping action. Another six men in the aft portion of the junk used sculling oars, two men to each of three oars. As they worked, the scullers chanted a rhythmic phrase; the oarsmen sang in time to their strokes.

No one indicated where the junks were bound.

IX

Ranald Taken South by Junk

En route to Soya from Rishiri Island, the junk skirted the coast of Yezo and crossed a large bay. Occasionally large ships could be seen in the distance. The Japanese seemed resentful or concerned, declaring firmly "American Ship!"; however, Ranald was able to determine from their appearance that they were not American.

As the junks neared Soya, other Japanese boats, flying the flags of the Matsumae, a quartered diamond in a square, came to assist them in docking at a landing. The party was received by men dressed in "mantles, generally of black silk, with their coat-of-arms figured on the back and on each sleeve; they also had on a pair of wide trousers." The two swords carried by some officers identified them as high-ranking samurai, since ordinary soldiers carried no swords, the next highest in rank one sword, and only samurai wore two. Often such swords were inscribed beneath the handle with the name of the owner and were believed to have a "life of their own," a spirit life guarding the owner. When a sword was taken in battle, its owner, dead or alive, was restless until the sword was recovered, it is said.

At the landing were curious Ainu residents, lining the sides of the road, saying nothing but bowing politely to passersby. Before the party disembarked from the junk, a superintendent of foot samurai, Kujuzo Oba, came aboard to greet Ranald cordially, thereafter escorting him under considerable guard to the Government House in the city.

Ranald appeared the next morning before the commandant of the post, Captain Toyoshichi Sato, flanked by an officer on each side. Sato politely shook hands with Ranald, then sat down.

Seated on a mat, the captain merely scrutinized Ranald and said nothing for some time. Apparently making a decision, he gave orders. Ranald was conducted to a newly built prison with two apartments, one for the guard, and one for Ranald, each carpeted with clean mats. Despite the imprisonment his captors were solicitous of his comfort.

Ranald replied somewhat haughtily through Tangorō that any prison was not to his liking, to be behind bars was a disgrace. Kindly in their manner, the officers interrogated Ranald about his needs. When he said he needed more room to walk, at least, more than the meager twelve by eight foot cell, they replied that they could leave the door open between the apartments by day, giving him twenty-four feet to walk in and, responding to his request for fresh air, the officers promised to leave the windows open in the evening.

Many officers filed by the cell to examine the foreigner, saying nothing. When they left, Tangorō came again with a box of sweetmeats, offered in the name of the *Oyakata* or Daimyo of Matsumae. Captain Sato sent no message or gift until the following day when, in Ranald's presence, he inventoried and examined his possessions. Captain Sato was a man of seventy-four years, appearing much younger but somewhat stern. When he entered the guardroom, all the officers and men bowed their faces to the ground, but Ranald stoically remained seated in his prison. The captain did not converse with Ranald other than what was necessary.

A week or two transpired, during which Ranald was treated kindly. An example of the Japanese preoccupation with secrecy was that Ranald was allowed to read his books but, whenever he asked for them, a guard produced a key to unlock a container. Apparently the common people, even officers, were not supposed to look at such books. Nevertheless, curious about the outside world, officers came to visit and try to converse through the interpreter. Ranald learned that there were about a hundred officers and men at Soya, with other garrisons not far distant.

Since the appearance in the late 1700's of foreign ships, and particularly in 1811 of a Russian ship led by Captain Golownin surveying the Kurile Islands and along the Hokkaido coast, the distant Shogunate had established forts and posts to guard strategic points in Yezo and the southern Kuriles. Japanese farmers were encouraged to move north as immigrants to bolster control over the northern islands, with an estimated 60,000 arriving between 1800 and 1821. Soya was a most strategic location, since Saghalien or Sakhalin in Russian hands could be seen clearly across the Soya Straits.

The officers and a doctor, Yoseki Kakizake, sent to examine Ranald, questioned him about America and the European countries. They revealed that Ranald was, indeed, being held temporarily—only until a larger junk would arrive to take him to Matsumae.

After many days of imprisonment, Captain Sato came with several officers to speak courteously with Ranald. The captain brought generous gifts of tea, sugar, pipe and tobacco, and told Ranald a large junk would soon appear to take him away. Preparing for such occasion, the next day the interpreter-guard Tangorō was sent home to Rishiri, bidding Ranald a tearful goodbye. Another man took his place, having a slight knowledge of English through contact with the shipwrecked men from the whaler, *Lawrence*, held on Etoforu Island off Yezo from June 4, 1846, to May 31, 1847, after which they were transported for release at Nagasaki.

When time passed and the large junk did not appear, the officers decided to transport Ranald south, anyway. Anxious to rid himself of reponsibility for the foreign barbarian, the commandant intended to risk the long trip to Matsumae by open boat. Ranald and his guards, officers and soldiers marched to the landing to board a small junk, similar to the one that transported Ranald from Rishiri Island to Soya. After a half day's journey sailors reported seeing a large junk heading their way, but far off; awaiting identification, the captain ordered the smaller junk to put in at a small fishing village. When it proved to be the expected seagoing junk, the smaller boat put about and returned to Soya. While the large junk, a freighter, discharged cargo and reloaded, Ranald was confined to quarters ashore once more until this task was completed.

When Ranald was taken from his cell to board the junk, the streets again were curtained off from the view of ordinary citizens. This time some of the curtains were white and emblazoned with the coat of arms of the Daimyo of Matsumae and Yezo.

The large junk rocked gently at anchor, draped as were the streets with white sheeting showing the daimyo's coat of arms. MacDonald wrote in his diary, "On the quarter deck of the vessel, for banners, along the guards, was a forest of spears, upright, with glittering steel heads, shining shafts, ornamented with gold and silver and mother of pearl, and appended were elaborate sheaths, of finest fur, for the spear heads."

Ranald went on to describe incredulously a long swab of hair or fiber suspended from the high prow of the boat, almost touching the water, "but an enormous . . . hair swab flopping, with the motion of the waves, into the limpid sea is beyond my comprehension—like a mote or hair in the lips it tickled me."

As did the other men aboard, Ranald entered the junk by crawling through an entry about three feet high that opened directly into a main saloon, where the officers were seated cross-legged on mats. Tea and refreshments were served to all, a farewell courtesy and social exchange, and several of the officers departed the ship thereafter.

Oba now rejoined the party as Ranald's guard, although Ranald was placed in a small cabin near the stern of the vessel. Oba indicated that, should Ranald attempt to escape, he would be knocked on the head with a sturdy iron rod a foot long conveniently hanging near the cabin prison . . . and then he would be bound hand and foot with cords. If he behaved, he could have the run of the deck.

This large junk was about three hundred tons burden, with a high, sharp bow, and an even higher poop deck. The main deck was elliptical with a rise in the deck amidship for cargo. The stern was square above the water. A large and heavy rudder with a tiller about twenty feet long guided the craft, manned by only one man. In the daytime the tiller man steered directly by compass; at night, the watch called out points from the compass below.

The ship had only one mast about forty feet high with a square canvas sail and a lugsail. The sails were reefed from below by securing the reef points to transverse bars on deck. The anchor was a grappling iron with four square flukes. "Weighing anchor" was achieved with a sort of Spanish windlass or capstan between the lower and upper decks and fixed to each— the beam being perforated with two holes through which the working poles were put. The halyards were rove through the upper deck and secured on the lower to bitts. About two dozen sailors formed the crew.

Once under way, the crewmen relaxed, eating and drinking, telling jokes and lying around while not on duty. In the main cabin was a Buddhist altar about three feet long and four feet high, made of an aromatic wood. The altar was decorated with pictures of men with shaven heads, with halos marking their holiness. At sunrise and sunset the captain and crew met for devotional services, kneeling before the altar. A small door in the altar was opened, whereupon the devout clapped their hands to petition the spirit within, crying "Namu Amida Butsu (Sacred Eternal Buddha)." Together the assemblage prayed, fingering pea-sized black beads, for about twenty minutes. Individual sailors also went into a small prayer alcove that had a checkered board overhead, to pray in the same manner alone. No one expected Ranald to join the prayers.

Since he seemed suitably impressed by the threats of his jailers and made no trouble, Ranald was given the run of the deck on the big cargo junk filled with salt fish and kelp. They sailed southward past the Rishiri Islands and little Yageshiri Island where Ranald had first practiced capsizing his boat, and along the western coast of Yezo to the major settlement of Matsumae at the southwest corner of the island. In general, the course was relatively close to shore, the navigators taking compass courses before crossing one bay after another, sometimes out of sight of land.

All in all, Ranald found the time to pass pleasantly, skirting the shores of Yezo. A north-south range of mountains was adjacent to the shore, indented

by numerous rivers that emptied westward. Some of the bays along the
west coast were so broad that the helmsmen steered out of sight of land for
ten or twelve hours at a time across the indentations in the coast. Running
low on provisions and water, the ship dropped anchor one day off a small
village of about forty houses. It might have been Otaru, where there is a
good anchorage. There the Iskari River, largest in Yezo, entered the sea
about fifteen miles northeast of the settlement. For some distance upriver
there were long drying sheds and houses for the fishermen. According to
an observer in 1880, Captain H. C. St. John of Great Britain, the banks
were artificially sloped to the water, making possible the use of a seine net
from shore. The salmon entered the river to spawn around the end of
August and, from then until the beginning of November, salmon were
caught and salted for export to the rest of Japan. Although the chief of the
village came on board and presented fruit to Ranald, no one would divulge
the name of this settlement.

As the junk circled around the Shakotan Peninsula, west of today's
Sapporo, Ranald caught his breath at the occasional sight of Mt.
Nisekoannupuri and Mount Yofeizan, sometimes called Ezo-Fuji. Skirting
along the land southbound, the ship traveled close enough to shore that
Ranald could see the steep cliffs and rugged terrain, the mountains descending with few exceptions to the shore, leaving little level land for settlement. Several significant rivers tumbled seaward, carving their own
precipitous valleys from an unforgiving shore. Small fishing villages straggled
along the mouths of the major rivers.

After a voyage of more than two weeks, the course changed toward
the southeast, passing near several small islands, and on September 7, fifteen days after leaving Soya, the ship entered the bay of Matsumae. Before
arrival at the dock the junk was decked out with small flags and the government pennant of Matsumae. The lances of the officers were planted as
in Soya, at regular distances around the poop deck. The arrival of the big
junk elicited considerable excitement, and dozens of fishing boats swarmed
close to see what was transpiring.

The Japanese admonished Ranald to stay below in the officers' quarters while the ship eased into her anchorage. However, Ranald was able to
monitor some of the goings-on through a crack in the partition. Smaller
boats came to assist the junk in entering the harbor, and one of the large
junk's crew boarded a small boat that took off toward shore, an emissary to
announce the arrival of the junk to the headman of Matsumae.

At that time, Matsumae was the dwelling place of the local Lord Matsumae,
after whom the entire peninsula was (and is) named. From the sixteenth

century until the Meiji Restoration, it was the capital city of Yezo or Hokkaido. Almost all of the trade from Yezo passed through Matsumae, and the few travelers coming from Honshu or elsewhere had to come first to Matsumae to obtain permission to proceed farther. The castle of Yoshihiro Matsumae, built in 1606, was destroyed by fire in 1854 with only the three story *donjon* and main gate escaping the holocaust, but it was rebuilt and lived in by the Matsumae family until the governmental change in 1868. In 1949, the castle again was partially destroyed by fire. The Matsumae castle was the most northerly and the last feudal castle to be constructed in Japan. There were a number of Buddhist temples, the finest *Kōsenji* belonged to the Jōdo sect and was founded in 1533 as the burial place of the consorts of the Matsumae daimyos. Another fine temple was *Ryu-ūn-in* of the Sōtō sect, the leading Buddhist denomination in the district. Only after the Meiji Restoration, when Hokkaido came under the direct governmental control of Tokyo, was the settlement of Matsumae renamed Fukuyama, its current name. Since the harbor was only a relatively unprotected open roadstead, a far better one was developing across the large bay to the east at Hakodate, today's terminus of the inter-island tunnel from Aomori City on Honshu, completed in 1988.

When Ranald hove into port, Lord Matsumae was governor of all Yezo, which only boasted 30,000 residents in 1800, on an island of perhaps 160,000 square miles. Most of them resided in the extreme southwestern portion, for the Matsumae Peninsula and the lands just north enjoyed a far warmer climate than the balance of frigid Yezo. However, typhoons often swept the peninsula, possibly leading to the eclipsing of the port of Matsumae by protected Hakodate.

Not long after the emissary from the junk went ashore, a group of boats full of Japanese officers and men appeared. Two appeared to be of high rank—ordinary crewmen were scurrying around to receive them, laying mats on the steps and all around the main cabin. As the important personages approached, the ship's company grew totally silent; only the slight sibilance of the boats could be heard by Ranald at his restricted peephole below. Sailors handed two camp stools from the smaller boat to crewmen of the junk, then the two important personages came aboard, greeting the officers of the junk. Following them, about thirty or forty other officers and soldiers gave formal greetings and were seated on mats around the main cabin. The officer in charge or chief was dressed in a pair of wide trousers of large patterned silk, held in below the knees by garters. At the ankle, these trouser legs were tucked into the tops of white linen shoes of a design similar to Indian moccasins. Over his shoulders was a handsome mantle of black silk emblazoned with the coat of arms of Lord Matsumae.

After the visitors were properly seated, all eyes turned toward the cabin where Ranald was confined. He moved from his peephole and awaited a summons to appear. Instead, two men rose and removed the entire partition that separated the officers' cabin from the main cabin. Ranald found himself suddenly the center of all eyes, like a specimen under glass. No one spoke or moved to present him to the dignitaries and, annoyed as he was by the dramatic impact of the unexpected exhibition of Ranald the prisoner, he rose to one knee, bowed and waved his hand to the assembled military men. No one responded by gesture or word.

Then the well-dressed chief, "a person about five feet six inches in height with remarkably large eyes, plump, and with healthy countenance," burst out in surprise, "Nippon-jin!"—"a Japanese person!" However, no further discussion of this revelation ensued, only a searching regard of Ranald's appearance. After a few moments, the chief turned to an officer and said "Nagasaki . . . go away, Taisho." (Taisho is a word for admiral.)

The appointed officer spoke then to a subordinate who slid on the mats, still on his knees, to a position beside Ranald. There he elaborated on the terse command. By hitting with a hammer with the right hand, bringing the left thumb and forefinger together as if holding a nail, he said "carpenter" and "ship." From this Ranald surmised that a junk was to be repaired for transporting him to Nagasaki, more than a thousand miles distant.

Through the interpreter Ranald queried, "Why take all that trouble? Why not allow me to remain among you?"

The chief's response was merely a loud laugh, "No! No!, Nagasaki, go away!"

Further conversation ensued, and Ranald was told that he would not sleep on board the junk, but that a house was being prepared for him ashore, that guards would come for him as soon as all was ready. The partition was replaced, and the dignitaries returned to shore. Thereafter, one of the sliding doors was removed, as the day was warm and humid. Ranald was given a pipe, tobacco, and tea, served to him by the lad simply called "musuko" (Japanese for "son" or "boy"), assigned in Soya to accompany Ranald and care for his creature comforts.

X

Prisoner at Matsumae

Dressed for the occasion, the junk officers escorted Ranald on deck about six thirty that same evening, where boats were waiting to take the party ashore.

Around the junk and across the splendid harbor were dozens of boats of all sizes—small skiffs and larger junks—decked out with flags and lighted paper lanterns as if bound for a parade. So dense were the boats that, upon leaving for shore, the small boat in which Ranald and six officers sat on mats was bumped by other craft. With the mountains looming darkly above the large bay in the half-light of evening, the legions of boats seemed like fireflies hovering above the water. Likewise on shore, the beach was crowded with residents, each carrying a colorful lantern, craning their necks to catch a glimpse of the prisoner, "this specimen," as Ranald felt from the scrutiny.

On shore MacDonald walked through an aisle formed by guards at attention. The junk officer Togoro Shinagawa, and Kujuzo Oba, superintendent of foot-samurai from Soya, solemnly marched with him to a palanquin or sedan chair, a *kago*, which Ranald entered. The curtains of the conveyance were lashed with cords so that their captive would not fall out. Ranald, inside and out of sight, was grateful to be away from the uncomfortable staring of the townspeople. He could see little except the vague outlines of streets, people, and buildings. The bearers, dressed only in loincloths and with strengthening bandages on their arms, and soldiers moved briskly along, soon leaving the lights of Matsumae and entering the country. With few lights now, boxed up in the conveyance and borne by two men at each end, Ranald could only surmise what terrain he was carried through by the sounds of water or rocks or the sensations of going up and down. Once the party crossed a stream so deep that the water came almost through the floor of the kago. At several points the party halted to change kago bearers. During such rest periods food was brought to Ranald, and the officers crowded around him, trying to communicate.

It was after midnight when the procession finally reached its destination, the town of Eramachi about ten miles north of Matsumae on the western shore, as Ranald learned later. Finally Ranald was permitted to leave the conveyance in front of a high wall, atop which were sharpened spikes of iron and bamboo, which Ranald said, "made me suspect that they were taking me to a prison or perhaps into a dark dungeon." Guarded by two lines of soldiers, he entered the building through a gate in this formidable enclosure, went down a long passage and found himself in a large room where he was confronted by the "Governor of Matsumae" (thought to be Captain Gorgoro Imai, commander of the company at Eramachi). The guards retreated, leaving the two men alone, and the Japanese took Ranald by the hand in friendly fashion, leading him to the far end of the room, where a glowing fire, tea kettle, cup and saucer "offered a cheerful welcome." The governor (or so Ranald believed him to be) motioned him to a short board bench.

The room appeared to be a residential apartment, not a prison cell; it was large with sliding partitions of light wood and glazed paper. The floors were covered with mats, and the room was warmed by two fireplaces, one in the center and one at the end.

Surveying his surroundings, Ranald was electrified to discover two English letters, I and C, written in charcoal on one of the walls. Above his head was a patch of new boards apparently covering an opening of about eighteen inches square. While Ranald tried to digest these astonishing sights, his host took him to the center of the room and showed him, written on a supporting beam for the room, the names written in pencil: Robert McCoy, John Brady, and John _____, the latter name indecipherable. Pointing to the boarded-up hole, the Japanese conveyed the information through signs and occasional words, especially "America," that fifteen Americans had tried to escape through that hole, were caught, handcuffed and had their throats cut. To illustrate the point more forcefully, the host drew his larger sword and made the sign of cutting a throat. He also pointed to the iron bludgeon hanging outside in the guard room, said "McCoy," and indicated that the man had been struck.

For the first time, Ranald felt fear descending over him like a clammy hand. He believed the former prisoners must have been those from the ship *Lawrence*, reported to have disappeared near Yezo in 1846 or 1847. Ranald was unclear as to the details, but now was convinced that here in this room or enclave the captain and crew of that ship had been executed.

The facts were somewhat different. The ship *Lawrence*, commanded by a Captain Baker, had been shipwrecked during a heavy storm, May 27, 1846, on the northeastern coast of Yezo. During launching of the lifeboats, the captain and several crewmen were lost, but George Howe, the second mate, and seven crewmen got away safely to land at Etoforu Island, one of the Kurile Islands, on June 2. (One of the crewmen died before reaching shore.) From June 4, 1846, to May 31, 1847, they were imprisoned on the island by the Japanese; thereafter they were taken by junk to Hakodate and later Nagasaki for repatriation to a Dutch ship, *Hertogenbosch*, in early December, 1847, which delivered the men to the United States consul at Batavia.

It was a year before Ranald learned the real identity of the prisoners, who had left the area only a month before Ranald's appearance. They were fifteen deserters from the whaleship *Lagoda*—eight Americans and seven Hawaiians—who had taken a boat and left while the ship was in the Strait of Tsugaru, the body of water separating the Matsumae Peninsula from Honshu Island. Upon coming ashore they were treated kindly, and imprisoned in the same room where Ranald now stood, awaiting transportation to Nagasaki. According to the laws of the time, "shipwrecked" (although these were deserters) foreigners were to be repatriated through Nagasaki.

The fifteen men proved to be unruly guests, quarreling and fighting among themselves. One Hawaiian hung himself in despair during the twelve months' confinement, and another died of natural causes. Despite the violent behavior of the men, the Japanese treated them well but firmly. When Robert McCoy and a second man tried to escape through the ceiling, they had not been executed, merely caged and more closely guarded. McCoy made additional attempts at escape, being then placed in a sort of stocks, his hands and/or feet locked into a restraining device. The Japanese must have been thoroughly happy to rid themselves of these contentious foreigners, and Captain Imai sought to frighten Ranald away from similar behavior.

Soberly nodding his head to the captain, Ranald indicated his understanding of the restrictions, whereupon the climate in the room changed again to one of friendly concern. Other officers entered the room, where underlings laid clean mats and deferentially seated them. Then one turned to Ranald and asked "Gozen?" or "do you want some rice?" Servants brought a tray with a bowl of rice and chopsticks and, although Ranald knew how to use them, contrarily he sat silently until the captain ordered a bamboo spoon and wooden fork to be brought in. (Ranald was allowed to keep these implements, bringing them with him to Nagasaki, but losing them later during the sinking of another ship.) In addition to the rice, a supper appeared of fish, pickles and boiled kelp, all served with style by four or five servants. Before presenting the dishes, a taster first sampled the food (tasters were garbed in mantles of an orange color).

In the face of uncertainty as to his fate and thoroughly alarmed by the admonitions of the captain, MacDonald still dared to say grace as a Christian before eating his meal. All the time he was eating, the Japanese company watched him, although in a kindly and curious fashion.

After the meal, the captain outfitted Ranald completely with a set of clothing and supplies: "four garments, like gowns, with large wide sleeves, viz., one, the widest of silk; one of light grayish cotton, of native manufacture evidently; one of some material—I don't know what to call it—lined with white cotton; and another of blue cotton, stuffed with cotton wadding; also a pair of Japanese trousers of cotton; two knives, a large and a small one, and a box of confectionery, with a presentation card consisting of a piece about the size of half a sheet of note paper, folded up in a peculiar form, the ends tied with bows of paper—paper very thin, fine and glossy. I was also presented with a bed and covering, a large gown thickly padded, and a pillow, varnished, of wood, about eight or ten inches long, bottom three inches wide, upper part two inches, and on that, a small pillow about the size of a man's wrist, apparently of rice husk; it had a drawer also. The governor kindly made a sign to me to sleep, and said 'Noo'—the Japanese, probably, for snooze. It was now about three o'clock in the morning, and I gladly did so."

Major changes would occur in this tranquil outpost of old Japan before twenty-five years passed. The island's 30,000 residents in 1800 would grow to 60,000 by 1870, still favoring the peninsula and lands slightly to the northward and across the bay to Hakodate. At the time of the Meiji Restoration in 1868, the island, which had been called Yezo or "wild" was renamed Hokkaido, or "north-south road." As soon as the change came from Shogun to Emperor, a renegade military man, Takeiki Enomoto, tried to hold Yezo as an independent fief, planning to break away from Japan. He held off the Japanese fleet for several months but, in June, 1869, was forced to surrender. In 1874, American geologist B. S. Lyman was employed by the Imperial government to explore Hokkaido and develop its huge coal deposits. Americans also assisted the Japanese in establishing modern farms, raising fruits, vegetables, horses and cattle; and in constructing the first railways in the areas south of Sapporo, declared capital of Hokkaido in 1886. The town of Matsumae was renamed Fukuyama, declining in importance from its days as the headquarters of the Matsumae family.

When Ranald awoke that following morning in his spacious and comfortable prison, he asked for his chest and books. At first the request was refused but, when he indicated that his religion had something to do with his request, they conceded and gave him his Bible only. Indeed, they made a shelf for it and, when handling the book, touched it to their foreheads as a mark of respect. His chest was sealed at the top and sides, the seals connected by strips of paper so that any unauthorized entry to the chest's contents would be immediately apparent. Only in the presence of several persons was it ever opened.

With considerable comfort MacDonald spent about three weeks confined to the Eramachi apartment. Before the time of his departure for Nagasaki, the servants brought him a piece of sailcloth from which to sew a bag for his personal belongings, and, of course, his chest was sealed for shipment.

When the day came for embarkation, the officers brought a scroll with a written order upon it, showing the exact positioning of each man accompanying Ranald. With pomp and ceremony the troop paraded about a quarter mile to board a shore boat that would take the party to a large junk anchored offshore. Residents and military men alike were garbed in festive fashion for the departure.

Some of the officers wore chain armor on their body and legs. The soldiers were ranked into individual companies, each under a chief and a different flag. Each soldier had his chief's coat of arms embroidered on each breast and on the back of his coat—a garment reaching to a point below the knees, with one sleeve of one color, the other of another, principally reds and blues. The coats of arms often bore figures of the sun and moon, while some were diamond shaped or had flowers. The flag of the Matsumaes was a square with a diamond quartered. Dangling on strings from the soldiers' backs were their head coverings, not worn on this occasion. These caps consisted of paper or japanned (varnished or lacquered) material, perfectly flat and padded with an opening near the top of the head for the hair to pass through.

The splendid parade ended at shore, where most of the military company and Ranald boarded a sort of barge, which was towed by several boats out to the large junk that would bear the prisoner to Nagasaki.

Arriving at the junk *Tenjinmaru*, Ranald found her surrounded by a swarm of other small boats and decked out flamboyantly, like the junk he boarded at Soya. Curtains surrounded the exterior, with portholes painted on them. Glittering lances bore flags of varying hue and design. The mysterious swab waved in the wind. Ranald found the scene both fascinating and phantasmagoric.

The decoration belied his treatment, however; below decks he was placed in a caged, small cabin, unable to leave it during the entire voyage.

Nevertheless, the officer in charge, Captain Tanemon Ujiye, presented him with a gift of small but delicious apples. Lest Ranald might get any ideas about escape attempts, small arms were piled near the door of his jail—light muskets similar to those of Americans.

Once at sea, after Ranald complained about the extent of his confinement, the captain ordered the grating to be removed that separated Ranald from others, but he was ordered to stay below at all times. The sea route along the western coast is much shorter but, possibly because of the pirates that rampaged through the Japan Sea, the junk traversed the longer route off Japan's east coast. This part of the North Pacific is often turbulent and stormy. Here the gentle Kuroshio current, a warm flow, does not skirt the shore until off the southeastern coasts. The northbound current is shunted aside by Japan's land area, veering eastward at an astonishing speed. The British explorer, Captain H. C. St. John of the Royal Navy, commented in his book about an 1880 voyage, *Wild Coasts of Nipon*, that "we dreaded this current. In reality, after once getting within its influence, we were never certain, if it came on thick or foggy, or at night, when the coast could not be seen, where we were going, at what speed we were being carried along . . . I have heard of vessels being carried dead to windward against a heavy gale of wind at a wonderful speed; other ships, thinking themselves close off the coast, suddenly finding they were far away to the south, being carried hither and thither amongst the islands and rocks." St. John went on to remember that, in the Korean Straits, where the Kuroshio meets the southbound counter stream from the Arctic, which rebounds off the Kurile Islands and follows the Sea of Japan, that "the meeting of these two streams, which is most remarkable,—the one so dark and deeply blue, the other of a pale green colour. They don't mix, but rub against each other. So decided is this, that on taking the temperature almost on either side of the ship, the difference was 14 degrees." He mentions being bound for Nagasaki on one occasion and, despite his best navigation, finding himself forty miles south of the Nagasaki entrance.

Despite these drawbacks, undoubtedly familiar to the junk's captain, the course continued along the eastern shore, as mentioned above. The winds were favorable—indeed so brisk and stormy that many sailors were seasick—but the voyage to Nagasaki lasted only ten days. During that time Captain Ujiye visited Ranald twice, and a doctor aboard the ship checked his health from time to time.

During this time Ranald MacDonald kept notes about the Japanese sailors and their customs, recording them formally only years later. He noticed that the inferior officers and soldiers ate in one corner of the main cabin while squatting on their heels, dining from varnished wooden bowls and drinking from a cup and saucer. Only chopsticks were used, even while eating soup. He noted, "The dishes were generally placed in trays about fifteen inches by twelve. In the centre bowl—generally the largest—was fish, boiled or broiled; in a smaller one, rice; in another of the same size, soup; in another vegetables; and in a smaller one, pickles. The vegetables used on the voyage were principally pumpkins, squash, cucumbers, and cabbage . . . Tea was taken by them regularly; sometimes mixed with rice. They used no sugar at their meals." The ship stopped three times, taking on fresh fruit, including mangos, which Ranald found nauseatingly sweet.

The sailors talked with Ranald, often furtively, as the crew seemed unsure as to how friendly they should be. There was no interpreter, but by now Ranald had picked up a smattering of Japanese. In the evenings after supper each soldier was issued about a pint of sake or rice wine. Ranald was surprised to learn that even these ordinary sailors were educated to read and write, having writing paper, pens and books.

Paper in the books was thin, doubled over and printed only on one side; some contained wood cuts of good clarity. The writing paper was almost transparent and much finer than that used by Europeans and Americans, while the pen was a brush of fine hair dipped either in India ink or ink made from cuttlefish. He noted that they wrote on rolled sheets, beginning at the right hand or outer end of the sheet, in vertical lines. In books the "footnotes" appeared at the tops of the pages.

All during the voyage MacDonald was forbidden to go on deck, only seeing the sights from the porthole or small window when the junk stopped for provisions. In harbor, the porthole was covered only with a curtain, while at sea, with boards against the weather. Only through cracks could he glean much information about Honshu. What he saw indicated a somewhat gentler landscape, with cultivated fields and hillsides, from that along the western shore of Yezo. Here and there could be seen the entrances to deep waterways. All in all, the ten-day journey, sans interpreter, was a purely business-like military style operation. Sailing southward for several days, the junk then veered southwesterly, crossing the entrance to a bay that stretched northwesterly to the horizon. A crewman gestured to Ranald and said, "Edo . . . Edo . . . ," (Tokyo Bay today). For the next several days Ranald saw frequent broad indentations in an otherwise rugged coast, indicating large bays. Passing through the Osumi Straits, the junk changed to a westerly, then northwesterly course. Off the extreme southwest tip of Kyushu Island were the large islands of Tanegashima and Yakushima, the former relatively flat and cultivated, the latter a circular maze of mountains as high as six thousand feet and densely forested. With Cape Nomo on the starboard bow the junk entered the bay that led to the teeming harbor of Nagasaki. Another mariner, Captain Sherard Osborn, in the ship H.M.S. *Furious* carrying Lord Elgin on a mission to Edo in 1858, described dramatically his own entrance to the bay during a fog:

"Thence, stretching far away to our left, rose peak, mountain, and table-land, until lost in the distance. Away to the north, a channel, dotted with islets, was seen between Gotto and Kiu-Siu [Kyushu]. It led to Hirando or Firando [Hirado] . . . For awhile heavy mists swept over land and sea, and we could only see a mile or so ahead. It was very tantalizing . . . presently there was a play of light along the surface of the sea; the hulls of our vessels came out sharp and clear. Then Japanese junks were seen; presently their sails and masts showed;—the fog was lifting, breaking, and dispersing. Down the mountains of Kiu-Siu rolled masses of cloud; out of every vale and valley came dense mists sweeping down . . . Poor cloudland fought at a disadvantage with the lusty youth of a morning sun . . . day, bright and beaming, burst fairly upon us with a shout of welcome. It was a glorious sight—mountain and plain, valley and islet, clothed with vegetation, or waving with trees and studded with villages."

As the junk on which Ranald was imprisoned sailed up Nagasaki Bay, he could see villages and richly cultivated gardens, flowers, fruit trees and fields.

More sinister was the multitude of gun batteries that were in place on the islands of Iwosima and Kamino-sima part way up the bay. Soldiers appeared ready to fire until they saw that the approaching junk was one of their own. The guns appeared to be of brass or iron, mounted on wheeled carriages. Government boats appeared in pairs.

Just as it seemed that the junk would crash into a rather forbidding shore topped by the peaks of Hiko-san (Hiko-san, Shichimen-zan and Hoka-zan, triple summits) and Tarutayama, or run aground on the island of Takaboko blocking the view of Nagasaki Harbor, the junk turned hard to the starboard and entered the last channel. The city came into view, nestled around the channel's end at the foot of steep hills. To port side appeared a rude collection of European houses on an island, Deshima Island, which Ranald later learned had been created by dumping fill on a shallow sandbar. There, connected by a bridge to the city, were confined the Dutch traders. During a visit to Nagasaki in June, 1859, en route to his post in Edo as head of a diplomatic mission, Sir Rutherford Alcock observed that Deshima was a low, fan-shaped strip of land, dammed out from the waters of the bay, the handle being towards the shore and truncated. "One long wide street, with two-storied houses on each side, built in European style, gives an air of great tidiness; but they looked with large hollow eyes into each other's interiors, in a dismal sort of way, as if they had been so engaged for six generations, at least,—and were quite weary of the view."

The main harbor was a full two miles long—a body of water perhaps a quarter mile wide between abrupt hills that rose to a thousand feet or more, and above them stood genuine mountains. Down every ravine came rushing streams, and on terraces and glades the residents had laid out small farms or gardens. Tropical trees and shrubs thrived: pomegranate, persimmon, palm bamboo, gardenia, camellia, ferns, and ivy. Alcock noticed that "the rare and much-prized stiphelia of botanists I observed, growing luxuriantly in many places as a creeper."

According to Captain Osborn, "nestling in the midst of green trees and flowery gardens, were the prettiest chalets seen out of Switzerland; children, with no clothes at all, rolling on the grass, or tumbling in and out of the water; whilst their respected parents . . . gravely waved their fans, or sat gazing upon the newly-arrived vessels."

Ten years before Osborn, when Ranald's junk entered, a chain of guard boats probably stretched across the entrance to Nagasaki Harbor. If any enemy managed to breach this battle line, it was said the commanding officers would commit *seppuku* rather than face the disgrace of having failed to stop the intruder.

The big junk from Matsumae continued on into the harbor without challenge, however, and dropped anchor in the outer harbor.

XI

Imprisoned at Nagasaki

No sooner had the anchor been set than boatloads of Japanese officials came on board, one of them Shirai Tatsunosin, an assistant to the governor of Nagasaki. The official strode into the cabin and sat cross-legged, flanked by an assistant and two "pale faced secretaries . . . with writing materials, and a large book like an atlas."

Among the delegation were at least two interpreters, Sakushichiro Uemura, an elderly gentleman, and Einosuke Moriyama, the latter a two-sworded or high-ranking samurai. At the request of Tatsunosin, Uemura asked Ranald for his name—in a kindly manner. Speaking through Moriyama, who looked up Ranald's words in an English-Dutch dictionary, then a Dutch-Japanese version, Ranald gave his birthplace (Oregon), said he had lived in Canada, and that he had sailed from New York.

MacDonald stated in his journal that "I was desirous that they should regard me as belonging to both nations (British and American) in order that in the event of a vessel of either of them visiting Japan my case might attract their special attention."

The interrogation went on (interpolated from brief mention in the journal):

"Do you have a father, a mother, any other family still living?"

"Yes, my father is with the Hudson's Bay Company in Canada, my mother, plus several brothers and sisters, residing with him [actually it is doubtful that Ranald knew exactly where his father was stationed]."

"Where is your ship, the one on which you came to Japanese waters?"

"I don't know. I left her, a whaling vessel called the *Plymouth*, off the coast of Yezo, and she proceeded northward. No doubt, by now she has returned toward America."

"Why did you leave the ship in a small boat? Didn't you think you would be drowned?"

"I left because I had difficulty with the Captain. We had bitter arguments, so I thought I would desert the ship and come ashore at Japan."

The officials looked at each other and talked about this event, then turned to him answering, "You must have a great heart."

"Do you believe in a God in heaven?" came the further query.

Ranald simply replied, "Yes."

This seemed to satisfy the interrogators. After a brief conference among themselves, the interpreter relayed the information that tomorrow Ranald would be taken before the governor of Nagasaki at the town hall.

However, the next day was inclement and the appearance postponed until the following day, when a large company entered the junk on which Ranald was confined. As each man entered, he knelt, bowed low and, without rising, slid to the sides of the cabin to sit on mats. Tatsunosin, however, walked in dignity to his seat and, as he sat, the rest of the men bowed low or salaamed to him. In response, he merely uttered a low grunt of acknowledgment.

After a brief conversation, Ranald was escorted from the junk to a shore boat, proceeding across a bridge of skiffs to the vessel, which then carried the party to the inner harbor and anchored a bit offshore to await the arrival of someone. Tea was served to everyone aboard except Ranald.

The inner harbor was perfectly landlocked, protected from all winds and permitting only a light swell from the ocean to enter. Brown fishing hawks swooped down to snatch fish from the water or surveyed the prospects from above, commenting shrilly. There seemed to be more hawks than seagulls in this latitude, perched about on the rigging of ships. To the left of the harbor was a bank rising to about a thousand feet; to the right in a valley lay the town of Nagasaki above a gentler, sloping shore.

At the entrance to the inner harbor was the island of Takaboko, which the Dutch called Papenberg (previously mentioned). Also in port were three large Chinese junks armed with formidable cannon, plus a large fleet of Japanese junks. Small boats bustled to and fro, the operators seeming less curious about foreigners like Ranald than had the residents of Yezo. On the southwest side of the town, just offshore by the tiny island of Deshima, a Dutch ship was anchored. Her captain leaned on the rail enjoying his pipe while gazing rather uncuriously at the new arrivals. A flagstaff held a snapping Dutch flag, marking the collection of hybrid European style homes huddled along a single street.

Ranald looked curiously at Deshima, about which he had heard much. It was tiny, only about five hundred yards long and narrow, with one street bisecting its length and another intersecting it and leading to the bridge. A few sailors in red shirts lolled about the landing place, and the bridge that tied the island to the shore was deserted.

Along the streets were the houses of the Dutch residents and their Japanese agents and retainers, plus stores for articles of Japanese manufacture. Another area, nearby but not on Deshima, was set aside for Chinese merchants to market the contents of the thirteen trading junks permitted into Nagasaki annually.

In 1859, ten years after MacDonald's visit, the crewmen of the ship carrying Lord Elgin on his treaty-making mission to Edo went ashore at Nagasaki and Deshima. They described an area called the Dutch Bazaar—where one could find tables inlaid with mother-of-pearl; bird and animal figures; cabinets on which golden fish or tortoise were inlaid; clever items of ivory, bone or wood; and marvelously beautiful porcelains and lacquerware in dozens of forms, the porcelain so delicate one was afraid to touch it.

At that time there also was a Russian bazaar at Nagasaki, about one acre in size, with booths on three sides manned by Japanese tradesmen. Nearly every article there was manufactured by the residents around Nagasaki. In his book about the Elgin expedition, Osborn says,

"At one stall we found microscopes, telescopes, sundials, rules, scales, clocks, knives, spoons, glass, beads, trinkets, and mirrors—all of native make upon European models—and the prices were so ridiculously small . . . and the entire workmanship was highly creditable . . . The Japanese clocks exhibited for sale were beautiful specimens of mechanism, and proved what we had heard, that the people of this country are most cunning in the fashioning of metals . . . The Japanese day being divided into twelve hours of unequal duration . . . the dial of their clocks was therefore different from ours."

However, Ranald was not to visit the Dutch island. Enjoying the pleasant sun, he waited. Soon a large boatload of officers and soldiers arrived from the outer bay and landed at the beach. Ranald's party came to life and followed them, debarking on a jetty with stone steps to be guarded by the military party that had come ashore.

About fifty yards from the beach the procession entered Nagasaki through a *torii*, a traditional gate about fifteen feet wide, thirty feet high, and topped with a curved cross beam. On each side of the street beyond stood soldiers with side arms. A palanquin awaited Ranald. As he was borne through several streets, he had a good view of the city. The ordinary dwellings were small, mostly one story, with peaked and overhanging roofs. They had windows of oiled paper encased in sliding frames; some roofs were of wooden shingles larger than those in America, others of red tile. Houses were neither painted nor whitewashed.

Distributed among the smaller homes were more impressive ones—two stories high of brick or stone. These had gardens in front, sheltered by a stone wall topped by broken glass.

Such Japanese houses consisted of a ground floor and a top story. The front and back of the lower floor were constructed of panels that were removed to admit air and light. Usually the back panels, formed of a light wood framework covered with translucent paper, were left in place to screen the cooking areas. The lower floor was raised about three feet above ground, then laid over nicely with fine mats. Shops were built similarly, except that the goods were exposed in shelves along either side, or stored in boxes or drawers. The merchants and customers sat on the floor to discuss purchases and prices. There were no shop signs.

Ranald saw no temples or pagodas, although he was told there were many in the city. On a small hill at the edge of the city, he saw white objects like monuments to the dead.

At the foot of a hill, the bearers stopped, lowered the palanquin, and Ranald stepped out. He was escorted by the guard up a series of large stone steps to an impressive residence, that of the governor of Nagasaki, Prince Ido of Tsushima, and entered the grounds through a gate to the scrutiny of "thousands of spectators." A porters' lodge or gatekeepers' structure stood near the entrance. The porters bowed low, touching their fingers to the ground. In front of the lodge was a stand of arms with a company of guards seated. Ranald's party entered a narrow alley between houses, a sliding low gate was opened, and the prisoner was conducted to a fenced area. There Ranald was ordered into a rudely plastered shed covered with graffiti and which had an elevated floor covered with dirty matting on which the guards indicated he was to sit. Replacing the soldiers were men in long black dresses, looking grim, wearing inferior swords and daggers, apparently jailers.

Time passed. Servants brought some food eventually and, although inwardly uneasy and too apprehensive to be hungry, Ranald ate the rice and fish to mask his fear.

About a half hour after the meal, the interpreter Moriyama appeared to tell him that he would appear soon before the governor to answer questions. He told Ranald not to be afraid, that he would be the interpreter, but that Ranald would be speaking under oath. Moriyama warned him that, before seeing the governor, on a metal plate at the door he would see an image of the "Devil of Japan" and that he must put his foot on it. Nonplussed by the description, Ranald replied that he would do so, because he "did not believe in images."

Waiting for his hearing was not a tranquil experience. From his shed he watched other prisoners pass by and enter another large black building surrounded by a courtyard with walls painted black. Periodically prisoners emerged from the gateway with their hands tied.

All too soon it was Ranald's turn. Moriyama entered with soldiers, who formed a double line from the shed to the entry of the forbidding courtyard. As he entered the gate he saw on the floor a round bronze plate about six inches in diameter; stooping down he saw engraved on it an image of the Virgin Mary and the baby Jesus. Since Ranald was not a Catholic, he said he had no qualms about placing his foot on the image and did so, to Moriyama's evident relief. Later Moriyama explained that, ever since the expulsion of the Portuguese Catholic priests by the Bakufu and the antagonism that ensued toward Christians (the Japanese apparently did not consider Protestants as Christians at the time), bronze plates with depictions of religious figures such as Mary and Jesus or Christ on the cross had been fabricated. Annually in Nagasaki on the first month of the year, all citizens were required to file past and place their foot on such an image as proof that they had not become Christian.

After this negation of Catholicism, Ranald passed through a sliding gate and found himself in a court where a prisoner was being tried for theft by a lesser magistrate. Glancing to the right, he was startled to see another court more impressively manned by Japanese men, dressed richly in stiff silk gowns with projecting shoulder pieces, each kneeling or sitting on mats along each side of a series of broad steps. At the top of the platform were more mats, behind which was a line of guards. Off to one side was a secretary with paper and inks. Moriyama directed Ranald to a position at the base of the steps, where he was to kneel on a shabby and dirty mat, while Moriyama ascended part way up the broad steps.

Observing the finery of the assembled company, the orderliness, and the cleanliness of other mats, Ranald determined to show courage and resist the demeaning manner in which he was treated. Instead of complying with Moriyama's request to sit or kneel, he kicked at the filthy mat and refused, saying that he saw no chair or seat fit for him.

Distressed, Moriyama insisted that he must sit on the floor as did the Japanese. "But I cannot," replied Ranald, indicating that he was dressed in tight European sailor's trousers, not a loose gown. When perceiving that Moriyama was worried for his welfare, the assembly looking sternly at this exchange, Ranald relented and knelt on one knee. Even this did not suffice, and the prisoner finally sat down.

Moriyama went on to instruct Ranald in proper etiquette, saying that, when the governor entered, he must not look at him but must bow low, to which Ranald angrily responded that he would not.

The door at Ranald's right opened. A soldier entered carrying a naked sword by the point, hilt up. It was a two foot blade two inches wide, slightly curved, with a circular bronze guard. Two or three other soldiers marched behind him, then came the governor himself. Ranald remained upright, and a shocked Moriyama commanded him to bow. Even though Ranald was flanked by armed soldiers and disapproving court members, he felt his best chance was to exhibit a bold stance and refused again. "I kotow to no man!" he declared angrily.

He said in his journal:

"Curious to read my fate at the hands of His Excellency, I looked him fearlessly but respectfully, full in the face. So did he me. I had just quickly, before that, looked around, and saw every one, even the soldiers, flat on their faces, the hands being placed on the ground, and the forehead resting on them. They all remained in this position for quite a time, say ten or fifteen seconds during which, in dead silence, the governor and I stared at each other.

"At length, rising from his sitting position, slowly, on his knees, and stretching forth his arms, resting on his hands on his knees, leaning toward me, the Governor addressed me a few words, deep toned and low, which though I did not understand them, I took, from his manner and look, not to be unfriendly. Afterwards—for I could not at the time—I asked Moriyama what he said. He answered: 'He said you must have a big heart.'"

Still standing the governor was, to Ranald, both an exotic and dignified figure. He exuded confidence and boldness, a portly man about thirty-five years of age, somewhat short but holding himself upright. He was dressed in a pair of wide trousers of figured silk, green with a flowery pattern, and a silk, belted, gown open to the ankles, over which was a blue garment of fine cotton like two pieces sewn together behind but open in front. At the shoulder the cloth was stiffened with starch or other substance to project like enormous epaulettes. Like other Japanese, the governor had a shaved head, except for a top knot. His hands were well-manicured, delicate and white. Of regular features, Prince Ido had a short, straight nose, and a well-formed mouth in a round, full and florid face. His eyes were large and black, not particularly oblique. Waving a palm leaf fan as he seated himself on the mat, he regarded Ranald soberly but not unkindly. This time Ranald bowed low to him, not quite touching the ground.

The assembled company lifted their heads, all business, as Prince Ido administered an oath to Moriyama. From notes placed before the governor, he queried Ranald, essentially with the same questions as before, while the secretary dutifully recorded the answers.

When the question again came about belief in a God in Heaven, MacDonald repeated a simple "yes."

"More specifically, what is your belief," came the query.

"I believe there is one God, that he is constantly and everywhere present," replied Ranald.

Prince Ido did not respond, but Moriyama pressed further, asking exactly *what* Ranald believed in respect to this God in Heaven.

Ranald began to recite the Protestant Apostles' Creed, remembering well the words from his Episcopalian teachings, "I believe in God, the Father Almighty, Maker of Heaven and Earth, and in Jesus Christ, His only Son, our Lord, born of the Virgin Mary." Moriyama jerked to attention, stopping this discourse abruptly. "That will do!" he said.

He proceeded to translate the reply, leaving out the part about the Virgin Mary and Christ. The official version of MacDonald's reply, as given by Moriyama, reads: "There are no gods or buddhas, [I] merely cultivate mind and will and reverence heaven in order to obtain clear understanding and to secure happiness. [I have] nothing else to declare." Any statement associated with the banned Catholic religion would have been abhorred by the Japanese. In this selective translation Moriyama proved his friendly concern for Ranald—the direct translation surely being potentially hazardous to MacDonald's reception by Prince Ido.

Seemingly satisfied with the responses to the queries, the governor, Moriyama and the assembled officials discussed MacDonald among themselves without translation. Arriving at a conclusion, Prince Ido turned again to Ranald and uttered his decision.

Moriyama translated, "A house will be prepared for you to live in and, if you are good, you will live better and better."

On his knees Ranald bowed politely to the governor, rose to his feet and bowed again. Prince Ido merely regarded him without response.

Guards conducted MacDonald out of the court and into a palanquin to be carried through the streets to a compound surrounded by a stone wall about six feet high, topped with broken glass. Within there was a cluster of houses, with a small garden in front; the houses were separated from the wall by bamboo railings or fencing. Ranald was placed in an older house that apparently had been newly repaired for his confinement. Everything was neat and clean, and the floors covered with mats. At the entry was a small room for guards, beyond which, partitioned from the guardroom, was Ranald's prison, his home for the next several months.

The front wall of this room had been removed and high bars substituted, about four inches thick and four inches apart. A wooden screen several feet high gave him privacy. At one side of his prison was a bathroom with facilities for hot- or cold-water bathing. In his main room, only about nine feet by seven feet in size, there were floor mats six feet by three feet wide with selvages of gauze, sleeping mats three inches thick of rice straw, a mosquito bar, brazier, and teapot and cup.

This type of prison compartment, according to William Lewis, an early twentieth century historian, was common all over Japan for the less serious offender.

MacDonald was fortunate to be classified thus. Since the initial days of the Tokugawa Shoguns at least three hundred prisons had been established for various offenders. Prison accommodations varied widely as to the social class of individual offenders, and there were distinct divisions between major and minor crimes. Punishment for major crimes might include: *oshikomé,* confinement in one's home for a specified period; *tataki,* fifty to a hundred blows with a stick; or *tsuihō* or *shikéi,* beheading with various additional indignities performed on the corpse after death or crucifixion. Minor offenses involved: *hissoku* or house confinement; *naga-chikkyo,* confinement to the offender's room for life; or *tégusari,* keeping the offender's hands tied with a chain for thirty to a hundred days. Those confined to jails were no better or no worse off than those in other medieval type prisons; in other words, they resided in unpleasant cells, often dark and drafty, with poor food. The daily ration of a jailed prisoner was about a quart of uncleaned rice and certain sauces, with occasional fish or other food.

Ranald's crime of intrusion into Japan was treated essentially as house arrest or *azuké*—confinement in some other house for an indefinite period of time, a minor crime's punishment.

Nevertheless the room *was* a cell, airy and light but small, and Ranald wondered how long he would be so restricted. That evening he dined alone on soup, rice and tea; the following day servants brought him a table about a foot and a half high.

When Moriyama eventually appeared to inquire about his welfare, MacDonald asked if he could get his books to read but Moriyama refused him. Asking for his Bible, at least, Ranald was told, "Don't mention name of Bible in Japan, it is a bad book!"

Although polite, Moriyama was cool and noncommittal, volunteering that, if Ranald was good, the governor would give him everything he wanted. Besides Moriyama and Uemura, nine interpreters stood by—one each day, taking turns. They did not converse, but merely translated whenever Ranald made any request, referring to a Dutch-English dictionary for clarification. Despite the contacts with nine men, it was Moriyama who captured MacDonald's affection after the initial twenty-day "quarantine" of contacts with the prisoner was relaxed.

Interpreters such as Moriyama enjoyed great influence. Ever since the establishment of the Dutch at Deshima Island for the purposes of trade, interpreters were trained and employed by Japanese officials in order to deal with the foreigners. Although such positions emerged as early as the foreign establishments in Hirado, it was somewhat later, after the entrenchment of traders at Deshima, that an interpreter class was created (major, minor, middle grade, lowest grade, apprentice, etc.) The numbers varied, but at the time of the Meiji Restoration in 1868 there were one hundred and forty interpreters in Nagasaki.

Annually in rotation one *ōtsūji* and one *kotsūji*, a major and a minor interpreter, were assigned to especially important duties, such as accompanying the Dutch on their obligatory journeys to Tokyo. According to Grant Kohn Goodman in *The Dutch Impact on Japan*, the interpreters at Hirado were not government employees but were employed by the Dutch. After transfer of the Dutch factory to Deshima, eleven men were made official interpreters, with their descendants (Yokoyama, Ishibashi, Sadakata, Nishi, Inomata, Takasago, Shizuki, Kimotsuki, Hideshima, and Namura) following after them in the profession. For several decades, knowledge of the Dutch language was restricted almost entirely to the interpreter corps at Nagasaki. At first it was merely a verbal knowledge, but a written conversion was developed by the late 1600's to teach the children of the interpreters, who would continue in their fathers' profession.

The duties of the interpreters, which included superintending the actions of the Dutch, had interesting side effects. For example, when the Dutch fell ill and were treated by their own physicians, the interpreters witnessed medical techniques unfamiliar to them. Inevitably some applied their newly discovered knowledge to their own people, leading to the eventual sanction of the study of foreign medicine by Japanese scholars. Goodman says, "The importance of the influence of these early Nagasaki medical pioneers cannot be underestimated . . . that practical application of Dutch medical techniques had successfully demonstrated how accurate Western science was."

This acceptance by the Japanese led to further inquiry into other sciences. For example, vigorous debates raged as to whether the world was indeed round, since this theory was at variance with the more widely read Chinese philosopher Chu Hsi. As Goodman said, "the significance of the work of the interpreters and their cohorts was to point the way for a later eruption of Dutch learning as a motivating force in the Japanese intellectual world."

Since the days of the Dutch in Hirado (England had only a brief appearance there), and later in Deshima, Japanese scholars and interpreters who were permitted to study about foreigners became steeped in Dutch philosophies. Their language was Dutch, the science and technology of Dutch extraction, the political opinions were Dutch, and the meager numbers of books available usually were in the Dutch language. Little wonder that these early seekers of knowledge believed—quite erroneously, as it happened—that the Dutch were the most powerful and largest foreign nation beyond the seas.

The isolation of Japan from the western world had been very effective. Except for the influence of pilot Will Adams and the brief contacts with Hirado traders from Britain in the 1600's, no known English-speaking persons had been "at large" in Japan prior to Ranald MacDonald. Several ships had attempted to penetrate the veil drawn over Japan by the Tokugawa Shoguns, with some forced to retreat from the shores under fire, but no official parties or individuals had been received by Japan. There were intermittent seizures of shipwrecked sailors, who—like MacDonald and the deserters from the *Lagoda*—had been brought promptly to Nagasaki, but most of these sailors tended to be relatively illiterate.

Ranald MacDonald was an exception, having received the best possible education afforded the sons of Hudson's Bay officers in Canada. He had graduated at a level of education approximating a modern-day high school. He was well-educated, indeed, for the times. Thus, his arrival in Japan was fortuitous—the messenger from abroad bearing news of an advanced civilization other than of Dutch extraction. In order to understand more fully the importance of MacDonald's appearance in Japan at that time, of his teaching of the English language and propounding English ideas, it is helpful to trace briefly the development of Dutch learning (then synonymous with "foreign" learning) by Japanese scholars.

XII
Development of Dutch Learning

According to Emil and Amy Lederer in *Japan in Transition*, the Japanese did not become entranced with the cultural heritage of the Occident, as Rome had come under the spell of Greek knowledge. Japan was too wrapped up in her own isolated and functioning world to place much importance, at first, on the intellectual advancements of Europe. Lederer proposed that it was the practical, pragmatic drive of Europe and America that broke down the isolation of the Orient and forced Japan to accept new ideas as well as new products.

In the 1500's it was the Catholic religion that first won a foothold, disseminating only minimally the culture of Europeans along with dogma. The priests' intolerance and unwise intrusion into Japan's political and social life so alarmed the Japanese that the Portuguese were banished from Japan. Somewhat by accident, the Dutch captured the right to trade with Japan, the only other nation permitted being China. After its repair and resupply by the Japanese following the shipwreck mentioned in Chapter VII, the Dutch ship *de Liefde*, under Captain Jacob Quaeckerneck, departed for Holland in 1605, bearing a permit from Shogun Ieyasu Tokugawa to trade with Japan. Shortly thereafter, the newly formed Dutch East India Company established a post at Hirado Island. Throughout the strife with the Portuguese, the Dutch maneuvered successfully to convince the Japanese authorities that they had interest only in trade, not converts. Although forced to relocate in 1641 to the dismal island of Deshima created from a virtual mud flat, the Dutch trod the line laid down by Edo as a condition for trade well into the nineteenth century.

For some years, bruised and concerned by their difficulties with the Portuguese, the Japanese frowned mightily on absorbing any facet of foreign culture through the Dutch. As stated earlier, the designation of a merchant on the social scale, even a foreign merchant, was at the bottom of any list. The Dutch were considered a necessary "evil," where certain supplies—especially a growing arsenal of European military equipment—

could be purchased, and where selected cliques of authorities could listen to the Dutch report on happenings outside their closed world of Japan. Shogun Iemitsu Tokugawa in 1630, through the Edict of Kanei, banned Western books mentioning any aspect of Christianity. The edict was interpreted by cautious underlings in the broadest sense. Even the official interpreters knew little of the Dutch language and culture outside of the economic vernacular.

Grant Kohn Goodman states that the first attempt at formal instruction seems to have begun in 1671, when a Dutch newspaper kept by the Deshima traders noted that, by order of the Japanese authorities, a number of boys from ten to twelve years of age (mostly the sons of the interpreters) were to be sent to Deshima for practice in reading and writing Dutch. There is considerable evidence that to enhance their own importance, the early interpreters indeed tried to cloister the knowledge of Dutch or Western thought, thus discouraging other students.

After interpreters happened to witness the practice of Dutch medicine in the households of Deshima, the first Dutch books to arouse intense curiosity were those on medicine. Before long, the Bakufu at Edo expressed official interest in matters of medicine, extending the curiosity to astronomy, gunnery, and mathematics. The propounded theory that the world was round and other Dutch theories angered the Confucian scholars, who still had the ear of the Bakufu and Shogun, for the most part. Yet as time went on, serious Japanese scholars began to perceive that the Chinese (from whom they had borrowed Confucian thought) might not be the real center of the universe, that there was a far larger world "out there," and that Western ideas were more practical than those of traditional Confucianism, which concerned itself chiefly with morals, household management and somewhat abstract philosophy. The ancient bonds that turned Japan inward were beginning to fray.

It was under the reign of Shogun Yoshimune that Western learning flourished for decades. In 1720, he relaxed the Edict of Kanei to allow certain Chinese books (including some scientific works written by the Jesuits in China and books on mathematics) and more Western books into Japan, especially those involving astronomy and other sciences. He expressed personal interest in the geography of foreign lands. Books, watches and maps were brought as gifts by the Dutch on their mandatory visits to the Shogun.

Curiously, one of the reasons for Yoshimune's interest was that the accuracy of the Japanese calendar was questioned. Since the government knew that a copy of an astronomical encyclopedia by Father Adam Schall still existed in Nagasaki, it ordered the book to be forwarded to Edo for scrutiny. If this foreign treatise was valuable, perhaps there were others that could be selectively used, he reasoned. Yoshimune also was fascinated by the possibilities of horses and weapons in war. Horses were imported from Korea, China, and Holland, and the Dutch ordered to give riding lessons to the Shogun's retainers.

By the middle of the 1700's a small but dedicated group of scholars, largely around Nagasaki but moving on to Edo, formed a group called *Rangakusha* or "Dutch Scholars." They were not necessarily interpreters, but included private persons—often lower-level samurai who occasionally were assigned by their overlords to engage in studies, especially those involving military advantage and medicine. In 1771, three medical scholars, Maeno, Sugita, and Nakagawa, all in the service of the Daimyo of Nakatsu, witnessed a human dissection after an execution in order to prove or disprove theories propounded in a Dutch anatomy book.

The infinitesimal band of Japanese scholars did not have an easy time of it. Books were still difficult to obtain, a dictionary from Dutch to Japanese or vice versa did not exist, and the political climate changed with the variations in the Bakufu. Zealous Confucians planted seeds of doubt in the minds of receptive officials about the heresy of Western learning, so that, on occasions, a scholar was summarily tried or executed. The tribulations of early scholars are recounted in books by two early Japanese authors: Gempaku Sugita, *Rangaku Kotohajime*, or *The Beginnings of Dutch Studies*, 1771; and Gentaku Ōtsuki, *Rangaku Kaitei*, or *First Steps in Dutch*, 1783. The latter became indispensable for those who studied Dutch.

As contacts with foreign ships increased toward the beginning of the nineteenth century, the Bakufu and feudal lords increasingly realized the need for more knowledge about the world. Between 1809 and 1817, the Japanese government commissioned the director of Deshima's factory, Hendrick Doeff, to compile a dictionary with the assistance of ten Japanese interpreters. When completed, two copies of the work—devoting itself to a Dutch-Japanese translation but not the reverse—were created; one sent to the Government Library at Edo, the other retained by Doeff (but later lost). A rough draft found its way in 1829 to the Dutch Royal Museum, Amsterdam.

Undoubtedly aided by the new dictionary, but also spurred by increasing curiosity about the Western world, the Japanese thronged to learn Dutch. Coming upon the scene in this auspicious time was P. F. von Siebold, ostensibly Dutch but really of German extraction. From 1823 to 1830, Siebold's home near Nagasaki was the center of instruction for Japanese students from many areas of Japan, and the Dutch language spread with his "graduates" to all of Japan. Siebold awarded certificates of proficiency to the best students.

Siebold's friendships with Japanese students led to tragedy for some. The Tokugawa edicts about secrecy and the opposition to Western learning by Confucians and doctors of Chinese medicine still were strong. Murdoch relates a dismaying incident in his *History of Japan*.

Accompanying a Deshima merchant on a visit to Edo, Siebold was lionized by scholars, who urged him to stay on in Edo to translate certain botanical works. But when the merchant van Sturler happened to offend the Bakufu in a trading matter, the climate totally changed. The close friends and interpreters of Siebold's circle suddenly came under hostile scrutiny—especially Otsuki, an official translator; "Wilhelm Botanikus" Katsuragawa (Siebold was wont to confer Dutch names upon willing students); and the Court astronomer Takaro Sampei Takahashi. The latter had shown Siebold a map drawn by the famed cartographer, Chukei Inō, in 1818 and engraved in 1823. (Inō had been a pupil of Takahashi's father, an astronomer to the Shogun.) To show a foreigner any maps of the country was a serious offense, but Takahashi had promised to supply one to Siebold in return for a copy of a fairly accurate Russian map of the world. An enemy betrayed Takahashi to hostile members of the Bakufu. Despite Siebold's attempted intervention on behalf of his cohorts and the support of certain daimyos, particularly Shimazu of Satsuma, Takahashi was imprisoned and Siebold was banished. Takahashi died in prison before his case was tried. For a time thereafter, in the 1830's, Dutch learning was in disfavor.

When the "scandal" died down, several of Siebold's former pupils gathered in Edo to form the "Downtown Club," while others more specifically interested in medicine organized as the "Uptown Club," founded by Noboru "Kwazan" Watanabe. Members were fascinated not only by science but also—somewhat surreptitiously—by military science. Watanabe was what one might call an "armchair scholar," a poet, an artist of some note, and capable administrator of his small Tawara fiefdom. Lively and gregarious, he organized intellectual discussion groups composed of those interested in sciences and the study of foreign countries. Possibly he was inspired by Nagahide Takano, a prolific translator of medical and science books. Murdoch claims that, before Takano died, he had translated or written at least fifty-two separate works, some of them several volumes long.

Takano, too, fell victim to reactionaries in the Bakufu, particularly to a foe of Dutch learning, Yozo Torii, son of the Confucian scholar Jussai Hayashi.

Takano's particular "heresy" was the writing of a pamphlet against the exclusion policy in 1838, before the Exclusion Edict of 1825 had been modified in 1842. Takano and his friends had heard that the American ship *Morrison* was to arrive for repatriation of Japanese castaways and that the Bakufu intended to order shore batteries to fire on it, a policy they disapproved of and felt would have unfavorable repercussions for Japan. Ironically the news was garbled, and the *Morrison* had long since come and gone in 1837, indeed having been turned back by the Japanese. For such unlawful criticism of the state, Torii brought charges against Takano and others, claiming that they were plotting military overthrow of the government. Takano's friend, Watanabe, popular among the cultural crowd, was the first to be arrested. Even though his cohorts, especially his fellow artists, struggled to gain his release and helped to smuggle creature comforts to him in his miserable prison cell, Watanabe was sentenced to confinement for life within his home. In poor health and threatened with further charges from the Bakufu, he committed *hara-kiri* in 1841.

Before his arrest, Watanabe had managed to warn Takano, who went into hiding for a time. Learning of the rough treatment of Watanabe, Takano surfaced voluntarily to take the blame for any misdeeds, since it was his pamphlet that had incurred the wrath of officials. Imprisoned in a common jail, Takano escaped in 1844 during a prison fire. A fugitive then, he wandered for six years, fed and clothed by friendly daimyos and sometimes earning money for translations, before he was betrayed by a former fellow prisoner to the police. During the attempt at re-arrest, Takano killed two officers before committing *hara-kiri* himself.

Still another distinguished scholar, Shuhan Takashima, was attacked by the influential Torii as a subversive. The Takashima family had been established in Nagasaki for centuries as holders of municipal offices and experts in gunnery. Shuhan Takashima succeeded his father and became a diligent student of military science. For this he had to turn to Dutch books and scholars. When he could not obtain better armaments from the Bakufu, he spent his own money to buy Dutch weapons, including mortars and modern muskets, while training two companies of infantry and a battery of artillery to defend Nagasaki. Particularly alarming to students of military science was the ease with which the British overcame China in 1840. Surely Japan would be next, they worried. Hakumin Aizawa maintained that Russia was the chief menace. If China were strong, Russia would invade Japan from the north, then use Japan as a base from which to attack China. If China were weak, Russia would overcome North China and turn upon Japan thereafter. Another worried scholar of military science, Shinen

Sato, felt that China's fall began with permitting European powers to gain an economic foothold. Shozan Sakuma and his student, Shoin Yoshida, trumpeted their concerns about England's intentions. Little concern seems to have been voiced about the United States, since the Americans had no visible territorial claims on Asia. Perhaps the United States was considered no threat or was so little known that its true power was not understood.

Impressed by Takashima's grasp of gunnery, Sakuma had studied for a time with Takashima's mentor, a high-ranking Bakufu official, Tarozaemon Egawa. Born of a samurai family loyal to the feudal lord Sanada of Shinano, Sakuma was encouraged in his studies by his lord. As a result of his probings into military science, Sakuma urged Western-style improvements in the nation's military defenses but was repelled by the idea of commerce with foreign barbarians. His appetite whetted by his readings, he continued his studies of the Dutch language so he might learn more. From the scientific treatises and instructions read in a Dutch encyclopedia, he learned to make glass and refine chemicals. By 1848, he was able to manufacture weapons, including small field artillery. To assist other scholars he published a new Dutch-Japanese dictionary, the *Halma*, taken partly from an eighteenth-century effort by Francois Halma. As his studies of Western learning progressed, Sakuma questioned the effectiveness of Confucian or Chinese literature as the criterion of learning, declaring that Western ideas were more practical.

Despite the concerns of such scholars about foreign invasion and their studies of military science for protection and not subversion of Japan, isolationist Torii condemned men like Takashima for even studying foreign disciplines. Fortunately, Torii himself fell from favor before he could destroy Takashima's career totally.

American historian E. Herbert Norman credits these nineteenth century scholars as the spiritual fathers of the Meiji Restoration, because of their dangerous and outspoken criticisms of the Shogun's neglect of military defenses. Japanese thinkers scrutinized not only military science, but also economics. Toshiaki Honda wrote: "As Japan is a sea-girt country, it should be the first care of the Ruler to develop shipping and trade. Through sending her ships to all countries, Japan should import such goods as are useful at home, as well as gold, silver and copper to replenish her resources. The country will grow weaker and weaker if it remains contented with the policy of supplying its needs exclusively with its own products. The weaker the country, the heavier will become the burden on the farmers, with the natural result that the farming population will become increasingly impoverished." (Quoted by Norman, *Japan's Emergence as a Modern State*, from a Japanese writer, Eijiro Honjo.)

As resistance to Western learning waned, private schools opened to disseminate Western learning, then almost entirely Dutch. Among them were Juntendō led by Taizen Satō in Sakura, Shōsendō led by Gemboku Itō at Edo, Nisshūdō led by Shindō in Edo, and—possibly the most important— Tamatamajuku founded by Shindō's pupil, Kōan Ogata. The latter was a physician, but his school—working largely from Dutch books—turned out influential graduates in education and politics, botany and gunnery.

Among the observations of early Japanese scholars studying Dutch was the cumbersome aspect of writing in Chinese characters, compared to the flow of Western writing. Some pointed out that, merely to learn the forty thousand characters of the Japanese language, scholars consumed a disproportionate amount of their working lives that could otherwise be devoted to research. The problem still plagues the Oriental countries in the modern world, with the difficulty of adapting the characters to typewriters, computers, and other business machines.

In 1842, the most powerful man in the Bakufu, Mizuno, Echizen no Kami, had ordered the dutiful Dutch traders at Deshima to provide models of European machines of possible use in Japan, along with pertinent books and journals. Toward mid-century Britain's prowess at war, now greatly feared since her victory over China, necessitated ferreting out what her plans might be. As occasional contacts with English-speaking people occurred, scholars were astonished to learn that Dutch was not the world's standard language; that, if any appeared to be destined to triumph as a broad communication medium, likely it would be English. Well steeped in Dutch, the Japanese needed now to master an entirely new language. The intellectual climate fermented with the need for able translators and interpreters.

Since it was in Nagasaki, the seat of Dutch learning, that new ideas and foreign knowledge were received most openly, Ranald MacDonald, no ordinary seaman but an educated gentleman in sailor's clothing, arrived as the answer to an unspoken prayer—a teacher of English. He was the key to understanding the barbarian Americans and British who were knocking at the closed door of Japan.

XIII

Ranald the Teacher

After twenty days of confinement, comfortable but in relative isolation, MacDonald was taken before Shirai Tatsunosin, a high military chief of Nagasaki and assistant to the governor and another unidentified magistrate. He was questioned again as to why and how he left his ship, answering in the same manner as before. These answers were compared for consistency with his replies given to similar questions at his first hearing.

In particular, the court asked him about the quadrant found in his possession, suggesting that he really intended to survey the coast, to which Ranald replied in the negative. Further questions came about his family; what was his father's business; whether the captain of the *Plymouth* would be punished for the desertion of a crewman; would an enquiry be made about Ranald after the *Plymouth* returned to her home port; and related matters.

The conclusion of the court was that "You must have a great heart to leave in a little boat."

Another period of tedious isolation ensued. After two weeks, the governor, Prince Ido, came to interrogate Ranald in his cage. Flanked by subordinates the governor produced a Japanese copy of an English atlas, asking Ranald to relate what course the *Plymouth* had taken on its voyage to the Sea of Japan, where it had stopped, details about the people and products at such places, etc. Ranald freely gave as much information as he could.

Ranald said in his journal, "When I pointed out Batan in the China Sea, as the last port at which the vessel I left had touched they observed it was a 'bad place.' They conversed a long time about it, using often the word 'padre.'"

Other queries included details about whaling and the number of vessels engaged in the business. A canny Ranald suggested that Japan would be a good place for whalers to obtain supplies, instead of forcing the foreigners to travel south to the Sandwich Islands or Hong Kong. He asked if the Japanese might consider opening trade with Americans or other foreign countries, to which the interrogators firmly said No! Interpreter Moriyama recited the Tokugawa edicts of 1825 and 1842 about forbidding ships from entering the harbors.

Ranald said, "I often, after that, spoke to him on the subject. His answer was invariably the same. He assigned, as the cause of the law, the revolutionary conduct of the Portuguese Christians early in the seventeenth century."

Within a few days MacDonald was examined at the Nagasaki Town Hall by Joseph Levyssohn, director of the Dutch factory, 1846-50. Essentially his questions were an echo of the previous Japanese interrogations. When he had finished questioning Ranald, he told him that the Dutch ship, *Josephine Catherine*, had left recently and it would be almost a year before he could be repatriated. He also expressed disapproval at the conduct of the *Plymouth*'s captain for allowing Ranald to leave the ship off Hokkaido (Ranald had told him the true situation, which Levyssohn did not reveal to the Japanese).

Finally satisfied that Ranald MacDonald was no threat to them, the Japanese settled down and left him to his extended confinement. Relationships became more friendly except for a horrifying incident: one of Ranald's guards permitted his wife and relatives to come to the jail to view the foreigner, for which infraction of rules the guard was beheaded.

Except for restriction of his liberty and the somnolent effect of confinement to the small quarters, Ranald was not unhappy. The Japanese returned his Bible, even honoring the book as "his God" by constructing a special shelf of respect or *tokiwari* on which to store it. They supplied bread, and provided pork in his diet every seventh day, even though religious Japanese ate no meat. How to make bread was remembered from Portuguese days, but most did not use products made of flour except for rare bakings of sweet cakes. From the Dutch factor Ranald received butter for his bread and, on special occasions, gifts of food. On New Year's Day, 1849, Factor Levyssohn included sixty-eight copies of the *London Atlas* newspaper and *Weekly Dispatch*, the most welcome and useful gifts of all, since they not only enlightened Ranald but could be used as reading materials during English classes.

During the seven months of confinement Ranald MacDonald received pupils sent to him to learn English, all of them interpreters (see Chapter XI). In addition to Einosuke Moriyama and Sakushichirō Uemura, his particular companions, twelve others received English instruction and engaged in conversation with Ranald about the outside world:

Nishi Yoichirō
Nishi Keitarō
Ogawa Keijurō
Shioya Tanesaburō
Nakayama Hyōma
Inomata Dennosuke
Shizuki Tatsuichirō
Iwase Yashirō
Hori Ichirō
Shige Takanoske
Namura Tsunenoske
Motoki Shosayemon
    (Spelled as reported by Lewis & Murakami, 1923, last names given first. Hori Ichiro believed to be incorrect; should be Hori Tatsunosuke, father of Ichiro.)

It was a vital breakthrough for these key men to receive instruction in English. As indicated in earlier chapters, until that time most of their knowledge of the outside world had been filtered through the Dutch, from Dutch factors and textbooks. Now Ranald MacDonald, a comparatively well educated man from a British background and schooling, provided not only a new language but also the concurrent ability to read books containing theories and facts sometimes divergent from the Dutch readings.

Indeed, whenever Japanese officials opened the matter of forging treaties with other foreign powers, the Dutch and Chinese naturally were opposed to them, since it would mean the dilution of the monopoly these two countries—and particularly the Dutch—maintained upon the trade with Japan, albeit through the restrictive confines of Deshima in Nagasaki.

During Ranald's imprisonment privileged Japanese came to stare at him in his cage, as one would view an exotic animal. Others came to share ideas. The latter, the scholars, reflected the ingrained mania for secrecy of the Tokugawa era. Ranald said, "they ever studiedly on their guard against saying too much in exposition of their affairs and general public or even private life."

Among his visitors were priests, some dressed in black, others in dark olive green, in reddish or Spanish brown. Their garments differed from ordinary Japanese dress only in the sleeves being wider and the dress longer. Such priests were perfectly bald; they never married; and all were vegetarian. Through discussions about religion, Ranald cautiously presented his Christian views in a general way, having "no special aptitude, nor training for the purpose; and it did not enter into my personal aims to incur any martyrdom for any Church's sake." His comments were couched in the broad agreement of a common humanity with the Japanese, and that church and state were not one, with the things of Christ not of this world. He learned that the Shinto priests worshiped an abstract deity, represented by the sun, and in a heaven, to which they would go if they were good during life. They had a devil whom they feared greatly; "when they imagine he comes across their course, they kneel, rubbing, at the same time, the palms of their hands together in sign of supplication to be spared from misfortune or evil."

Other than being mystified by their penchant for sudden execution of miscreants breaking their laws, or the respectability of suicide as expiation for misconduct, Ranald was tolerant of the differing faith, saying:

"We—of the so-called Christian Church, may regard such Theism as an imperfect religion, and, in effect, essentially heathenism, like that— said—of the Chinese, *Quaere!* Are we right? By what rule—law—should we so condemn our brother? As God made *him*; and has ever in his wanderings through the desert of life, from generation to generation been his Preserver and 'Way of life,' so he is today! Is it for us to condemn our fellowman? I am no controversialist in religion. What I have in this way, I cherish, and try in my own weak humble way to live up to, in faith in Christ—as a Christian in profession and heart—and I thus speak because this have I learned my duty to Man as to God."

Renowned author William Elliot Griffis writes, "On winter nights, Ranald's cage became a house of reception, lit with wax candles on low square stands. Men of all orders came to see and talk with the first teacher of English in Japan." It was the interpreters who were closest to Ranald's heart, with whom he spent hours almost daily in teaching and discussion. The interpreters, who already had a gift for languages, learned English rapidly but had some difficulty in pronouncing certain consonants. The letter "L" was a sound unfamiliar to them; they pronounced it as "R." They tended to round out a consonant at the end of a word by adding an "I" or "O" and pronounced all letters, contrary to certain English combinations where letters are silent in the verbal expression. MacDonald was pleasantly surprised at the students' ability to absorb English grammar readily. Part of the teaching was by rote: MacDonald read materials to them in English, and the students read English back to Ranald so he could correct pronunciation, explain the meanings of words, and instruct them in grammar. The English instruction was facilitated through the intermediary use of the Japanese-Dutch dictionary used by the interpreters. The precise meanings of words, one language to another via Dutch, had to be threshed out in endless discussions.

In the absence of any Japanese dictionary or book of instruction in Japanese, Ranald himself had nothing from which to learn except conversation. Within a short time he was able to converse in "pidgin" Japanese, however.

As time went on, Ranald was able to use these teaching sessions to disseminate information on British and American life. He told the interpreters of the principles of constitutional government practiced in Great Britain and the United States, while not openly criticizing the restrictive regime of the Tokugawa. The structure of Great Britain, with a single authority represented by the King or Queen, plus other elected officials was perceived to be somewhat similar to that of Japan (although not really factual). The American principle of government being *given* its powers by the people, instead of vice versa, was more difficult to fathom.

In turn, Ranald MacDonald acquired in bits and pieces an overview of what was transpiring in Japanese life, sensing the yearning of many Japanese to join the family of nations in trade and social intercourse but recognizing that exhibitions by his pupils of excessive interest was possible cause for reprimand or worse.

In the last years of the nineteenth century, when Ranald MacDonald wrote his journals from memory, he said of the Japanese:

"As to their wonderful progress in civil life and government within the last few years, I am not surprised.

"From what I saw of them, their aspirations—scarce concealed though studiedly covered—were, to my view, even then, in that direction. I felt at the time, that some such change, possibly soon, would come—come, not *over* them, as from some external force, but from within themselves—in process of that inherent principle of progressive national life, in evolution, which from the very *origin* of their nationhood has—uniquely, as a sort of 'chosen people'. . . they are truly a wonder among the nations; commanding, in their present position, the respect and admiration of the world."

By the time he wrote this, decades later, Ranald himself realized the impact his teachings had made upon history, but—except for a few acquaintances on both sides of the Pacific—the world did not recognize his contributions. In retrospect MacDonald wrote:

"Here, in reference to this incident of my having been the first, during their hermit seclusion, to be teacher of English to the Japanese, and in that was the first instructor—apostle in a sense—of English thought, influence, and power for good, to this people—then in darkness in such matter—the following questions suggest themselves."

MacDonald proceeded to provide the answers to his inner questions. He was convinced that the Japanese made him a teacher of English because of their recognition of their position at the time, a tenuous one, in the family of nations. In receiving his teachings and their "incidental advocacy of international relations on the general principles of comity of nations," they were but following their own desire to make changes. Ranald believed that the enlightenment provided through his conversations with intellectuals and interpreters at his Nagasaki prison gradually reached the heads of government in Kyoto and Tokyo, influencing those in power to accede to the demands—made soon after MacDonald's departure from Nagasaki—of Commodore Perry, representing the United States, and of Great Britain's envoys, for trade treaties.

MacDonald's own beliefs were expressed by a Japanese-Canadian, Reverend K. T. Takahashi of Montreal. In 1888, Ranald's old family friend, Judge Malcolm McLeod, had discussed the story of Ranald's adventure with Takahashi, who said:

"The special reason for which the narrative is interesting to us Japanese is the light which it throws upon the inner current of thought which was gradually changing its course then, in Japan."

Indeed, the fateful arrival of Ranald MacDonald on Japanese soil did affect the ongoing intercourse with the Western world.

XIV
Preble to the Rescue

While Ranald was languishing in prison enjoying a reasonably comfortable life except for lack of exercise, the ship *Lagoda*, shipwrecked off the
Hokkaido shore, had been reported missing and her crew presumed
drowned. However, on January 25, 1849, Robert Browne, Consul for the
King of the Netherlands, Canton, wrote to U. S. Commissioner, J. W.
Davis, at Whampoa, China, that he had received rumors in August, 1848,
that an American vessel had wrecked near Matsumae in June, 1848, and
eighteen survivors had been captured by the Japanese. Further, Browne
had been told the survivors were in Nagasaki by September, where they
were still being held prisoner. According to the Dutch Factor Levyssohn of
Nagasaki, the sailors had been interrogated by the Japanese authorities. He
listed their names.

A spokesman reported that the ship had left New Bedford, Massa-
chusetts, on August 25, 1846, to whale around New Zealand and
Kamchatka in the Pacific. On June 2, 1848, the ship was filled with 1,300
barrels of oil and turned home. During a fog, it struck a shoal in the Japan
Sea and sank. The crew abandoned ship in five boats, two of which were
swamped and their occupants drowned, while the remaining three reached
Hokkaido's shore after drifting for five days. (The survivors actually were
deserters. See account in Chapter X.)

Browne reported that, even though there was a Dutch merchant ship
in Nagasaki Harbor at the time the sailors arrived, the Japanese would not
release them without specific permission from Tokyo, about a forty-day
round trip for a messenger. Therefore, the crew remained in prison. Nothing was said about MacDonald, since he was presumed dead.

Davis passed Browne's information along to Commodore David
Geisinger, chief officer of the U. S. Squadron, East Indies, on the United
States flagship *Plymouth* in Whampoa. Wasting no time in pursuing the
matter, Geisinger wrote to Honorable J. Y. Mason, Secretary of the Navy,
Washington, D. C., on January 27, 1849:

Sir: In my communication No. 12 I had the honor to inform the department of my intention to despatch the United States ship Preble to Shanghai, and the intermediate consular ports, about the first proximo. The Preble was accordingly under sailing orders, and on the eve of departure, when I received a communication from the Hon. J. W. Davis, United States Commissioner to China, that induced me to change her destination. She will proceed forthwith to Nangasacki, Japan, and will probably be absent about three months.

The enclosed correspondence between Mr. Davis and myself, to which I have the honor to invite your attention, will fully inform you of the particulars of the shipwreck of the American whaler Lagoda, of New Bedford, and of the detention by the Japanese authorities of the survivors of her crew.

Commander Glynn is instructed to proceed in the Preble, under his command, to demand the release of these prisoners, and they will doubtless be surrendered to him at once. He is also instructed to make known to Mr. Levyssohn, the Dutch superintendent of trade at Decima, the high appreciation in which his humanity and generosity toward these sufferers are held.

I have the honor to be, very respectfully, your obedient servant,
D. GEISINGER,
Commanding U. S. Squadron, East Indies

The ship *Preble* then was in Hong Kong, undergoing repairs. On January 31, 1849, Geisinger gave sailing instructions to Commander James Glynn, requesting him to sail as soon as possible to Nagasaki. There he was to obtain the release of fifteen seamen, the survivors from the *Lagoda*, and deliver them to Shanghai. He asked Glynn to convey the profound thanks for the Dutch Factor's assistance and directed that,

> . . . should it be objected by the Japanese at Nangasacki that these prisoners cannot be delivered up without previously obtaining authority from the court at Yedo, you will at once proceed to the bay of Yedo, and avail yourself of the earliest means of entering into communication with the imperial court.
> . . . Should you ascertain from that government, or from any other reliable source, that there are other American seamen in confinement in Japan, you will, of course, demand their release and surrender. In your correspondence or intercourse with the Japanese, your conduct will be conciliatory, but firm.
> . . . The protection of our valuable whaling fleet and the encouragement of the whale fishery are objects of deep interest to our government . . . be prompt to aid and promote these objects.

Glynn left Hong Kong on February 13, but, a few days out of port, sailing against a strong current, was making little progress, when a sailor came down with smallpox and Glynn returned to Hong Kong. By March 7, it seemed everyone was well, but then another case appeared, delaying the ship again. While in port, Captain Glynn read a copy of the *Seaman's Friend* of December, 1848, concerning Ranald MacDonald. This was the first indication he had that MacDonald might still be in Japan, but Glynn thought it likely he was dead since the rudder from his boat had been found. Finally the ship sailed on March 23, proceeding with all haste to Nagasaki, arriving in the outer harbor on April 18, 1849.

Out from the port came a small boat with persons waving large mats to indicate "go away, go away," but Glynn gave the order to continue. The boats then planted themselves in front of the *Preble*, hastily moving only when it appeared the larger ship would run them down. One boat pulled alongside and threw three folded papers, stuck into the split end of a piece of bamboo, on board the *Preble*, but Glynn ordered them thrown overboard as an improper way of communication. After communication had been established later, the papers again were proffered and translated, saying, in essence, to anchor in the outer harbor and stay there until further notice, that "very disagreeable consequences might result in case this order should not be strictly observed." When the ship anchored to await developments, the boats came closer with their almost naked crews making loud cries of objection. Each boat flew a gray flag and a small blue flag with "Chinese" characters on it saying "Imperial Service."

Later that day a boat came to the *Preble* with Moriyama on board, accompanied by seven others. Boarding the *Plymouth*, he said his purpose was to inquire why the ship had come, and why Commander Glynn had not anchored where he was told by the paper thrown on board. Glynn took this somewhat brusquely, objecting to the proposed site as unsafe and inferring that he intended to anchor in the protected inner harbor, and that he had important business with the Japanese government. Moriyama and his men departed, ostensibly to seek the advice of a superior.

Without waiting for Moriyama's return, Captain Glynn proceeded beyond the Isle of Papenberg, bound for an anchorage, only to meet Moriyama's boat returning with the message, "anchor anywhere."

Later that day a Nagasaki military chief, Shirai Tatsunosin, came aboard to question Glynn. Glynn was asked if he had verbal or written orders to come to Nagasaki, and from whom. When Glynn replied that he had written orders, Tatsunosin asked if the retrieval of his countrymen was his sole purpose in being at Nagasaki, and how Glynn had learned of the imprisoned *Lagoda* crew. Only as the discussion ensued did Glynn learn that Ranald MacDonald indeed was being held, and that two seamen of the sixteen from the *Lagoda* had died.

Tatsunosin freely discussed the prisoner problem and left the three papers for Glynn's mate to copy. He left to discuss with the governor of Nagasaki whether permission must be obtained from Tokyo or whether the prisoners could be released.

On the following day a different high military chief, Matsumora, met with Glynn in a pleasant but somewhat vague interview about the release of prisoners. Among the odd questions asked by Matsumora was, "How old are you?" Glynn replied, after some humorous discussion with his crew, and later on asked Matsumora whimsically, "How old is the Emperor?"

Three days passed. On April 22, Matsumora with Moriyama interpreting consulted with Glynn, saying that the governor would send a reply "another time—not now." An exasperated Glynn declared, "Three days ago I sent a written communication to your governor. What is the reason that a verbal instead of a written reply is sent to me? I do not want a verbal message or a messenger. I must have a *written answer* to my demand for the liberation of the shipwrecked seamen, that I can show to my superior officer and to my government the official reply, and also to show that I have done those things I was ordered to do."

Matsumora replied, "By the usages and customs of Japan, we come to speak to you now by word of mouth."

Further wrangling continued about the propriety of the manner of handling Glynn's demand for release of the prisoners. Matsumora stubbornly admitted that he was not even sure the governor had yet written to the Emperor, and, if he had, that it might take thirty to forty days to receive a reply.

Without progress, another day went by. Tatsunosin returned to rehash most of the same reasons why the prisoners were not being released. However, Tatsunosin did reveal that the Dutch Factor Levyssohn had urged the governor to release the men, and that Levyssohn would see him a couple of days hence (not now because he was ill).

Glynn's patience had worn thin. He exploded, "Stop! Your policy is very apparent. Now, I do not want to know what you 'think;' you have had ample time, certainly, to think. I can think, also. I have thought a great deal. It is time that matters should come to a crisis—that something definite was arrived at. I have been here five days—a time full enough for the governor to have come to some determination, and to have sent me a reply to my letter. You put me off from day to day on the merest pretences, and up to this moment you refuse to let me know if my demands are to be denied or not. I want a 'positive promise' as to whether I am to get the men or not. Under such a promise I will give two days; more I must not, cannot give. Will you give me this promise?"

Still the Japanese procrastinated, unwilling to make a decision himself. Eventually the conference ended without resolution.

Meanwhile, at his prison, holding English classes, Ranald MacDonald heard cannon shots in the town. Startled he asked the interpreters with him if a new governor had arrived. A veiled look came over their faces, smiles of embarrassment showing deceit, as one replied in the affirmative—looking at his cohorts for support. Having so declared, the students left abruptly. One returned to the bars of Ranald's cage and confided that a foreign ship had arrived, and that the guns were being fired to signal troops in the interior that auxiliary soldiers would come into Nagasaki.

Ranald was consumed with curiosity about the ship, but no one enlightened him further. The following morning there was a pile of papers resting beside his solitary guard. When queried, the man said that the papers contained lists of the soldiers that had arrived from the interior, precisely three thousand five hundred of them.

Ranald pondered the reasons for leaving such lists at his particular door, and doubted the existence of that many soldiers. The guard offered the information that the usual strength in Nagasaki was only three to four hundred men and that, as needed, troops were summoned from the interior. Remembering other conversations, Ranald questioned the high number of troops. He knew that there were few forts, that the troops were equipped with matchlock rifles with steel barrels of good quality, but that their gunpowder was inferior and they preferred powder imported from the West. What manner of threat was being planned against the mysterious ship?

Three days passed before Moriyama came by to tell Ranald about the ship, an American ship! Ranald was so excited that he could scarcely breathe. His mind whirled, especially since he was not certain that the Americans would be aware of his imprisonment, or be notified of it. Moriyama said that the captain had asked for his liberation.

On April 25, Moriyama appeared to say that MacDonald must go to the Nagasaki Town Hall the following morning to pay his respects to the new governor that had arrived—coincidentally—since the *Preble* docked. Unknown to Ranald, the new official had visited MacDonald's cage or prison without being identified, his purpose not clear. That night Ranald slept little, tossing and turning on his pallet. On the morning of April 26, Moriyama came to show MacDonald a letter, translated into English, which seemed to be a communication to Commander Glynn, requiring him to leave the harbor of Nagasaki as soon as the prisoners had been received. Moriyama asked what was the relative importance of Commander Glynn, whereupon Ranald related, in order of ranking: the people (which Moriyama could not comprehend), the President of the United States, Secretary of the Navy, Commodore, Post Captain, and Commander. "Commander" seemed to be sufficiently important to win the interpreter's respect.

Tense with excitement, Ranald entered a palanquin that morning to be carried to the Town Hall. Despite his comparatively kind treatment by the Japanese, and the fascination of teaching the interpreters, trading ideas with them, MacDonald had begun to wonder when—if ever—he would be released. Imprisonment definitely had worn thin. The palanquin stopped at the same court or hall at which Ranald had first been examined. He entered the anteroom or shed, clad in a plain, clean Japanese gown, to await an audience with the governor. Within a few minutes he was amazed to see thirteen other Americans enter the shed under guard, all appearing very subdued, pale and thin. He soon learned that these were the survivors of the *Lagoda*, about whom he had been told but had not known the place of their imprisonment, a location somewhat distant from Ranald's cage. Ranald said later that "I was fully under the impression that the fifteen men . . . were still in Japan, and doomed to perpetual imprisonment; and that I believed that their liberation depended entirely upon the success of my efforts to return to civilization and send them relief."

Through the interpreter, the new governor told the men about the arrival of the *Preble*, and that he had decided to release them all to the American ship, but that first they must go to the Dutch Factory on Deshima Island. One can imagine that the men's hearts leaped with joy at this news, all the while behaving in the restrained manner required of them as prisoners. The men returned their profound thanks to the governor and left the court.

Each was borne to Deshima in a palanquin. One by one, the seamen joined in a lively sea chantey, "O o-ly-i-o cheerly man," as the happy procession went through the streets of Nagasaki, crowded with spectators, to cross the covered bridge to Deshima. At the Dutch end of the bridge, the men alighted, were searched and released to Chief Factor John Levyssohn. So accustomed were they to Japanese ways that they knelt before Levyssohn, who gruffly exclaimed that they should arise, that "This is a Christian house!"

In high spirits, the seamen compared stories with MacDonald and related their experiences to Levyssohn, who entertained them with a proper dinner, at a table with chairs, silverware, meat, bread, and Dutch Java coffee—their first European meal in months. After the celebration, the fourteen (other sources say fifteen) men embarked on the ship *Preble*, where an officer interviewed the seamen and MacDonald, later filing reports with the U. S. government where they are found in Executive Document No. 84, House of Representatives, 31st Congress, 1st Session. When Ranald was interviewed, Captain Glynn handed him a copy of the Reverend Damon's article and of his own obituary.

Ranald said in his memoirs that possibly the Japanese authorities wanted to get rid of him because they had already kept him for several months. He said, fervently, "Conjecture, however, is idle at this point. So it happened; and all for the best! God be thanked! There *is* a Providence that shapes our ends."

His mission accomplished, Commander Glynn sailed out of Nagasaki for Macao, where the seamen were put ashore to pursue their own ends as best they could. Ranald MacDonald promptly signed onto a ship bound for the southern seas.

On May 11, 1849, D. Geisinger, commanding U. S. Squadron, East Indies, wrote to the secretary of the Navy, Washington, D. C.:

> Sir: I have the honor to inform you of the arrival of the Plymouth at this port on the 9th instant. The Preble reached here from Japan on the 2d, and was dropping down the Woosung river, on her way to Macao, as the Plymouth passed up.
>
> The Preble had visited Nangasacki, in pursuance of my instructions of January 31st, and relieved from confinement the seamen of the American whaler "Lagoda," and an adventurer named Ranald McDonald, who left the whaler Plymouth, Captain Edwards, of Sag Harbor, New York, on the coast of Japan, and was also in confinement there. I shall leave in a few days for Macao, and on my arrival there will be enabled to inform the department more fully of the result of the Preble's cruise.

On June 18, 1849, from Macao Roads, Commodore Geisinger continued his report to the secretary of the Navy:

> Sir: Transmitted herewith, for the information of the department, are copies of the depositions of the seamen brought by the Preble from Japan, and of the memoranda made by Commander Glynn of his various interviews with the Japanese officials at Nangasacki, &c.
>
> The honorable Secretary will perceive that the cruise of the Preble was altogether successful. The release and surrender of these seamen, under these circumstances, is probably the first instance in which the stubborn policy of the Japanese has yielded to the demand of foreigners . . . The original representation of the seamen of the "Lagoda," that they were shipwrecked mariners, was an expedient to obtain sympathy and the means of rescue. The truth is, they deserted the ship, and allege, as their excuse, the harsh treatment they experienced on board.

XV
Sailor and Gold Digger

From June to August, 1849, Ranald MacDonald resumed his life as a sailor aboard ships of unknown destinations or ports, wandering—it is said—throughout China, India, Java, and elsewhere in the Orient. According to his own notes, he arrived at Singapore on August 19, sailing again on August 22 on the *Sea Witch*, which wrecked off the coast of India near Madras. There in the distant, warm waters of the Indian Ocean he had to swim for his life, a knife in his belt against the circling sharks, a packet of possessions, and a few original notes about his Japanese adventure held above his head. (From these paltry remaining notes and the vivid scenes crowding his memory, he told of his imprisonment and impressions to McLeod in 1853, amplifying and rewriting those adventures four decades later between 1889 and his death in 1894.)

Perhaps in 1851 or 1852, he turned up in Ballarat, Australia, site of the rich gold fields discovered between July and December, 1851. Exactly when he arrived is not established, but until he departed Australia in 1853, he was part of the tumultuous gold fever that affected every facet of life in southeast Australia. Since life at Ballarat is well documented, we can project his lifestyle of that period with some accuracy.

Australia was a young, raw nation when gold was discovered in California in 1848. Her government was hard put to assimilate the restless men and women sent to that continent. Some were the dregs of society—hard-core criminals banished from England. Others were decent people whose chief misfortune was to be poor, to have been debtors or convicted of crimes like stealing bread for their children. Still others were the soldiers and administrators sent (often unwillingly) to that distant land to govern the fermenting mixture of settlers, criminals and mere adventurers, their imaginations now titillated by the reports that reached Australia of fabulous gold strikes across the Pacific in California. Freemen schemed to gain passage aboard ships bound for California; others schemed even more mightily to acquire and sell passage on ships, vessels often highly unseaworthy.

Meanwhile, the government downplayed reports deliberately, fearing an exodus of settlers from Australia—men and women sorely needed to work the land, explore the interior, and expand its commerce if Australia was to function. Curiously, reports of gold finds in Australia itself regularly trickled into Sydney or Melbourne, but were given minimal importance by the press and the government for the same reasons.

The first rumors of gold were just that, circulated by a conniving thief and convict in August, 1788, to gain attention. The man literally had manufactured his gold specimens by melting down pieces of old gold and mixing them with dirt and rock. Much more reliably, surveyor James McBrien wrote in his reports in 1823 that there was gold in the Bathurst district of New South Wales. Nine years later, Polish explorer Count Paul Strzlecki reported a find between the Blue Mountains and Bathurst and notified the newspapers about it. When he exhibited specimens in London, England, brought from Australia in 1844, a renowned geologist, Sir Roderick Impey Murchison, proposed that England mount a serious mineral survey—again ignored by the government (the provinces of Australia were crown colonies of England at the time).

Meanwhile, others continued to come up with nuggets, gold dust, and promising mining strata. It was Edward Hargraves, a miner or "digger" (as the Australians termed prospectors) from California, who found the gold. Some say that he went to California with the specific purpose of learning how to recognize gold-bearing strata and how to extract the gold efficiently. In 1850, he wrote to a friend that, from what he had seen in California, he was convinced that there was gold in parts of New South Wales. He returned to Australia in January, 1851, with the firm purpose of prospecting in his homeland. Although thought to be mad for wandering, seemingly in aimless patterns, through the bush, Hargraves found specks of gold in pannings on the Lewis Ponds Creek in New South Wales. He is quoted widely as exclaiming to his aboriginal helper, "This is a memorable day in the history of New South Wales, I shall be a baron, you will be knighted, and my old horse will be stuffed, put in a glass case, and sent to the British Museum."

Returning to Guyong to make up a California-style gold cradle, Hargraves went back to the same general area and on Summer Hill Creek found real pay dirt—four ounces of the glittery stuff. In March, 1851, he showed his gleanings to the Colonial Secretary, E. Deas Thomson, and received his finder's reward of 10,000 pounds, a life pension, and an appointment as a commissioner of lands—for by 1851, the Australian government had perceived that, if gold were discovered "at home," fewer men would leave Australia for California.

The gold madness began and with good results. A boy found an eleven-ounce nugget, and an aborigine picked up a 106-pound nugget, then the largest in the world—Kerr's Hundredweight, it was called.

Such excitement gripped the colonies that, Melbourne, four hundred miles from the gold fields, was becoming a ghost town, with laborers, lawyers, policemen, doctors and government workers thronging onto the ships bound for Sydney or clambering over the lonely hills separating them from instant riches. They carried wash basins, tin cooking pots and collanders to sift out the hoped-for nuggets from sand. Manufacturers could not turn out picks fast enough, so some hopefuls went with hoes and shovels. In the country, sheep farmers were unable to get help for the annual shearing of an estimated fifteen million animals; the wool business, so essential to Australia's economy, was endangered. However, the farmers soon learned that even more money was to be made in supplying the would-be diggers with food.

Melbourne authorities offered a reward for anyone finding gold within a 200-mile radius of their city in their own province of Victoria. By mid-July James Esmond discovered gold near Clunes; on July 29, gold was found only twenty miles from Melbourne; and in August the fantastically rich finds near today's town of Ballarat and also Bendigo were located, touching off a massive gold rush that lasted for decades. Whether Ranald MacDonald had been to the New South Wales diggings first, or came directly to Ballarat, he indeed was in Ballarat as a digger.

With countless others, he may have left his ship crew-less in Melbourne or Geelong harbors to trek the eighty miles to Ballarat. According to an account in the *Sydney Morning Herald*, diggers came on foot with picks, shovels, tucker (food supplies), and miscellany hanging from their shoulders—soft-handed office workers beside calloused sailors, only a very few boasting animals to haul their gear or carry their women. Those women who came to Ballarat endured the most miserable of existences, even largely ignored by their husbands who were too busy and too tired to pay much attention to their wives' insurmountable problems of obtaining household supplies, water, or decent shelter.

Business in the cities came to a standstill, and entire hamlets became ghost towns as the procession of diggers traveled across the dry hills to Bendigo, Castlemaine, and Ballarat. The wife of the governor of Van Diemen's Land (Tasmania) complained that, if any piece of furniture broke, it stayed broken as no one was there to fix it. Any boat, however small, was commandeered or stolen by those eager to cross the channel to Victoria and get on the trail. In London, Charles Dickens, editor of the weekly

Household Words, reported that from ten in the morning to late at night would-be diggers clamored for any passages available on departing ships. A startling result of the gold fever was that, since transport to Australia now was so feverishly desired, it was foolish to freely carry convicts to that continent. The banishment of prisoners to Australia was discontinued in 1852. In May, 1853, an American businessman in Melbourne reported that there were between six and seven hundred vessels of all kinds in that harbor alone. Cargos of needed supplies and tools were a part of the incoming commerce, since local manufacturers and suppliers could not begin to stem the outflow of goods, nor did they wish to.

The diggers came from everywhere—Germans, French, Americans (a large percentage), Poles, Britons from many colonies, and later Chinese. A suave, tough, extremely capable young American brought coaches on ships to found the Cobb and Co. stage lines, similar to those of Wells Fargo.

The Victorian government lost no time in assessing licenses for digging, a highly unpopular monthly tax of thirty shillings a month—whether the digger found gold or not. The theory was that the tax would deter a few diggers from entering the fields, thus controlling the vast numbers bound for instant riches. It did not. Trouble was not long in coming, as diggers rebelled, culminating in the Eureka Rebellion of 1854. However, that brief but bloody uprising occurred after MacDonald had left Australia.

For MacDonald and the other diggers the work was grueling, the climate uncertain. During the day, the sun usually shone and in the low mountains, higher than sea-level Melbourne, the temperature was acceptable. However, by evening a chill wind often blew in from the south coast, so blankets and cookfires were welcome. In winter, snow sometimes fell in the Ballarat and Bendigo hills, with the frigid southern sea just beyond the horizon.

After the first discoveries around Ballarat, most mining was alluvial or merely washing gold from the dirt and gravel. Occasionally a digger chanced to find large and small nuggets. However, the first phase of mining was not profitable for most diggers and some drifted away. After an enterprising digger went beyond the layer of clay that had discouraged earlier men, the real treasure was uncovered. But it required hard work. One had to create a tunnel opening that would not collapse, and continue the downward digging, shoring up the passageway. Clever sail-like devices at the surface shunted air into the mines. Working in the dark and often mucky mines, one digger called it "wombatting," after the digging marsupial animal common to Australia. In fact, it was water that often defeated the diggers—lack of it on the surface for panning, too much underground for tunneling. It seemed that a vast underground lake or river lay beneath Ballarat. Nevertheless, in 1852, the gold taken from the Victoria goldfields totaled twelve million pounds, a tidy sum, indeed. At Ballarat in 1858, the largest nugget ever found anywhere was uncovered, a whopping 2,216 ounce chunk. This, the Welcome Nugget, eventually was sent on to London after being exhibited for some time locally. Total production figures in the earliest days of Victoria mining are uncertain, but modern statisticians project that 630 tons of gold were taken from the fields between discovery and World War I.

The digger came home from his underground labors with his gold in a matchbox. After resting and drying out, he often placed the gold on a shovel above a fire to remove the moisture from it, then reclaimed the dust with a magnet for his safebox.

In *A History of Australia*, Marjorie Barnard quoted William Hall in an 1852 book, *Practical Experience at the Diggings of the Gold Fields of Victoria*, describing the scene at these homecomings—MacDonald undoubtedly among them:

"The scene around us was singularly picturesque and striking—thousands of tents of every possible shape and size, whose snowy whiteness contrasted strongly with the dark thickly wooded hills in the background. In front of the tents the cooks for the day were seen busily occupied at the fires preparing supper for their parties who returned tired and hungry. The appearance of the men as they came home, their shirts and trousers stained with clay, one carrying the tools, another the gold, and the others armed to the teeth, escorting the latter. Their sun-burnt countenances, large whiskers and moustaches, and cone-shaped hats, gave them the appearance of Italian Brigands, and the broken, hilly, and mountainous country around seemed to confirm that impression. As night approached rockets and blue-lights ascended in every direction, and for upwards of an hour the discharge of fire-arms was incessant, then all became silent, silent as the city of the dead;—not a footstep or voice was heard in that vast assemblage."

In 1853, when MacDonald left the area, there were no hotels, no theaters, no places of amusement where men could congregate; yet in 1854, there were all of these amenities. Tent cities and crude "humpies" housed the earliest diggers—a "humpy" consisting of a scooped-out hole in the ground with an above-ground structure and roof perhaps three feet high, the walls made of earth, gravel, stone or timber. At least they provided warmth during chill nights.

Australian historians have conjectured that the diggers were too tired and too busy to consider crime worthwhile; however, theft and violence were not wanting. Ranald MacDonald was known then and later as a man of courage but mild manner; if one treated him well, he responded in kind. However, he could be a formidable and stubborn foe (one remembers his stalwart approach to the Japanese authorities). In the diggings he became involved in a controversy with another digger, a total stranger to him, and—upon being attacked by the man—he proceeded to thrash him, knocking him out. Giving the matter no further thought, Ranald returned to his digging. Later that evening he heard a "rap on his cabin door" (it must have been a humpy to have a door). Standing outside was a group of men holding an honor belt. Handing it toward Ranald, the men informed him that the belt had belonged to Ranald's assailant, a man who was the champion fighter of Australia. Since Ranald had defeated him, the men said he was entitled to the belt. Somewhat astonished Ranald declined with thanks.

Boxing was popular, however, in Ballarat and elsewhere in Australia. As soon as buildings were erected, possibly as early as 1853, MacLaren's Boxing Saloon in Ballarat featured amateur matches to entertain the diggers. (See paintings in the book *S. T. Gill's Australia* by Geoffrey Dutton, Macmillan Company of Australia, Ltd.)

By 1853, the alluvial gold was becoming scarcer; the equipment needed to go deeper and deeper required considerable capital investment. The thirty-shilling license loomed ever larger when the digger's income plummeted. Chinese diggers began to arrive, resented intensely by the diggers of largely European descent, plus a goodly number of Americans. The stage was set for trouble in Ballarat.

With digging becoming a more serious business, Ranald MacDonald the sailor returned to the sea. It was time to work his way home, to contact his parents and become reacquainted with the homeland from which he had fled a decade earlier.

XVI
Home to Canada

Signing on a ship bound for Europe, Ranald MacDonald sailed away from Australia and the South Seas, never to return. Since he spent the next few years without any known income, it is probable that he did make a stake from his gold digging in Australia.

His circuitous route back to North America took him across the vast watery wilderness of the Indian Ocean, around Africa's Cape of Good Hope, and along the western shore of Africa, stopping for supplies at exotic ports. Either MacDonald's ship entered the Mediterranean and docked at Rome, or Ranald left the ship to make his way there.

It was enlightening for MacDonald, well versed in European history through his British education, to compare the ancient Roman ways and the shadowy but flourishing civilization of Japan. After his visit in Rome and a fling in Paris, Ranald worked his way to London, where—although there are few details of the trip—he must have checked on his family's whereabouts at Hudson's Bay Company offices, because it is known he visited one of his brothers at school in Surrey. Thereafter he visited Scotland to revel in the history of Clan Donald, before sailing to Canada. Often in later years, when he wrote his memoirs and the manuscript he hoped would be published as a book, he romanticized his Scottish ancestors. He spoke of his father as "in his young manhood was of the handsomest of the sons of men—and *debonair;* eagle-eyed, and with the thews and eclat of his mountain race." When he was a restless youth of St. Thomas, Ontario, he said of himself, "I felt, ever, and uncontrollably in my blood, the wild strain for wandering freedom; *im primis* of my Highland father of Glencoe."

In the *Washington Historical Quarterly* of 1918, William S. Lewis quotes John McDonald of Garth, who lauded the clan:

"It is asserted in the Highlands of old Scotland that the McDonald's [*sic*] are coeval with the family of Old Noah, etc.; that they had a boat of their own on Loch Lomond, independent of the ark, by which the chief of the clan saved as many as the boat could safely hold, of course the finest and fairest of both sexes. Hence the superiority of that race over all others ever since. Be that as it may, they have not, at any rate, fallen off, either in peace or war, from any of the race of Adam." (Contained in L. M. Masson, *Les Bourgeois de la Compagnie du Nord-Quest*.)

He continued to say that Clan Donald, referred to in ancient history as "Siol Guinn," is the principal house of the earlier Clan Cholla of A. D. 125. The clan claims immediate descent from Somerled of the Isles, in the twelfth century, a Gael ruling over the mixed Norsemen and Gael of Argyllshire. From one of his sons, Reginald, came Donald, from which Clan Donald is derived, the principal branch of which is the MacDonalds of Clanranald (hence our Ranald's name).

The exploits and adventures of the Argyllshire clansmen that so intrigued Ranald included his great-grandfather's battles with Montrose in 1645, and his grandfather John who narrowly escaped with his mother and brother Donald from the pillages of William of Orange at Inveriggan in 1692.

Ranald's father Archibald was born on the south shore of Loch Leven in Northern Argyllshire, the youngest of thirteen children. He had studied medicine in Scotland before he was appointed clerk and agent in 1812, by Lord Selkirk of the Selkirk Colony that came to Red River, mentioned in an earlier chapter. North American history is rife with other McDonalds and MacDonalds, many of whom were related as family or clansmen to Archibald and Ranald.

His trip into nostalgia complete, Ranald moved on to Canada. Turning up at the home of his stepmother, Jane Klyne McDonald, in St. Andrews, he gave her a considerable fright since Ranald was supposed to be long dead, drowned in the Japan Sea. Once recovered from her astonishment, his stepmother greeted him affectionately. Ranald was dismayed to learn that his father had passed on a short time before on January 15, 1853, after a short illness. The news of more than a decade unfolded, as Ranald became reacquainted with his family at Glencoe Cottage in St. Andrews, Quebec.

Archibald, Jane (who was pregnant), and their children, Mary Anne (ten), John (seven), the lively twins, Donald and James (five), Samuel (three), and little Joseph (eighteen months), had left Fort Colvile on September 21, 1844, a time when Ranald was roaming the world's oceans and completely "lost" to his ever-growing family. Delayed by unseasonally high water on the Columbia, the party, traveling by canoe, arrived at Boat Encampment on October 10. Transferring to horseback, with some on foot, the party set off into the high Rocky Mountains across Athabasca Pass.

Snow began to fall at the higher elevations and Jane, due to deliver a baby within a month or so, must have wondered at the wisdom of the passage. An effervescent Archibald, however, was buoyant about the prospect of going East to his retirement. In her biography of Archibald McDonald, *Exile in the Wilderness,* Jean Murray Cole relates, "the most stalwart of men found the beauties of the mountain scenery small recompense for the hardships of the tortuous crossing through the rugged, snow-clad summits of the Rockies. That late in the season fresh snow had already begun to fall and the horses, when they were not tripping in mud holes or stumbling over the upturned roots and gigantic tree trunks that lay across their path, struggled through drifts which frequently engulfed them up to their haunches or slithered on icy patches that flung them, packs and all, back down the precipitous inclines that reached to the height of land over which they must cross. As far as the eye could see there seemed to be no end to that vast, endless ocean of mountain peaks. More often than not, choosing the least of the evils, the miseries of struggling over the uneven terrain on snowshoes seemed preferable to the pitfalls of riding on horseback, however sure-footed the animals might be on a normal trail."

The men of the company helped to carry the little boys through the worst of it, but Jane made her own way, heavy with child, to Jasper House. After a short rest, the party pushed along by canoe on the Athabasca River, challenging the onset of severe winter weather. But little Benjamin MacDonald, who would figure in the pioneer mining and ranching life of British Columbia and Washington state, made his appearance on November 23, 1844, in the wilderness west of Fort Assiniboine.

Finally Archibald McDonald and his party were stopped, veering south to spend the balance of winter at Rowand's post, Edmonton House. During a damp, cold winter at the edge of the North Saskatchewan River, three of Ranald's little brothers died of scarlet fever before he ever could know them—little Joseph and the twins, Donald and James. Although severely stricken, the other children and Archibald (who also came down with the fever) recovered sufficiently that by June 5th, the family set off for Cumberland House to attend the Northern Council meeting, to which Governor Simpson had summoned Archibald.

En route Jane finally fell ill, having nursed her family through the fever and borne with stoicism her unimaginable grief over loss of the little boys. A worried Archibald canceled his plans for the Northern Council and made for Red River by the shortest possible route. Weather even in summer continued to resist their progress, with wild storms and hail the size of eggs.

Fleeing the storms, they put in at Fort Alexander on Lake Winnipeg's eastern shore. From Norway House, since the regular fall boats to Montreal had no room for the McDonald family, they fell in with the family of George Gladman for a harrowing and unpleasant voyage, enduring narrow escapes and the intransigence of Gladman's family, via Fort Frances, Fort William, and the Sault to Windsor, Ontario, and Port Stanley just south of St. Thomas, bypassing Red River entirely.

With relief, they found their old friends, the Edward Ermatinger family, waiting at St. Thomas to succor them. Other old Hudson's Bay friends also welcomed them in St. Thomas. After much-needed rest and warm sympathy for the losses the McDonalds had endured, the family proceeded to Buffalo and nearby Cobourg to visit with John Dugald Cameron, with whom McDonald had first traveled west in 1821. Finally they reached Montreal.

Meanwhile, sons Alexander (fifteen) and Allan (thirteen) had come east from Red River with Peter Skene Ogden in 1844, to attend school and live at the Chambly rectory. In a small home at Chambly, near Montreal, the McDonalds set up temporary residence; and—except for Ranald—the whole family finally was reunited when Archibald Junior returned from college in England soon thereafter.

By 1847, Archibald officially retired from Hudson's Bay Company service, purchasing a large farm near St. Andrews East, naming it "Glencoe Cottage." With their children around them, and their many friends swirling through the place, Archibald and Jane enjoyed an idyllic life—actively involved in the Anglican congregational activities and in the social life of the community. Old Hudson's Bay cohorts, George Simpson, Duncan Finlayson, John McLeod and George Barnston lived within easy visiting distances; Edward Ermatinger lived in Montreal during the legislative sessions; and Frank Ermatinger came by on vacation. For his administrative background in the West, McDonald was consulted on the Oregon question and became active in other political endeavors of the local area. Life was good.

In May, 1852, Archibald McDonald drew up a new will; believing Ranald to be dead, he left no provision for him. Within seven months he was dead.

Ranald received the news of his father with sadness and perhaps a bit of guilt. Except for the letter given to Captain Edwards that Archibald never received, Ranald apparently had not contacted his father in all his wandering years. During this visit, for the first time Ranald discovered that Jane was not his birth mother. However, as far as both were concerned, the bond was as enduring as if he were her "blood" son. As a measure of her feelings, when Jane died Ranald discovered she had included him in her own will, making him a bequest of $400, the same as that given to the widow of Archibald Junior, Ranald's immediate younger brother, who had died of exposure in 1868 when his sleigh fell through the ice on the Ottawa River, drenching him in the frigid waters.

With seven brothers and a sister, Ranald had a joyous reunion, since all except possibly Alexander were in or near Montreal. Four of them he had never seen. Little Angus, only six years old when Ranald reappeared in the family, listened wide-eyed to the tales of adventure spun by his handsome, rugged oldest brother. For about four years Ranald lived around St. Andrews, cementing his family relationships. Upon the recommendation of Malcolm McLeod, he was made a member of the Masonic Order of St. Andrews, Quebec. It was here, too, that the old family friend, Malcolm McLeod, listened raptly to Ranald's stories of Japan—of intrigue, friendship, mysticism and the well-developed society of that little-known place. Here began McLeod's conviction that Canada must build roads or railroads through to the western coast, in order to trade with the Orient. He was to maintain that theme in articles and speeches for the next several decades, until the completion of the Canadian Pacific Railroad and the establishment of steamer service to the Orient on Canadian Pacific lines. In fact, the first of several versions of Ranald's journals was written by McLeod in 1853, as the story was related.

"In this way, my Japan of 1848-9 had a very intimate connection with the CPR in 1886, with its steamship line with Japan and China—a perfect success," Ranald was reported to have declared.

As delightful as the settled life was for Ranald, surrounded by a loving family after so many years alone at sea, he became intrigued by the prospects of finding gold again. Reports reached St. Andrews of gold being found on the lower Fraser River, with prospectors ever moving north along the Columbia and its tributaries into the northern wildernesses. Once again, it was time for the adventurous Ranald to move on. Bidding a loving farewell to his mother Jane, for so he regarded his stepmother, Ranald went in 1857 or 1858 to join the thousands of gold seekers in British Columbia. With him was his brother Allan. The MacDonald brothers traveled by ship to Panama, crossed the Isthmus, and reboarded another ship for the voyage to Vancouver. They stopped off to visit Governor Douglas, since the latter had been a lifelong friend of the MacDonald family and Jane Klyne was related to Douglas' wife. From Victoria, they followed the increasingly well-worn path to the Cariboo country of the upper Fraser River.

Not to miss all the fun, younger brother Benjamin left St. Andrews in 1862, when he became eighteen years old, to join his brothers. (The Benjamin MacDonald credited with finding gold in the Horsefly country of the Cariboo in 1859, and often believed to be Ranald's brother, was another MacDonald who, oddly enough, had a ranch south of Cache Creek, only twenty miles from where Ranald and his younger brother eventually ranched.) Their brother Alexander already was serving the Hudson's Bay Company in the West. In the years ahead, he undoubtedly visited his siblings in the Cariboo from time to time.

During a stop in San Francisco, who should Ranald encounter on the street but his old employer, Captain Edwards of the *Plymouth*. He was overjoyed to learn that Ranald was still alive and invited the two brothers to his palatial home to hear the whole tale, for he had prospered in the California gold fields. He said he had never fully settled up with the ship's owner after that particular voyage; having heard of the California gold strikes, he took himself off to the West as soon as he could decently escape. He offered Ranald some payment for his share of the whaling proceeds, which Ranald declined to accept.

Entering the Columbia River, the ship called at Fort Vancouver. Some historians have stated that Ranald wanted to see about his claiming a part of the government's settlement with Chief Comcomly, since Ranald was his direct descendant. (Archibald earlier had attempted to file Ranald's claim while the latter was off at sea.) However, in a letter to Malcolm McLeod in 1889, after McLeod inquired about pursuing the matter, Ranald professed to have barely heard of any such claim, saying he could not remember even where he had heard some rumors about it, possibly from his mother.

XVII

In Japan, Meanwhile

While Ranald MacDonald was seeking wealth in Australia, visiting in Europe, and becoming reacquainted with his family in Canada, world-shaking events transpired in far-off Japan. Because of incomplete communications, Ranald only knew what he read in the newspapers and could not have known that his students, his interpreters, played a crucial role in the arrival of the Americans in force. Years later, when the details of Commodore Perry's visit and the subsequent journals of Townsend Harris were published, Ranald would learn of his ex-students' part in the historic meetings.

As part of his Japan assignment, Glynn was supposed to sound out the Japanese on their readiness to negotiate for trade; however, there is little indication that he got beyond negotiating for the release of prisoners. Yet the reports of Commander Glynn filed with the U. S. government about his meetings in Nagasaki with Japanese officials did not go unnoticed. Glynn himself urged President Fillmore to take further action and suggested that the leader of a Japanese expedition should be a ranking naval officer of tact, maturity and judgment. The best person was deemed to be Commodore Matthew Galbraith Perry, in his late fifties, a member of a distinguished naval family (including Oliver Hazard Perry, hero of the War of 1812). Perry had a long history of achievements, including assignments that had been essentially diplomatic in nature. He was a stickler for detail, a careful planner, and a strict officer; nevertheless, his crewmen and officers respected him as much as feared his wrath. The discipline aboard his ships made for relative safety in tight quarters.

Perry was a handsome man, powerfully built, his heavy eyebrows emphasizing the authority that shone from his eyes. Although given the delicate task, possibly even dangerous, of a Japanese expedition—instead of his preferred request of assignment to the more benign Mediterranean— Perry threw himself into preparations for the voyage, reading every scrap of information about Japan that he could find. The brief account given by

Ranald MacDonald to Commander Glynn, forming part of the Congressional Record, undoubtedly was a part of the background reading.

A dozen ships were assigned to his command: three of the Navy's best steam frigates, the *Mississippi, Princeton* and *Allegheny;* three storeships, *Supply, Lexington* and *Southampton;* one corvette, the *Vermont;* sloops of war, *Vandalia* and *Macedonian;* with the additional ships already in East India that would join the expedition, the steamship *Susquehanna,* and sloops *Saratoga* and *Plymouth.* At the last minute the *Powhatan* was substituted for the *Princeton.* Expensive gifts for the Emperor and other dignitaries were a part of a considerable cargo. It was a self-sufficient naval force prepared to stay stubbornly in Japan until some agreement might be reached.

Perry signed A. L. C. Portman as his Dutch interpreter and, since he needed a Japanese interpreter, he sought out S. Wells Williams, who had some knowledge of the Japanese language and who had sailed on the *Morrison* in that abortive attempt at rapprochement with the Japanese in 1856. Williams was living at Canton, operating a printing office, and only received the request from Commodore Perry on April 9, 1853, to sail with him on the 21st when the latter arrived in Canton en route to the Ryukyu Islands and Japan. Williams agreed to go, despite his professed misgivings about his ability to speak more than "gutter" Japanese learned from relatively ignorant and unlettered Japanese sailors (and even that nine years earlier). He could not leave, however, until early May, so Perry went on ahead to the Ryukyus, leaving Williams to catch up later on the *Saratoga* out of Macao.

(In 1856, Perry's version of his expedition was published by order of the U. S. Congress, with his friend, Dr. Francis L. Hawks, serving as editor. Perry first had asked his interpreter, S. Wells Williams, to assist him but Williams refused because he had been appointed to the U. S. Legation in China and, quite possibly, because he intended to publish his own diary, about which Perry did not know.)

Williams joined Perry at Okinawa (then Napha) in the Ryukyus (widely called Lew Chews or Luchus then) on May 26, 1853, moving aboard the flagship *Susquehanna* on June 2. After a month's visit at Okinawa, the expedition sailed for Japan on July 2, with only the *Susquehanna, Mississippi, Saratoga* and *Plymouth,* leaving the *Supply* in Okinawa and the *Caprice* to sail back to Shanghai. The other ships had not appeared yet. On July 7, the squadron was about forty miles off Cape Izu. Williams said in his diary:

"One small craft seeing us coming up rapidly took in sail, turned about and pulled away for Vries Island as if its existence depended on their haste . . . Mount Fusi rose in the distance . . . the mist concealed the coast and hid us too, probably, from the people. The remarkable white rocks along the coast were hidden by the same cause, but a few guns which were ordered to be scaled made our presence known, perhaps, by those who could not see us. The sight of land diffused a feeling of exhilaration through the whole company, and certainly the dim idea any of us could have of the results of this visit upon us or the Japanese was calculated to excite our minds."

Perry's account adds, "The steamer, in spite of a wind, moved on with all sails furled, at the rate of eight of nine knots, much to the astonishment of the crews of the Japanese fishing junks gathered along the shore or scattered over the surface of the mouth of the bay, who stood up in their boats, and were evidently expressing the liveliest surprise at the sight of the first steamer ever beheld in Japanese waters."

The ships moved on past Vries Island or Oshima toward Cape Sagami, the guns aboard loaded and crews ready for action if hostility was encountered. At one point a fleet of about a dozen boats bearing large banners of Japanese writing came from shore, unsuccessfully attempting to intercept the swift American squadron. Once off the city of Uraga, on the western side of Edo Bay, the Americans dropped anchor.

No Japanese was allowed on board any of the fleet; Commodore Perry's orders were explicit. He had weighed the experiences of the ship *Columbus*, when it had been in the same bay July 20, 1846. Then, Japanese were permitted freely aboard and, consequently, Perry believed, were contemptuous of the status of the commander, Commodore Biddle. This time, only suitably high-placed functionaries were to be allowed to negotiate and then only with Perry's flagship *Susquehanna*. The expedition's ships also were fully on guard, commanding the shore batteries with their naked guns.

Williams asked a man in one of the boats that crowded around to return ashore and request a high-ranking officer to come out to the ship and receive a letter for the Emperor. In good English a well-dressed man, Tatsunosuke Hori (today believed to be Ranald's interpreter incorrectly identified as Ichiro Hori), announced, "I can speak Dutch," which thereafter appeared true, but no further English. Questions about the fleet and its purpose fairly burst from the man, who was permitted aboard—along with a companion whom he claimed was Saberosuke Nakashima, a vice-governor of Uraga. The commodore did not address them, but kept to his cabin, leaving the negotiations regarding the letter to Lieutenant Contee.

The Japanese interpreter was directed to inform a dignitary that the commodore had been sent by the United States on a friendly mission and had brought a letter from the President of the United States to the Emperor. Perry through his aide stiffly demanded that a person of proper authority be sent on board to receive it.

Thus began a series of sparring matches between the Japanese, of ever greater rank, and the aides to Perry. In his account of Perry's expedition, prepared in 1855 and 1856 in conferring with the commodore himself, Francis Hawks said:

"The Commodore, also, was well aware that the more exclusive he should make himself and the more unyielding he might be in adhering to his declared intentions, the more respect these people of forms and ceremonies would be disposed to award him. Therefore he deliberately resolved to confer personally with no one but a functionary of the highest rank in the empire . . . As a man, he did not deem himself too elevated to hold communication with any of his brethren . . . But in Japan, as the representative of his country . . . he felt that it was well to teach the Japanese, in the mode most intelligible to them, by stately and dignified reserve . . . to respect the country from which he came . . . The Japanese so well understood him that they learned the lesson at once."

However, the tone of the Japanese response was monotonously singular, too, repeating that the fleet must take the letter to Nagasaki, the only place where Japanese laws allowed its reception. Perry steadfastly but politely maintained his position, that he was on a friendly mission, that he wanted this letter to be received there in Edo Bay, and that it was for the Emperor alone.

The Japanese ashore were not asleep. Boats full of men lay offshore and at a respectful distance from the fleet's guns. Ashore there were beacon fires on every hilltop and along the shores, and the deck watch could hear the tolling of a great bell, presumably a signal of some sort.

On July 9, the highest officer at Uraga, Yezaimon Kayama, was permitted aboard with his two interpreters and several attendants. The governor, or so he called himself (there is some doubt as to the accuracy of his statement) was resplendent in a black gauze jacket with his crest emblazoned upon it, brocaded trousers, and a lacquered hat (Americans later called it "japanned") with the same crest.

Ongoing conversations were achieved with Kayama speaking in Japanese to interpreter Hori, who translated the matter into Dutch for Portman, who translated it into English. Conferring with commanders Buchanan and Adams, and Lieutenant Contee, Kayama reiterated the view of previous conferees, that neither he nor others were willing to take the letter, because the laws of the land demanded that intercourse with foreigners must be at Nagasaki. Just as adamant as the Japanese, Perry's officers re-stated the official position that the documents were addressed to the Em-peror and that, if necessary, Commodore Perry would go ashore with a strong force and deliver the letter in person. Somewhat startled, Kayama replied that he would send a communication to Tokyo, asking for further orders, but that it would take four days to receive a reply since Tokyo was a considerable distance away. Through his officers Perry (apparently moni-toring the conversations from his cabin, but not appearing) stated that he would wait only three days. To emphasize the importance and validity of the communiques from President Fillmore, the letter was shown to Kayama in its elaborate box.

Hawks observed that the Japanese emissaries were required to use language involving the same level of importance for the President of the United States as that used when referring to the Emperor. Alert interpret-ers had noted the previous difference. Hawks said, "In a country like Ja-pan, so governed by ceremonials of all kinds, it was necessary to guard with the strictest etiquette even the forms of speech."

On Tuesday, July 12, three days after the initial conference with Kayama, Perry sent surveying boats up Edo Bay with the steamer *Mississippi* accompa-nying them for "protection," in reality a power ploy by Perry. He believed correctly that the movement of the larger ship nearer to Edo would elicit a response. Three large boats approached the *Susquehanna* from Uraga, thirty crew members in the largest boat and thirteen in each of the other two. The boatmen were dressed in loose blue gowns with white stripes.

The advance boat bore a black and white flag, indicating important officials were aboard; soon could be seen Kayama dressed elegantly and seated, with his immediate party, on mats. The two interpreters were Hori and Tokushumo Hatshisuko [Williams called him Tokoshiuro]. Receiving the party were Captains Buchanan and Adams. The balance of that day and the next were taken up by negotiations as to how and where the letter was to be handed over, and obtaining assurances that the proper rank of Japanese official was to receive it. Perry demanded a "high officer of Yedo, holding rank in Japan corresponding to the rank of Admiral in the United States. This officer shall be accredited, *viz.*: possess a writing properly signed by the Emperor, authorizing him to receive the said letters. Of this writing or letter of credence shall be made a copy, translated into Dutch, and the same copy be transmitted to the Admiral before the interview takes place."

The details eventually were resolved and, despite the formality that was maintained scrupulously, there was polite entertainment, as well. The official party was offered whisky and brandy, food and tours of the ship.

On Tuesday, July 14, the Japanese had completed a building ashore for the acceptance ceremony. Stretched between wooden posts were ornamental screens—forming decorative panels, on which appeared the imperial crest alternating with a pattern of a scarlet flower with heart-shaped leaves. Bright scarlet banners hung from nine tall poles, waving gracefully in the breeze and dipping to the ground. A forest of streamers and flags gave the whole area an air of festivity. The Japanese soldiers, drawn up as a regimental guard, were in special dress—a short, sleeveless gown, gathered at the waist with a sash. When Kayama and his sub-governor Nakashima appeared to escort Perry's party to shore, they, too, were garbed in very rich clothing, gowns embroidered with gold, figured lace.

The Americans were not wanting in ceremony, with all on board in proper uniform. Perry also took no chances at subterfuge, managing to anchor his steamers so their guns could rake the beach if any treachery ensued. Going ashore in fifteen boats were about three hundred Americans, including marines, musicians, officers and ordinary sailors, all heavily armed. Williams vividly describes the procession ashore:

"As soon as Commodore Perry landed all fell into procession; Captain Buchanan, who was the first man ashore, had arranged all in their places so that no hindrance took place. The marines, headed by Major Zeilen, led off, he going ahead with a drawn sword; then half of the sailors with one band playing between the two parties. Two tall blacks heavily armed supported as tall a standard bearer, carrying a commodore's pennant, and went next before two boys carrying the President's letter and the Full Powers in their boxes covered with red baize. The Commodore, supported by Captain Adams and Lieutenant Contee, each wearing chapeaux, then advanced; the interpreters and secretary came next succeeded by Captain Buchanan and the gay-appearing file of officers whose epaulettes, buttons, etc., shone brightly in the sun. A file of sailors and the band, with marines under Captain Slack, finished this remarkable escort."

Already seated, the two Japanese dignitaries arose as the commodore entered. They were Toda, Prince of Izu, and Ido, Prince of Iwase. Interpreter Williams described their dress: "The upper mantilla was a slate-colored brocade kind of silk, made stiff at the shoulders so as to stick out squarely; the girdle a brown color, and the overall trowsers of purplish silk; the swords were not very rich-looking. The coat-of-arms was conspicuous on the sleeves, and some of the undergarments appearing, gave a peculiarly harlequin-like look to his dress, to which the other envoy was accordant."

Ranald's old student Hori and Governor Kayama were seated on mats. Hori asked if the letters were ready to be delivered, and stated that Prince

Toda was ready to receive them. The commodore waved the two boys forward, bearing the splendid boxes containing the letters, and the two black sailors or marines, the honor guard, escorted the boys. The President's letter, the commodore's letter of credence, and three other letters from the commodore to the Emperor were thus delivered to the Japanese. Accompanying the letters were translations in Chinese and Dutch. An "imperial receipt" was given to Commodore Perry, through Hori and Kayama, with the assistance of Dutch interpreter Portman.

Commodore Perry, through the interpreters, indicated that he would leave in his ships within two or three days, offering to take any answers from the Emperor with him, which Hori did not comment upon. But Hori asked whether the commodore would return in a year with all four vessels. Hori received the reply that Perry would, and possibly with additional ships. The brief conference, lasting only about thirty minutes, was over; the two envoys had barely moved or spoken during the interview, but now that the ceremony was over, they relaxed a little as if glad that it all went satisfactorily.

Perry returned to his ship while the bands played lustily. The procession to the ship included the Japanese dignitaries, except for the two princes, and sixty or seventy Japanese boats with soldiers manning them. Governor Kayama, his assistant Nakashima, and the interpreters were invited on board and entertained modestly by the captains and the commodore's aide.

After exchanging presents during the following fortnight, the Perry expedition weighed anchor and left Edo Bay on July 17, arriving at Okinawa a week later. The curtain surrounding Japan had been lifted a few inches, with the participation of Ranald MacDonald's own student, Tatsunosuke Hori.

XVIII
Perry Returns

In leaving Japan without an answer to the letter from President Fillmore, Commodore Perry was deferring to the protocol of the Japanese; in meetings with foreigners and portentous decisions they moved slowly. However, he had a second reason; several vessels promised by the Navy department had not appeared, and he needed all the ships he commanded in East Asia to protect American interests in China, which was undergoing political turmoil. Furthermore, the elaborate presents for the Emperor of Japan were not available, but stowed aboard the *Vermont*, one of the missing ships. Perry wanted to be prepared for a long stay in Edo Bay, with full supplies and armament, to await a reply from the Emperor—if waiting was what would be required. The Perry fleet left for Okinawa and Hong Kong, where interpreter Williams left the ship.

On January 18, 1854, Commodore Perry, the interpreter S. Wells Williams, and others again left Hong Kong for the Ryukyus, where they would rendezvous with other American ships and set out for Edo Bay. Detained at Okinawa by business matters (arrangements for storage of coal for the fleet, for quarters devoted to ill sailors or for those not needed, for supplies, etc.), Perry sent part of his fleet to sea on February 1, planning to catch up later. Captain Abbot left with the *Macedonian*, *Vandalia*, *Lexington*, and *Southampton*. His negotiations completed, Perry left on February 7 with the steamers *Susquehanna*, *Powhatan*, and *Mississippi*. A storeship, *Supply*, was to divert to Shanghai for coal and livestock, then join the fleet at Edo Bay.

Before leaving Okinawa, Perry received word that the Emperor of Japan was dead, and that—through the Dutch superintendent at Nagasaki—the Japanese requested the Americans to delay their visit. Although sending his formal condolences through the Dutch superintendent, Perry resolved to continue with his voyage.

On a cold, windy afternoon the bluffs of Izu came into view. By morning of February 11, the navigators discovered that the ships were in the

Bay of Shimoda, instead of Edo Bay; furthermore, the *Macedonian* had gone aground and had to be towed off. After these setbacks the fleet anchored for the night and moved past Uraga to the "American Anchorage" above Sarushima. The *Southampton* already was anchored and the *Lexington*, *Vandalia* and *Macedonian* sailed into the bay with the three steamers, Perry now using the *Powhatan* as his flagship. The *Susquehanna* was slated to return to China soon. The expedition would languish for three months in a sea of diplomatic stagnation, eventually winning the concessions for which Perry came.

For the first twelve days the officials were involved largely in a stalemate about where the Emperor's reply to President Fillmore's letter should be received. The Japanese were adamant that Uraga was the best place, after first suggesting Kamakura. Captain Adams, through the interpreters, conveyed Perry's firm decision to stay where he was at an anchorage out of the dangerous winds. Clearly the Japanese really wanted Perry's ships farther away from Edo, as the present anchorage was only about twenty miles from the city. The envoys, who included a prefecture official, Kahiyoye Kurokawa, seemingly higher in rank than 1853's Kayama, pleaded their case good-naturedly and accepted the hospitality of the ship's company. Williams noted that, on February 14, "The younger interpreter came today about two o'clock with a party of friends . . . whose object was chiefly to see the ship. Among them was a third interpreter from Nagasaki who spoke considerable English with a good accent"—undoubtedly another of Ranald MacDonald's pupils since, as far as we know, he was the only person to teach English in Nagasaki up to that time (just five years after Ranald's departure). On February 16, Hori, interpreter from the 1853 visit, came aboard on a social visit; on the 18th Nakashima, a familiar visitor of 1853, was the emissary repeating the tiresome insistence that the ships should go to Uraga. As the stalemate continued, Commodore Perry suggested through Captain Adams that perhaps he should proceed to Edo and receive the letter there, a statement which caused the Japanese to blanch and declare the suggestion impossible.

(The author believes that Perry did not realize that he was negotiating at Edo with the Shogun's messengers and not the Emperor's. At the time, the Shogun was the political ruler. The Emperor largely confined himself to spiritual matters. In 1868 the shogunate system was overthrown by the Emperor's political supporters—the Meiji Restoration. However, in the final negotiations, the Emperor was consulted at Kyoto.)

On February 24 during another unsatisfactory conference in Uraga between subordinate Captain Adams and a high-ranking official (Hayashi,

Prince of Daigaku), the commodore moved his squadron yet closer to Edo near the town of Kanagawa, so close that he could hear the striking of Edo's bells. Edo's structures could be seen, stretching along a hillside for some distance. Lighter surveying boats that had been mapping the bay for world-wide charting purposes, as well as America's interests, went so close that the sailors could see the seawall. That evening there were many fires on shore and huge curtains were stretched along the shore, in the Japanese fashion of screening any activity from the populace, and—in this event, the landscape from the Americans.

In all of these conversations Perry's seeming recalcitrance was a studied one; he wanted to make the point clear that the Americans would not be maneuvered as the Japanese wished. Further, his stiff formality and intransigence were calculated to emphasize the position that the United States would not accept the same treatment as that afforded the Dutch, but demanded conferences—country to country on a footing of equality among nations.

On February 25, another of MacDonald's students, Gohachiro Namura came aboard. His excellent English immediately was noted by Williams, who said: "[he] enunciates better than either of the others." He came aboard with Kayama and another interpreter. After some verbal sparring, again about Uraga, the Japanese suddenly gave up the point, saying "Well, then, can you go ashore here [not far from the village of Yokohama] this afternoon and pick out a suitable place?" Without delay Kayama's party, captains Buchanan and Adams, Williams, and others, went ashore about five miles from the ships. A farmer's wheatfield was suggested for the site by Kayama, who dispassionately commented that he would demolish three or four houses there to make room for the conference buildings. The farmers, on their knees and of low condition, were not consulted on the matter.

Upon receiving the report of his men, Perry concurred in the selection of site, especially since the anchorage itself was excellent and afforded a good command of the shore for the ship's guns—in case of treachery during the forthcoming ceremonies. Feverish construction ensued on shore, and on February 27, Perry moved his ships to a line abreast just a mile offshore.

During this period there were social contacts. On March 1, Captain Buchanan gave a dinner for Kayama and friends, including interpreter Namura. Interpreter Williams commented that Kayama "acting in all respects with perfect propriety. This officer certainly exhibits a breeding and tact in all the novel positions in which he is placed that reflects great credit on him and shows the culture of the social parts of the Japanese character." After the dinner, in the Japanese custom, guests were given the remainder of the food served to take home. It was noted that Namura added two spoonfuls of syrup to his ginger before he stowed his parcel in his capacious garments.

Captain Adams gave Kayama a letter written by a Japanese refugee, a youth named Sentarō, now called Sam Patch. Presently a crewman on the *Susquehanna*, the man was a sailor rescued from a shipwreck earlier and now was appealing, hesitantly, for repatriation to Japan. Considerably amazed to receive the letter, Kayama requested a meeting with Sam Patch; when it did occur a few days later, Patch was paralyzed by the fear of losing his head on arrival in his own country. Facing the Japanese officials, Patch refused to talk or to stand up, remaining prostrate on the deck, until Captain Adams ordered him to rise while reminding him that he was perfectly safe as a crew member on an American ship. Adams said he would be entirely willing to see Patch repatriated, but asked for a guarantee that Patch would not be punished for his unplanned absence from Japan. The Japanese scoffed at the idea of Patch sustaining any harm from the situation, but Patch refused to leave the ship, after all.

About this time Einosuke Moriyama joined the interpreter corps. One of his first queries was about the health of his benefactor and teacher, Ranald MacDonald. Of course, all Perry's men knew of MacDonald was that he was a sailor repatriated during the voyage of the *Preble*, and, as background for his trip, Perry had read his brief statement entered by Commander Glynn into the Congressional Record. Williams indicated that Moriyama was "a new and superior interpreter . . . He speaks English well enough to render any other interpreter unnecessary, and thus will assist our intercourse greatly . . . He examined the machinery and at last sat down at dinner in the ward room, giving us all a good impression of his education and breeding."

Commodore Perry and his scribes were busy putting together a draft for a treaty to propose to Japan. The Japanese undoubtedly had been working toward the same end, or at least deciding what to reply to overtures. Kayama and his interpreters, among them Moriyama, frequently conferred with Perry's men concerning proper details of the forthcoming meeting, such as designs of flags, receipt of credentials of the participating officials, etc. Meanwhile, the treaty house rose—a rather stark building of unpainted wood topped by a peaked roof, enclosing a sizeable reception hall. The exterior walls were covered with dark cloth on which there was a colorful design, said to be the coat of arms of Izawa, Prince of Memasaki. Extending from each side of the building were yellow canvas screens, divided into panel-like squares by black painted stripes. A pier was constructed of straw bags filled with sand.

The fateful day—March 8, 1854—came. Early in the morning workmen and minor officials bustled around on shore, making final preparations. Only a small military honor guard appeared, instead of the considerable military force that had attended the 1853 ceremony. Large crowds of spectators pressed forward to barriers outlining the conference grounds. Hawks' narrative reads, "Bands of flag-bearers, musicians, and pikemen maneuvered in order, here and there, glistening with their lacquered caps, bright colored costumes, crimson streamers, showy emblazonry, and burnished spears . . . Soon a large barge came floating down the bay, from the neighboring town of Kanagawa. This was a gaily painted vessel with its decks and open pavilion rising high above the hull. It had very much the appearance of one of our western river steamboats. Streamers floated from its three masts, and bright colored flags and variegated drapery adorned the open deck above. This barge bore the Japanese commissioners . . . these dignitaries disembarked in several boats and hurried to the land. An immense number of Japanese craft of all kinds, each with a tassel on its prow and a square striped flag at its stern, gathered about the bay."

Commodore Perry's emissaries, too, sported elegant dress in keeping with the importance of the occasion. Officers wore frock coats, caps and epaulets, and were equipped with swords and pistols. The sailors were garbed in blue jackets, trousers, and white frocks, and armed with muskets, cutlasses and pistols. Even the musicians were armed.

The party of about five hundred Americans in twenty-seven boats landed in precise order, followed by the commodore in his barge, under a salute of seventeen guns. With bands playing, the commodore walked to the ceremonial house through an honor guard of marines posting bayonets. As the Japanese officials entered the house from a welcoming position at either side, the American ships gave a salute of twenty-one guns in honor of the Emperor, then a seventeen-gun salute for Prince Hayashi, and the Japanese flag was posted from the masthead of the *Powhatan*.

The interior of the structure was carpeted with thick mats. Benches covered with red cloth extended along the sides with like-covered tables in front. The room was heated by copper braziers of burning charcoal, supported upon lacquered wooden stands; and hangings on the walls—especially representations of cranes—gave a decorative effect. Moriyama introduced each of the five high commissioners and several other dignitaries to Commodore Perry, and tea and confections were served to all. Commodore Perry and his party then adjourned to a separate room where the five commissioners waited. Moriyama was the chief interpreter for the occasion. The five were: Prince Councilor Hayashi, the chief of the commission, a handsome, courtly man;

Prince Ido of Tsushima, tall and heavy, with a lively demeanor; Izawa, Prince of Memasaki, an elegantly dressed dandy of about forty with a good sense of fun; Udono, a member of the board of revenue or Mimbusco, a man of Mongolian appearance; and Michitaro Matsusaki, position undetermined, a sickly, nearsighted, elderly man. Kurokawa, Kayama and interpreter Hori also were there. Unknown to the Americans, the repatriated refugee, Manjiro Nakahama, who had spent several years in the United States, England, Hong Kong and Macao before being returned safely to the Japanese, was sitting undetected to double-check the statements being translated back and forth.

After pleasantries were exchanged, the Emperor's reply to President Fillmore's letter was presented, written on a scroll of coarse paper. A Dutch translation signed by Einosuke Moriyama (nothing was said about a written English translation; perhaps Moriyama was not that fluent), but not the signed original, was presented. Essentially, the Japanese letter agreed to kindly treatment of shipwrecked sailors, supplies for ships in dire need, one port for trade to be chosen later, and an adequate supply of coal to be maintained there. The document suggested that it would take five years to complete the arrangements for such a port, but that some trade could commence before that and prices for articles could be determined by Kurokawa and Moriyama. Perry accepted the document, then returned it, requesting that it should be signed by the high commissioner and delivered to him the following day. The American draft of a treaty and an explanatory letter, in Chinese, English, and Dutch, were handed to the Japanese, emphasizing that a treaty between Japan and the United States would be a desirable achievement. Moriyama readily translated the proceedings, moving back and forth from one delegation to the other, always remaining upon his knees as proper submission to his commissioners, who outranked him. Perry included in his remarks to the commissioners that he had been sent by his government to make a treaty, and if he did not succeed, possibly the United States would send more ships to make one. His none-too-veiled threat was couched in his wish that everything would be settled soon and that he could send two of his ships off to intercept any others already en route.

Extending to the delegates an invitation to visit his ship, and after requesting and receiving permission to bury a deceased sailor at Yokohama at a site adjoining a temple, Perry assumed the negotiations were over for the day and repaired to his ship. During the negotiations, the lesser members of Perry's party had been entertained with food and drink.

The following day Kurokawa and Moriyama delivered to the *Powhatan* an official copy of the Imperial reply to the President's letter, signed by four commissioners. Also discussed were the formalities of exchange of presents the following March 13, the obtaining of provisions, permissions to go ashore for walks, and—more formally—which ports were to be opened for trade. Perry indicated through Captain Adams that, despite the 1853 letter asking for one trading port, now he (Perry) wanted five. Interpreter S. Wells Williams was critical of what he construed as Perry's arrogance, going beyond the requests of the U. S. government. Fillmore had asked for good treatment; Perry demanded a treaty and obscurely threatened them if they did not sign one. Such discrepancies were not mentioned, apparently, by the Japanese. Moriyama declined to suggest possible ports, observing that the entire matter was contrary to the laws of the land and the idea would take some time to resolve.

Elaborate gifts for the Emperor, delivered on March 13, included such things as history books, a lifeboat, velvet cloth, perfumes, wines, china, and—most exciting to the Japanese—a telegraph with three miles of wire, plus a one-fourth size miniature steam engine, track, tender and car. The latter was set up and became immensely popular with the citizenry. Even though it was scaled down so that it barely supported a child of six, adults gleefully boarded the train, sitting on the roofs of the miniature cars. It was quite a sight to see dignified Japanese, robes flying, riding the train, laughing convulsively in half embarrassment, half enjoyment.

Kurokawa and Moriyama visited the ship almost every day, dealing with myriad details of the treaty, as well as current needs for supplies, monitoring of sailors on shore leave, etc. On March 17, Commodore Perry went ashore for a meeting with four commissioners, Hayashi, Ido, Izawa, and Udono, this time with minimal ceremony. The prior day the commissioners had sent a counterproposal to Commodore Perry, agreeing to furnish supplies but suggesting—for the time being—that the Americans should trade at the Port of Nagasaki and, in five years, maybe they could open another port for trading with passing ships. Perry insisted that one or more ports other than Nagasaki must be designated, and those opened within sixty days. The details of treatment of shipwrecked sailors were discussed.

On the request for an open port in the Ryukyus and on Hokkaido the Japanese delegation stalled, tenaciously holding Nagasaki as the only immediate place for commerce. The commodore was just as insistent that the Americans would NOT be treated in the same servile manner as that accepted by the Dutch and Chinese. Perry suggested the five ports should be: one on Honshu Island, possibly Uraga or Kagoshima (Hawks must be in error there, because Kagoshima is in southern Japan on Kyushu Island); one on Hokkaido Island; and a third on the Ryukyus, probably Okinawa; with two others to be designated at a later time.

After much discussion through the intermediary Moriyama, the commissioners and Perry agreed upon a port in the Bay of Shimoda—if the holding ground was found to be satisfactory—but that an answer about Matsumae (Hokkaido) and the Ryukyus could not yet be made. March 23 was set as the date for a further conference. At that time Kenzhiro Hirayama, believed to be an assistant to Kurokawa, and others came to the *Powhatan* to deliver the assent of the Japanese commissioners, signed by Einosuke Moriyama, that ships of the United States could be supplied at Hakodate (near Matsumae and with a more protected harbor) starting September 17, 1855.

Thereafter the tensions between the two countries were relaxed markedly and, the very next day, Commodore Perry and others went ashore at Yokohama to receive the Emperor's gifts—not just to Perry, but to carefully listed other officers (the Americans had specifically designated the recipients of their gifts, as well). Prince Hayashi read aloud the name of each recipient and his gift, translated dutifully by Moriyama into Dutch and by Portman into English. Among the significant gifts were lovely lacquered ware, porcelain cups decorated with figures and flowers in gold, and rich cloths. Perry was presented, in addition, with three matchlocks, two complete sets of Japanese coins, and two swords—more ceremonial and indicative of respect than valuable. Finally, in an old Japanese tradition, sacks of rice were presented—one to two hundred of them.

After the gift ceremonies, the entire company was entertained by sumo wrestlers, giant athletes as they are yet today. Among them were two or three of the most famous wrestlers of Japan, including Koyanagi. Hawks says: "They were all so immense in flesh that they appeared to have lost their distinctive features . . . Their great size, however, was due more to the development of muscle than to the deposition of fat . . . and capable of great strength. As a preliminary exhibition of the power of these men, the princes set them to removing the sacks of rice to a convenient place on the shore for shipping. Each of the sacks weighed not less than one hundred and twenty-five pounds, and there were only a couple of the wrestlers who did not carry each two sacks at a time."

Williams described the wrestling exhibition: "The match then began, two and two coming into the ring. First, squatting on their feet, opposite each other, the two began to rub themselves with dirt on the palms and arm pits, and then advanced to the centre in a steady step. Here, each stretched out one leg after the other, holding his knee with a close grip and planting his foot in the earth with a heavy groan, or grunt, several times, again rubbing his hands in the gravel like a bull pawing the earth. All this took up a minute or more, and then each, seizing the other's shoulders, endeavored to push his antagonist over; one butted his head with all his force against the other's breast, while that one only tried to throw him by turning his body, and generally succeeded in doing so, he coming to the ground with a thump that showed the force exerted. In only one case was there anything like wrestling . . . It was a curious, barbaric spectacle, reminding one of the old gladiators."

By the next day, March 25, Moriyama conjectured that Hakodate might be available as early as March, 1855. Perry indicated, then, that he would visit Hakodate after leaving Edo Bay, requesting the assistance of interpreter Namura for the trip, a MacDonald student mentioned earlier who had been a part of the interpreter corps for the Perry negotiations from time to time. Moriyama suggested an additional interpreter, because of the different dialect at Hokkaido.

The matter of a resident American consul was discussed, which was not very palatable to the Japanese, but Commodore Perry agreed to just one consul residing at Shimoda (the first man to be appointed would be Townsend Harris). Moriyama would carry that information back to his superiors.

While maneuverings and ratifications were taking place ashore in the Japanese halls of authority, Commodore Perry and his squadron commanders returned the hospitality afforded them by the Japanese earlier. Invitations went out to about seventy Japanese people for a banquet, performances by minstrels, and tours of the ship. The biggest hit of the affair was the preparation of four large cakes, each bearing a miniature flag of the coat-of-arms of each commissioner. Prince Matsusaki expressed the goodwill of all when he threw his arms about the commodore's neck, stating over and over, "Japan and America, all the same heart." Of course, the glow of wine consumed copiously contributed to the effusiveness.

The following day a more restrained negotiating team pursued the clauses about ports, consular residence, and shore leaves for sailors. The Japanese agreed, in principle, to opening three ports, Hakodate, Shimoda, and Okinawa (Napa or Napha), and to one consul stationed in Shimoda a year to eighteen months hence. With most points now covered, drafts were prepared. On Friday, March 31, 1854, Commodore Perry went ashore to the treaty house to sign three drafts of the treaty written in English and delivered them to the Japanese commissioners, together with three copies in Dutch and Chinese, certified by interpreters Williams and Portman. The Japanese commissioners, in turn, handed to the commodore three drafts of the treaty signed by the four commissioners appointed by the Emperor to act officially. Two copies in Dutch, the only mutual language (except for Moriyama's good, but still limited English), were signed—by Moriyama for the Japanese, by Portman for the Americans.

The Perry expeditions had been remarkably successful. Japan was now open to the Americans, albeit on a limited basis. Basically the treaty provisions covered the following points: (1) peace; (2) ports and supply privileges; (3) assistance for shipwrecked sailors; (4) freedom for shipwrecked men during their stay; (5) shipwrecked men and American citizens residing in Shimoda and Hakodate could travel seven Japanese miles from a central location in each; (6) consideration for trade matters; (7) permission for American ships to use gold and silver coins, as well as goods, for purchase of Japanese products; (8) certain provisions must be procured through a Japanese agency only; (9) that any privileges granted to another country would also apply to Americans; (10) American ships were allowed only at Shimoda and Hakodate, unless in dire distress; (11) the consul to live at Shimoda; and (12) the treaty was to be ratified by the President of the United States and by the august Sovereign of Japan, and ratifications exchanged within eighteen months from the date, March 31, 1854.

Upon completion of the signing, Commodore Perry presented Prince Hayashi with an American flag and gave gifts to the other commissioners. A banquet followed, toasts were drunk, and admonishments given by the Japanese to not move the ships any closer to Edo. Nevertheless, at a later conference with Moriyama and Hirayama, the two agreed to accompany Perry on the *Powhatan* during a brief cruise toward Edo, not landing there. The squadron left the "American Anchorage" on April 10, returning the 13th. Little by little, since the treaty signing, the various ships of the squadron were putting out to sea for other destinations; on April 18, Perry and the remaining squadron steamed out of Edo Bay into Shimoda, where they stayed for almost a month, exploring the shore and becoming acquainted with the local residents, before proceeding to Hakodate. During this period the interpreter Hori officiated, as required, as well as Moriyama—who had traveled down to Shimoda to assist in supervising the compliance with treaty conditions.

During Perry's stay at Shimoda, two fugitives appealed for asylum, one being Torajiro Yoshida under his assumed name Manji (who had fallen from favor years earlier along with Shozan Sakuma; both were scholars and had been willing to entertain modern notions—ideas that fell contrary to the Shogun's politics of the time). Manji and the other fugitive, Koōda Isagi, first sent the following letter:

> Two scholars of Yedo in Japan, named Isagi Koōda, and Kwanouchi Manji, present this letter to the high officers and others who manage affairs. That which we have received is meagre and trifling, as our persons are insignificant, so that we are ashamed to come before distinguished persons; we are ignorant of arms

and their uses in battle, nor do we know the rules of strategy and discipline; we have, indeed, uselessly whiled away our months and years, and know nothing. We have heard a little of the customs and knowledge of the Europeans and Americans, and have desired to travel about in the five great continents, but the maritime prohibitions of our country are exceedingly strict . . . We have decided on a plan, which is very privately to request you to take us aboard of your ships and secretly carry us to sea, that we may travel over the five continents, even if it is disregarding our laws . . . When a lame man sees another walking, or a pedestrian sees another riding, would he not be glad to be in his place? How much more now, since for our whole lives we could not go beyond 30 degrees east and west, and 25 degrees from north to south, when we behold you come riding on the high winds and careering over the vast waves, with lightning speed coasting along the five continents, does it appear as if the lame had a way to walk, or the walkers an opportunity to ride! We hope you who manage this business will condescend to regard and grant our request; but . . . if this matter becomes known, we shall have no place to flee, and doubtless must suffer the extremest penalty.

Unfortunately, when the men slipped aboard with the collusion of a crewman, their small boat drifted away. After Perry had heard their case, he dared not give them shelter, since it might interfere with the amicable dealings just completed, but he did attempt to return the hapless men to shore without discovery. However, apparently the boat had been discovered and the refugees identified, for later the next day, Moriyama came to inquire about "two demented Japanese." The flag lieutenant was vague, putting the matter off as a mere casual visit and assured Moriyama that the men were back on shore. Later, however, a party on shore leave walked past the local prison, recognizing the two would-be stowaways being held in a small cage-like prison. The prisoners smuggled a note written on a piece of board back to the *Powhatan*:

When a hero fails in his purpose, his acts are then regarded as those of a villain and a robber. In public we have been seized and pinioned and caged for many days. The village elders and head men treat us disdainfully, their oppressions being grievous indeed. Therefore, looking up while yet we have nothing wherewith to reproach ourselves, it must now be seen whether a hero will prove himself to be one indeed. Regarding the liberty of going through the sixty States as not enough for our desires, we wished to make the circuit of the five great continents. This was our hearts' wish for a long time. Suddenly our plans are defeated, and we find ourselves in a half-sized house, where eating, resting, sitting, and sleeping are difficult; how can we find our exit from this place? Weeping, we seem as fools; laughing, as rogues. Alas! for us; silent we can only be.

Isaga Koōda
Kwansuchi Manji

Upon learning of their imprisonment, Perry sent a lieutenant to see what could be done to alleviate their condition, but found the prisoners had been transferred to Edo and the local prefecture had no further authority over them. As Ranald MacDonald once had yearned to gain entrance to Japan to learn about that country, so, too, these two scholars' only apparent crime was a thirst for learning about the outside world.

On May 13, Perry left with a reduced squadron of ships for Hakodate, arriving May 17, to the consternation of local officials—who had not been notified about the treaty and were understandably agitated. Interpreter Namura and the official Hirayama had not yet arrived with instructions. However, communication was established through Williams and Portman, presumably, and the company was cordially received. After the officials read in Japanese a copy of the new treaty, they were much relieved. Interpreter Williams was pleased to receive the "considerable practice in Japanese." The ensuing days were passed pleasantly, with crewmen permitted to go ashore for shopping, walking and general entertainment. Since it was stated that the trip from Edo to Hokkaido would take at least thirty days, Perry bided his time until Hirayama came. Finally, after a grueling journey through snow and cold (the route lies over a considerable mountain range), Hirayama arrived on June 1—not with Namura, as far as can be learned, but only with a lesser official, Junnoshin Anma.

The arrival was an anticlimactic one, since the local dignitaries and Hirayama's party came aboard with an interpreter, Ayasaburo Takeda, who spoke no English or Dutch, but could write Dutch only. Little more was accomplished then or thereafter beyond that already settled with Hakodate officials. Perry's ships left two days later to return to Shimoda, staying there until June 25 to settle the finer points of the regulations and agreements promulgated by the treaty—all of which was facilitated through the linguistic abilities of Moriyama. Apparently the latter was appointed to serve in Shimoda permanently, as Townsend Harris encountered him there upon his arrival in 1856.

So closed an important chapter in world affairs, with the two Perry expeditions consuming one full year (less a day). Of the fourteen interpreters coached in English and instructed in the ways of the Western world by Ranald MacDonald in 1849, at least three—Moriyama, Hori, and Namura—participated in the fateful events that led to trading, social and economic intercourse between the United States and Japan.

XIX

MacDonald in the Cariboo

In the gracious Victoria home of Governor Douglas, Ranald MacDonald, his brother Allan, and the governor discussed with interest the happenings from abroad. The Japan treaty was signed; Perry's report to President Fillmore had been made public. Townsend Harris was in Japan to negotiate a trade treaty.

Closer to home, though, were the electric happenings in the Cariboo—that broad, rolling plain that lies between the Rocky Mountains and the Coast Range one hundred fifty miles "as the crow flies" from Vancouver, British Columbia. Gold had been discovered on Fraser River sandbars. Prospectors were swarming into the area and working ever northward, hoping to find the source of the free gold in the rivers.

Partly because of the gold fever, partly because of territorial pressures from the United States, the British sought to strengthen their ties to the area now known as British Columbia. The Hudson's Bay Company had founded Victoria on Vancouver Island in 1843, receiving authority from the British government later to encourage colonization. An old and warm friend of the MacDonalds, James Douglas of the Hudson's Bay Company, was made governor of the new Vancouver Island colony. The international border had been established in 1846 at the forty-ninth parallel, just south of today's city of Vancouver. (Ownership of the scattered islands of Puget Sound and the Strait of Georgia was still to be decided—in 1872, when the border was established by an imaginary line through Haro Strait.)

When the probability of a major gold strike loomed, Britain established British Columbia as a colony in 1858, with New Westminster designated as the capital in 1859. Douglas' authority was expanded to include all of the new colony. (British Columbia was not to become part of the Dominion of Canada until 1871, however, and then only under the condition that a railroad would be constructed to the west coast. See Chapter XXIII for the influence of Ranald MacDonald's wanderings in the Orient on this event.)

After a pleasant visit with their father's old friend, the MacDonald brothers bought supplies and joined the trek to the gold fields. There were no good routes, just a choice of difficult trails—a dangerous, rigorous, seemingly endless journey. (In 1858 and yet today, more than a century later, the actual access via the trails or roads totals close to four hundred miles.)

Prospectors working the lower Fraser River sandbars near Hope, a hundred miles east of Vancouver, clawed their way upriver looking for the mother lode. "Upriver" was all but impassable—the Fraser Canyon, that raw gash in the Coast Range, had defeated water travelers a half century earlier. In 1828, George Simpson himself, with Archibald MacDonald, Ranald's father, had experienced a rare trip downriver, barely emerging unscathed from the fury of the boiling rapids. Soaring six to eight thousand feet, the mountains rose steeply on either side of the river leaving few ledges to traverse—just treacherous paths through unstable avalanche deposits of rock and dirt. Prospectors fell into the Fraser from the ledges or, attempting to use canoes or rafts, were swamped in the turbulent waters. Occasionally local Indians picked off prospectors with their bows and arrows. Scarcely a day passed without dead bodies floating downstream into quieter water.

A safer but longer foot or horse trail, the old Hudson's Bay fur brigade trail of the Coquihalla, detoured far east of the Fraser to Kamloops before it returned to the river. Still other prospectors followed the Fraser River upstream from Fort Langley, up the Harrison River into Harrison Lake to its northern end, then trekked along a demanding and complex route to Lillooet and beyond, by trail, rivers, lakes and portages. Lesser numbers of miners proceeded east up the Columbia River and through the Cascade Mountains to eastern Washington, then turned north to the Grand Coulee country destined for Canada's Okanagan region and the Fraser.

Large numbers of the wealth seekers were Americans, many from the California gold fields, who arrived at Whatcom (now Bellingham, Washington) and went overland to the Fraser River. Outfitting stores sprang into being at Whatcom. To avoid losing the outfitting business and governmental revenues, and to initiate some control over the prospectors, Governor James Douglas, taking his cue from the Australian gold rush, decreed that prospectors must obtain a license costing ten shillings or five American dollars before proceeding into the Cariboo. This assured that newcomers logically would proceed from Victoria or New Westminster up the Fraser River past Fort Langley, stocking up on supplies in British Columbia. An estimated twenty-five thousand miners flocked into the region by any means, but mostly by steamer, to search for gold.

For the early years of the gold rush, the Harrison to Lillooet route was the most popular foot trail. In an effort to improve access to the Cariboo, Governor Douglas offered miners his cooperation in cutting a trail from Harrison Lake north toward Lillooet Lake. The steamboat *Otter* made its way to the north end of Harrison Lake, disembarking two hundred and fifty prospectors/trail builders. A rude hamlet called Port Douglas (named for the governor) sprang up a short distance north. Prospectors paid $25 each for the privilege of working on the trail, in return for which Douglas promised free provisions and, when the trail was completed, the return to each worker of the $25 deposit in the form of provisions delivered to the site, so the prospectors could proceed.

Preferring to be merchants, Ranald and Allan MacDonald jumped into the supply business at Douglas, where hastily erected buildings became stores and hostelries, with supplies brought in by raft or canoe. In 1860, Commander Richard C. Mayne, during his explorations of Vancouver for the British, came to Douglas from Port Pemberton at the time the MacDonald brothers were in business there. He mentioned the fine, hard road (the result of Douglas' prospectors pressed into service, no doubt), a rare treat after the walking they lately endured: "when we reached the four-mile house from Douglas, they were so far in the rear, and it was getting so late, that we decided to halt there for the night. Next morning we crossed 'Sevastopol,' as the steep hill which lies behind Douglas is named, and reached the port. Douglas, too, had improved somewhat within the year which had elapsed since I had seen it. The restaurants were decidedly better, and things generally cheaper. The saw-mill in the gully leading down the mountain was finished, and had been at work for some time, while the mule-trains were larger and more numerous. Except, however, as a resting-place, or point of arrival and departure, Douglas does not promise to become of much consequence."

As gold interest moved northward, so did the MacDonald brothers, joined in 1862 by little brother Benjamin, age eighteen. Having participated in the gold madness of Australia, Ranald was more interested in supplying prospectors than in being one, although he did engage in mining ventures in the Horsefly country from time to time. Likely, he was prospecting on the Thompson River as well in 1860, for gold commissioner Cox said that seven miners on Lake Kamloops were realizing three pounds, six shillings per day; and, a friend on the Thompson River reported that he easily gained one pound per day with the rocker, "but it should not be forgotten that he was an old Ballarat miner," and that others should not expect that much.

Leaving Allan to operate the Douglas store from 1859 to 1860, Ranald operated a ferry across the Fraser River at Lillooet, where the stream was relatively narrow as it murmured through a chasm formed by broad mesas or precipitous benches like stair steps up the mountainside. Prospectors toiled laboriously from Douglas along the Lillooet River, boarding boats, rafts or canoes, on Lillooet Lake, Anderson Lake and Seton Lake, and portaging or walking from one to the other. From these high lakes they descended to cross the river, and promptly faced equally rigorous ascents. Then the country began to open into high, rolling plains interspersed with pleasant forests and trout-filled streams. Summer days were not too bad, except for hordes of black flies. Winter was another matter. Snow lay several feet deep upon the Cariboo, driving game into hiding and fish beneath thick ice. Blizzards howled across open stretches, and the temperature often plunged below zero. As always, the availability of supplies measured how fast the prospectors could work northward.

In May, 1859, after following "color" up the Fraser Canyon and tributaries that seemed promising, five prospectors, Peter Dunlevy, Jim Sellers, Ira Crow, Tom Moffit, and Tom Manifee, made a modest strike at what became Horsefly River east of today's Williams Lake. At almost the identical time a loner named Benjamin MacDonald (not Ranald's brother) paddled up the Quesnel River to prospect, since the search for gold was narrowing down to the wilderness near Lake Quesnel; he, too, found color. The old Hudson's Bay Company's Fort Alexandria became the main supply point for these early prospectors, shortly thereafter supplanted by Quesnel Forks or today's Quesnel.

Early in 1860, W. R. "Doc" Keithley and either J. P. Diller or George Weaver (stories differ), plus John Rose and Benjamin MacDonald, found gold at Keithley Creek. The returns were not high, but the geological formations were markedly similar to those of the California diggings familiar to them. Attempting to keep their find secret, the party stayed in the wilderness and worked until they were forced to send several men for supplies. Although they said nothing, the prospectors hanging around the store were astute enough to figure that there was some reason for the men's return into the wintry wilderness. By spring goldseekers were spread throughout the area south of Quesnel Lake, especially around Antler Creek. There is considerable evidence that Ranald MacDonald might have been among them. A town sprang up like magic.

Robin Skelton, in the book *They Call It the Cariboo*, says that, "In July 1861 Antler had sixty houses and boasted luxuries hardly to be found elsewhere in Cariboo. Champagne was sold at $12 a bottle, and theatrical

troupes such as Watson and Taylor's Minstrels were performing regularly
. . . a group of suddenly rich miners decided it needed a race course. Several racehorses were ordered from England and arrived in Victoria in 1861
. . . a four-furlong course was laid out straight, edged with stones . . . A
thirty by forty foot 'Casino' was built at one end . . . Fred W. Ludditt
believes that it was a visit by Sir James Douglas to one of these early meetings that so impressed him with the wealth of the Cariboo that he began
his plans for the great Cariboo Road."

By September the town contained ten saloons, seven general stores, two
blacksmith shops, a sawmill, a shoemaker and a butcher shop, according to the
Victoria newspaper. All this less than a year after the discovery of gold. In the
summer of 1861, the aggregate yield of Antler was valued at over two thousand
British pounds per day, and even some new hands took out gold valued at
twenty pounds each day. When the bedrock was laid bare, in places there were
lumps of gold valued at ten pounds or more. Two men took out 3,750 pounds
worth from May, 1860, to the summer of 1861.

Meanwhile on November 3, 1860, presumably abandoning Allan's
store and Ranald's ferry, the MacDonald brothers went into the packing
business from a claim on one hundred and sixty acres of land, identified as:
"P/R 12, Lillooet, situated on the Bonapart [sic] River, as shown on the
accompanying sketch," of the Ashcroft district, Bonaparte River Area.
However, pre-emption was not completed by Certificate of Improvements
and Crown Grant. In the gold rush days, this location was at the crossroads of the high trail from Lillooet and the difficult but soon to be improved Cariboo Trail up the Fraser Canyon. Historical notes indicate that
the ranch lay just north of property filed upon by George Dunne (later an
operator of Hat Creek House), the same property claimed by Sophie
McLean as the widow of Donald McLean. Ranald's ranch, therefore, was
probably that piece of property later proved up and filed as Lot 95, by M.
Veasy, April 17, 1873. Above this property straddling a steep mountainside
was a second claim filed by Ranald and Allan on April 23, 1869, and also
not completed, probably the later Lot 643. The later claim must have been
filed as a speculative one for minerals, as the terrain is of little use for
anything else.

At any rate, Donald McLean, a stern but honest Hudson's Bay Chief
Trader from Kamloops, moved adjacent to Ranald's ranch in 1860 and
opened McLean's Restaurant, which later was owned by George Dunne.
McLean's old restaurant building is preserved today at Hat Creek House
Provincial Park, having been moved there from the Dunne property.
McLean was known as a brutal man, but a good farmer and manager. A

prospector reported that McLean had the best farm in the colony: "The enterprising and industrious proprietor has valuable stock of cattle, especially some fine shorthorns. Here we replenished our stock of flour at the competitively low price of two shillings per pound. Fine turnips, cabbages and scarlet runners were growing hereabouts."

Traveling through the area in 1861, Governor Douglas admired the country around the Bonaparte and Chapeau rivers (Hat Creek's original name), saying it was beautiful and picturesque—a grateful spectacle to the traveler because of its green hills, crowning slopes, and level meadows, and of great value as a grazing district. He mentioned that McLean was stocking his ranch with excellent cattle of the best American breeds.

Donald and Sophie had many children, including three sons who were to become outlaws of the worst sort in later years; however, Ranald does not mention any difficulties with McLean. Straddling the Cariboo Trail a few hundred yards after its junction with the old high trail from Lillooet, which ran over Pavilion Mountain and down Hat Creek to the Bonaparte Valley, Ranald's ranch served as a marshaling point for the supply business opened by the MacDonald brothers. They utilized long strings of pack mules and horses. Such pack strings could number more than two hundred animals trudging unlinked, each knowing its place in line and following a lead animal, usually a white, belled mare.

Intermittently the two brothers prospected for gold themselves—Ranald continuing to favor the Horsefly district opened by Keithley. He may have been correct in his conclusions, for that river traverses the Quesnel Highlands, a low range of mountains sheltering Richfield and Barkerville where the major gold strikes were made.

The key discovery was made by William "Dutch Bill" Dietz, who worked northward with a party of miners from Antler Creek in February, 1861. Camping beside a small creek that became known as Williams Creek, they spent a cold night. According to the *Victoria Chronicle* of November 5, 1863, the party had quit for the night and cooked their dinner. Later Dietz wandered back to the creek where the bare bedrock was exposed in the stream. Swirling a pan of gravel from a point near a ledge, he found gold worth a dollar a pan. Excitedly he returned to share the news with his two companions, but they were unimpressed, and determined to return to Quesnel Forks. Dietz reluctantly went with them to Antler, where he coerced three other men to backtrack with him to Williams Creek, first acquiring additional supplies and equipment.

Several days later, when one of the party returned for more supplies, Antler's miners were convinced that Dietz's party was onto something and several followed the man when he set out for Williams Creek. The color was good everywhere and, since the take was routinely running a dollar or more per pan, additional miners swarmed into the new diggings staking out claims where sometimes eight feet of snow covered the ground. Around these diggings arose the town of Richfield, called Elwyntown at first to honor Thomas Elwyn, gold commissioner of the Cariboo.

The fifteen-foot layer of blue clay in the creek, at first believed to be bedrock, was probed with unspectacular but steady results. Several creeks in the same vicinity yielded amounts consistent with the original discoveries. The "Big One" was yet to come . . .

Merchants in Victoria were clamoring for a chance at the rapidly developing supply business in the Cariboo country. Some—mostly those who had not *been* there—favored a route from the Chilcotin Plateau along the the Homathko River south, to join with a harbor to be established on Bute Inlet, located at the northern end of the Strait of Georgia. Not to be dissuaded, this group of Victoria merchants sent surveyor Robert Homfray and a party of six men to explore from Bute Inlet into the rugged interior. Homfray returned somewhat "white-knuckled" after losing his canoe and never reaching his destination at Fort Alexandria.

Still operating from his ranch at Hat Creek and the Bonaparte River, Ranald MacDonald embarked on an exploration on May 24, 1861, to assess the country from Fort Alexandria to the west coast—in hopes of finding a better route to the goldfields from the ocean. It was said that Ranald also had in mind the concept of eventually trading with the Orient through such a seaport, routed from the Cariboo. Accompanying MacDonald on horseback with four pack horses for supplies were John G. Barnston, a barrister and son of a Hudson's Bay factor; Gilbert Tomkins; J. B. Pearson; and R. P. Ritchie. Parts of the trail were along a route similar to that traveled by Colin McKenzie in 1860 and Sir Alexander Mackenzie in 1793 across the Chilcotin Plateau to Bella Coola.

After several minor mishaps and delays, the party reached Lake Anahim in early June (Barnston says in an account in the *Victoria Colonist* of August 16, 1861, that this was presumably "McKenzie's Lake"). The party obtained a native guide and was camped in the Coast Range by June 12, descending to the Bella Coola River the following day.

There the guide deserted them without warning. The river was running swiftly—swollen and full of dangerous dead trees. Incoming streams, though shallow, were rushing torrents over boulder-strewn streambeds. Leaving the horses with Pearson and Ritchie, the other three men continued on foot, arriving in the Bella Coola village of Naniclouf. Two days later by canoe, MacDonald and his party ran down the Bella Coola River in six hours into North Bentinck Arm. They put in at the village of the Kungotos, friendly Indians who freely gave them information about the area. According to them, the trail along the river between their village and Naniclouf was good.

MacDonald, Barnston and Tomkins left the village on June 24 for a grueling two-day paddle upstream—a trip that had taken only six hours with the current. Reunited with Pearson and Ritchie, the party returned without haste to Alexandria. Barnston reported:

"The Ballakoolah [sic] River can, we consider, be made navigable for light draught steamers as far up as Naniclouf, and perhaps for some distance above. From the village, pack trains could make Alexandria or the mouth of Quesnelle River in 14 or 15 days. The trail to Quesnelle River, if one were made there, would probably have to diverge from the Alexandria trail at Chesikut Lake, about 73 miles from Alexandria. The trail runs the whole distance from the Fraser to the coast range on an elevated tableland, and is studded in every direction with lakes and meadows. The feed for animals is good and plentiful. The streams are numerous but small and shallow, in fact, with one or two exceptions, being mere creeks. There are some swamps which would have to be corduroyed."

He went on to describe the route further, as fairly level and with no insurmountable obstacles, concluding:

"We all consider that if a road were made from the Ballakoolah Inlet (North Bentinck Arm) to strike the Fraser somewhere about the mouth of the Quesnelle River, and from thence into the Cariboo, a great saving in the cost of transportation would be effected . . . if that part of the country turns out to be as rich in gold as is expected, goods can be laid down quite as cheap if not cheaper at Fraser's Lake or Fort George than they can at present be obtained at Williams' Lake, 60 miles this side of the Forks of Quesnelle. Fraser's Lake is actually nearer the coast than Alexandria."

MacDonald and Barnston proceeded with a plan for a toll road over the proposed route, and joined forces with a group of capitalists from San Francisco. In a report to Edward Green, Esq., dated January 1, 1862, at Victoria, Vancouver Island, MacDonald and Barnston laid out their proposal and reasons for the endeavor.

"In compliance with your request we beg leave to submit the following remarks as a Report upon the proposed Road from the Bellacoola Inlet, or North Bentinck Arm, to the Northern Mines of British Columbia:

"The road would be about two hundred miles long, that is to say, from the head of the Inlet to the point required on the Fraser River."

The report continued with a review of the terrain, largely contained in Barnston's report to the *Colonist*. It continues:

"As regards the practicability of the road all we need say is this—that at eight different times during the last summer parties consisting of two, three, or more persons, have been over the route.

"All of these parties succeeded in getting through without difficulty, and agree with us in saying not only that a good practical Road, or Mule Trail, (that is to say, *ten* feet wide as required by Government) can be made at a comparatively small cost, but that when made, a very great saving in the cost of transportation will be effected."

MacDonald and Barnston put forth economic reasons for the trail: the harbor at North Bentinck Arm would be very safe and roomy, the site was favorable for building wharves and docks, there was superior timber nearby, excellent possibilities of establishing fisheries existed, and copper and gold had been found in the rivers nearby. They also mentioned that Bella Coola would be only two hundred miles from the southern tip of Queen Charlotte's Island, on which copper deposits had already been found.

The writers cited comparative data on distances to be saved over the Port Douglas route (158 miles shorter), the savings in transshipment points (only three for the Bella Coola route and fifteen for the Port Douglas route), and the speed of travel (seven days less than the old route). They pointed out the failure of explorations from Bute Inlet and via the Nass River.

"The town of Bellacoola would become the depot for the supply of the Northern Mines, and would also be a starting point for pack trains . . .

"Victoria is, as it always has been, the only Depot for British Columbia." MacDonald and Barnston had pointed out that none of the river ports such as Yale, New Westminster, or Lytton were commercial depots; "merchants at Victoria, inasmuch as by establishing branch houses or agencies at Bellacoola . . . would in fact, in this way, deal DIRECTLY with Cariboo traders . . . Victoria will be . . . the main depot for the coast trade."

The entrepreneurs estimated that four hundred and fifty tons per month of goods would pass over the new road. At a rate of 1-1/2 cents per pound, that would bring in $81,000. Less expenses, the two estimated a net profit for six months of $66,000.

The report concludes with the farsighted view of a trans-Canada road (or railroad) by this route. (Malcolm McLeod, a prime mover for the building of a trans-Canada railroad, noted later that "I had written to him [MacDonald] advising the route in question, in connection with the Leather [Yellowhead] Pass route which I was then writing on in the Canada Press.")

In regard to a trans-Canada road, MacDonald and Barnston said:

"Before concluding this report we may mention that it has also occurred to us that at some period not far distant a road will be made across the Continent, connecting the British Provinces of the Atlantic Coast with the Colonies on the Pacific. Such road there is every reason to believe will pass through the Red River and Saskatchewan country, and through the Rocky Mountains via Jasper's House, and Tete Jaune Cache; thence down the East branch of the Fraser to Fort George; thence, provided the Coast Route be opened, there is no doubt that it would go to the North Bentinck Arm. So that it appears to us probable enough that the future town of Bellacoola will yet be the terminus of the much talked-of Pacific Road through British Territory."

The logic of the proposal bore fruit and a company organized for the construction of the road. On April 5, 1862, the Prospectus for the company listed "nominal capital" of $60,000, divided into two hundred and forty shares of stock of two hundred and fifty dollars each.

In the prospectus was the clause: "The Government of British Columbia has granted to Mr. Ranald McDonald [sic] an agreement for a Charter, authorizing him to levy a toll of *One and a half Cents* per pound upon all goods transported over the Road, and a *half dollar* per head on all cattle, for the term of five years from the completion of seventy miles of the Road.

"This agreement, which also provides for the conversion of the Trail into a Waggon-Road—in which event a new Charter will be granted, giving an increased rate of toll and an extension of time—has been assigned to the Company by the said Ranald McDonald."

Application for shares were to be made at the office of Edward Green, Wharf Street, Victoria.

XX

Barkerville, the Big Strike of the Cariboo

Seemingly an entirely sound venture, the Bella Coola road never got started despite the keen support by Victoria merchants for either the Bentinck Arm Company or the Bute Inlet Company. Neither of these companies were financed by the government, but each was proposing to construct a road and thereafter to charge good prices for freight hauling to and from the Cariboo. During 1862, Alfred Waddington and a crew of seventy men struggled to construct a road inland from Bute Inlet, reporting in November that they had built twenty-three miles of trail and blazed another forty, while under harassment from the local Indians.

The Bentinck Arm Company awaited the report of Lt. Palmer of the Royal Engineers, who had been sent by the government on a survey of the country between Fort Alexandria and Bella Coola. Palmer's report was highly unfavorable because of the region's "high continuous elevation, and from the general absence of good soil and pasturage in the districts which it traverses." Palmer's party, too, experienced the Indians' curiosity and hostility. Palmer reported the disappearance of pannekins (pans and cups, usually tin), knives, and even the inverting eyepiece of the theodolite (a surveying instrument). Palmer said that the Indians believed that, when he took sightings with his sextant, he was communicating with some almighty power to determine whether or not the current smallpox outbreak would be serious.

Developing routes to the western coast of Canada would become the top priority of the Victoria government after the major gold strikes at Richfield and Barkerville, beginning in August, 1862. The Bentinck Arm and Bute Inlet schemes, however, were eclipsed before birth by the urgent necessity of improving access to the Lake Quesnel area. Even if the trails sought by MacDonald or Waddington would have proved more efficient, the existing Cariboo Trail was favored since it already was *there* and only needed improvements—with liberal assistance from the government— to become the Cariboo Wagon Road.

The central figure of the great Barkerville gold strike, Billy Barker, was an ordinary sailor who jumped ship to join the Cariboo gold rush. Believing the gold to be lying beneath the persistent layer of blue clay (considered to be the "bottom" by most miners), Barker dug deeper and deeper—not without enduring some derisive remarks by fellow prospectors. At a depth of fifty-two feet, Billy Barker struck it rich on August 21, 1862. Around the Barker diggings (whose claim included six other men) grew Barkerville. Reportedly Barker and his companions extracted $600,000 before impossible winter weather forced a halt. Barker soon dissipated his share in riotous living at Victoria, but the find was to initiate a true bonanza for others. Among them could have been Ranald's brothers, Allan and Benjamin (who had joined his older siblings in 1862), for they had an interest in the fabulous Cameron claim near Barker's strike.

John C. Cameron, later known as "Cariboo" Cameron, and his family came from Ontario. Newly married with a baby that died five days after they reached Victoria in March, 1862, the Camerons were grubstaked by an acquaintance, Robert Stevenson, for the trip to Barkerville. Stevenson had some capital and guaranteed a loan of $2,000 worth of supplies for Cameron from the Hudson's Bay Company store. Both men came from Glengarry, Ontario, but had not known each other there; they just formed a sudden friendship. Stevenson went on to Antler, where he had previously purchased a building, and set up a commission business—grubstaking packers and selling the goods they packed in at a ten percent commission, a lucrative enterprise. Stevenson reported clearing $11,000 in just four months.

Cameron, meanwhile, arrived in Antler but reported to his friend and benefactor, Stevenson, that his supplies were still stored at the forks of the Quesnel River because he owed $1,400 to packer Allan MacDonald. A generous Stevenson paid off MacDonald so Cameron could get his goods to Richfield, where he and his wife built a small house. After staking and working some unsatisfactory claims, Cameron decided to follow after a miner named Ned Stout who had located farther down the canyon near Barker's find.

Stevenson entered the picture again shortly thereafter, organizing a gold exploration company that included Cameron and his wife Sophie; a Dr. Crane (who had told Stevenson about the possibilities on Williams Creek, but lost his share with the company due to an altercation shortly after filing the claim); Ranald's brother, Allan MacDonald; Richard Rivers; and Charles and James Clendenning. Stevenson reported in his diary that Cameron almost did not join the party as they went to stake their claim, because it was a Friday and he had some superstitious feeling about Fridays. Nevertheless, Stevenson wanted to call the company's claim "The Cameron" when it was staked on August 22, 1862. Cameron's original superstitions seemed to be correct, at first. A shaft sunk to twenty-two feet produced no results. The Clendenning brothers gave up and went to Victoria on September 26. Poor Mrs. Cameron died on October 23, 1862, of typhoid fever—certainly not an auspicious beginning. On another piece of ground, the remaining company members sank a shaft, encountering water at fourteen feet. Allan MacDonald was disgusted at this point and sold his one-eighth interest (the interest belonging to him and brother Benjamin) either to a Mr. McGinnis or possibly to Stevenson and Cameron.

Engaging a helper, William Halpenny, the group continued on down and struck it very rich at twenty-two feet on December 22, on a wintry day considerably below zero. The claim proved to be excellent all the way to bedrock at thirty-eight feet. Secure in their knowledge that they had a good strike, the men decided to keep the news quiet for a time.

Now began a bizarre trip initiated by Cameron, who wanted to return his wife's body to Ontario for burial. Despite the rumors of smallpox raging from the north down to Victoria, Cameron, Stevenson and a party of twenty-two men set out on January 31, 1863, with Mrs. Cameron's frozen body on a toboggan, fifty pounds of gold dust, and supplies, without so much as a trail in the deep snow and in temperatures as low as thirty-five degrees below zero (with a wind chill factor in gale force winds of considerably below that). Some hours later, fourteen men returned to Richfield, but eight continued—without tents to sleep in, and losing their matches and running out of food for a time. Four more men turned back, but Stevenson, two men known only as French Joe and Big Indian Jim, and Cameron eventually made it to Victoria, passing numerous graves due to the smallpox epidemic between the Quesnel River and Lillooet. Stevenson reported seeing Indians lying in their tents actually black from smallpox. Yet the party itself somehow was spared.

At Victoria, John Cameron gave his wife's body to the undertaker, subsequently burying Mrs. Cameron in the Quadra Street cemetery. (Still later, in the fall of 1863, Cameron returned again from Barkersville, exhumed the body and brought it to Cornwall, Ontario, via the Isthmus of Panama and New York City. At the latter place, customs officials believed Cameron was smuggling gold into the country and the coffin had to be opened, revealing Mrs. Cameron's body perfectly preserved in alcohol. This process had to be repeated once more in Cornwall to disprove rumors spread by local gossipmongers that Cameron had sold his wife to a Cariboo

Indian man and that there was no body in the coffin. Despite such apparently ugly neighbors, Cameron stayed on in Ontario, but returned to Barkerville with his second wife in 1888, dying there before the year was out. He is buried in the cemetery at Camerontown near his original claim—a part of Barkerville, which still is a lively town today and preserved as a historic district.)

To return to early 1863: after attending to Mrs. Cameron's temporary burial and other matters in Victoria, Cameron and Stevenson returned to Barkerville to work their claim. They eventually took out over one million dollars for the company, of which Cameron's share was $350,000.

Disgusted with the whole Cariboo gold rush, Allan MacDonald had left the area in 1862 as already related. Within two weeks of his departure, his brother Ben received a letter from a former partner of the mine, Bob Dexter, who must have bought in later than the original group. Dexter advised Ben not to sell his interest in the mine because he, Dexter, had already been offered $50,000 for his one-eighth interest. Of course, it was too late; Allan MacDonald already had concluded the sale.

Traveling from Barkerville to Lillooet and Montreal, Allan took over the family farm left to him by Archibald on the condition that his mother Jane would have a home there as long as she lived. However, Jane preferred to move into St. Andrews, purchasing a small home that she called "Little Glencoe." Allan became an officer in the militia called up to quell the disturbances in Manitoba led by Louis Riel, and later returned west to become the Indian agent at Que 'Appelle in southern Saskatchewan. He was to become involved in intense land speculation when it seemed that the Canadian Pacific Railway might pass through that area.

History does not record the feelings or regrets of Allan and Ben MacDonald for having sold their Barkerville mining interest too soon, nor of Ranald for having deigned to buy in. Ben continued to pack mule trains from Lillooet to the gold mines until the fall of 1863, when he took part of his train to Walla Walla, Boise, and Kootenay, working in those new mining camps as a packer and restaurant operator. By the fall of 1864, he returned to Fort Colvile, then operated by his cousin, Angus MacDonald, and thereafter lived and worked in Washington for eight years. In about 1864, he helped to build and owned an interest in the first steamer, the *Forty-Nine*, that operated on the Columbia River above Kettle Falls into British Columbia and in supplying the Big Bend mining country of the Kootenai River. The steamer was so named because it crossed the international boundary on its route. Funds for building the craft came from the Oregon Steam Navigation Company, and some of its inner workings were from the old Willamette River steamer, the *Jennie Clark;* the parts were hauled into the interior to where the *Forty-Nine* was constructed. Its first voyage from Marcus near Fort Colville began December 9, 1865, and the steamer proceeded with considerable difficulty as it encountered ice between the Lower and Upper Arrow lakes.

In 1872, Benjamin left Washington and returned to Quebec to marry Elizabeth Pyke, the daughter of a prominent clergyman. Those who remained, prospered in Camerontown (a designation later to disappear as the area all became known as Barkerville). Cameron was exceedingly generous with his cohorts, acquiring additional claims near his own strike, then later assigning them—apparently without receiving remuneration—to friends before he left Barkerville for the East. An unidentified diarist, whose work is in the Kamloops archives, was a Cameron shareholder and wrote: "When Cameron left Cariboo [Cameron and Stevenson left October 6, 1863] the Cameron claim was what I would call well opened up. We worked on the claim over two years after he left and I think he made a present of all his interests to his friends and the people that held the ground, for I was on the claim till we quit working it and never knew of any money being sent to him, and the claim was paying big for a long time. The pay in some parts of the creek was very high. Pay on the Cameron was 40 to 300 feet wide."

Cameron had made presents to his family, as well, but he himself eventually died broke there at the site of his original claim shortly after returning in 1888, as already related.

After Ben left, Ranald MacDonald continued to pack from his ranch in the Bonaparte Valley, in between his visits to the Horsefly country for prospecting. Ben and other relatives inferred years later that Ranald had made good money at mining—indeed, his cousin Christina MacDonald Williams claimed he had taken out $65,000 in Cariboo gold, but had lost it to unscrupulous investors or speculators.

Pressure from Victoria and New Westminster merchants for improvements continued to rise as traffic along the difficult Cariboo Trail increased. As early as 1862, Governor James Douglas set forth a plan to build a real wagon road to the gold mining areas, one that would circumvent the need for portages and water segments. Before that, he personally made a trip along the existing trails to assess what was needed. Thereafter, when appeals to the British government did not produce the necessary capital, Douglas went ahead with the road anyway, raising the money privately and with loans.

The route selected was formidable—that of the Fraser Canyon, where the V-shaped passage allowed only ledges and stingy benches on which to place a road. In October, 1861, the Royal Engineers had completed a survey through the canyon, and during 1861 contractor Gustavus B. Wright started work on forty-seven miles of road to link Lillooet to Clinton, a difficult stretch that passed over a 4,000-foot mountain. This road was generally considered rugged and unsatisfactory, although an unidentified miner differed in this opinion after he went to the Cariboo gold fields in the spring of 1862, traveling from Lillooet to Lightning Creek near Barkerville. When he returned in November, he stated that C. B. Wright had contracted to improve the Cariboo road from Fort Alexandria to Lillooet and it was a "fine road" with mile posts planted all the way. Those mileposts later were to hatch a crop of "mile houses" or inns for travelers, some of which still stand.

In 1862, the Royal Engineers started on the first six miles of road from Yale to Lytton, where a path was dynamited from the cliffs or hung out over the grumbling river far below on wood cribbing and bracing to create an 18-foot-wide road that could handle wagons and teams. Other work was under way for two hundred and forty miles from Clinton to Soda Creek. Construction continued along the canyon, with different stretches contracted to different companies. South of Chapman Bar, six miles were built at a cost of $47,000; twelve miles from China Bar to Boston Bar for $75,000; and thirty-two miles from Boston Bar to Lytton for $88,000 (the last twelve miles completed in two months with more than four hundred laborers).

Then there were the bridges: Alexandria Bridge, 300 feet long, was completed in September, 1863, for a cost of $45,000; Spence's Bridge was finished in 1864, by Thomas Spence for a mere $15,000. Both of these structures were toll bridges for a time.

In 1864, a road was begun from Quesnel to Cottonwood, thence on into Barkerville, Camerontown, and Richfield in 1865, by G. B. Wright, the initial contractor for the Clinton road, which had now been bypassed. It was said that he used as laborers three hundred Chinese (out of the total force of five hundred and twenty), paying the Chinese $45 a month. All workers had to be fed and sheltered, of course, by these contractors. The Cariboo Road was something of a miracle—three hundred miles of road from Yale to Barkerville had been built in four years! Long stretches of the road, which went right through Ranald MacDonald's ranch, are easily visible today.

Meanwhile, in the spring of 1862, a party of one hundred and fifty prospectors set out from Ontario for the gold fields. At today's Winnipeg, they purchased Red River carts, those ungainly but useful conveyances used for north-south freight hauling about the time Ranald MacDonald was a schoolboy in the Red River settlement. With horses, carts and basic provisions, they reached the Rocky Mountains and transferred their gear to pack animals. Having crossed the heights, at Tete Jaune Cache they were able to reprovision and some traveled down the Thompson River on rafts to Kamloops. The most determined of the Overlanders, as they became known in history, continued on westward to join the Cariboo Trail at what is today's Cache Creek; others stayed in the fertile and pleasant valleys near Kamloops. Still others had chosen at Tete Jaune Cache to take to the Fraser River and approach Quesnel from the north, a few making it through.

The road from Kamloops to the Cariboo Trail, however, became a favored thoroughfare from the east and south—from the Okanagan Valley trails, the Coquihalla trail, and all variations on the Hudson's Bay Company's old fur routes.

Meanwhile, Alfred Waddington's supporters had never given up the idea of a trail from Bute Inlet—and now some were talking about a transcontinental railroad that would go through that area. In March, 1864, when Waddington's construction party came to Bute Inlet to begin work, they found that local Indians had broken into a supply shed and stolen flour. According to an account in the *British Columbia Chronicle*, Waddington's agent wrote down the names of the thieves they could identify, and, to warn the Indians from repeating such offenses, declared that, if they did not desist, the whites would send terrible sickness into the country. Remembering the smallpox epidemic of 1862 in which thousands died, the Indians assumed the white men meant the dreaded smallpox. With little regard for their own safety after making such rash statements, the road workers continued steadily up the Homathko River for about thirty miles, establishing a ferry operated by a Timothy Smith, and working on toward the main construction camp. About four miles above that was an advance camp where Brewster, the foreman of the camp, worked with three helpers.

On the evening of April 28 or 29, 1864, it seems that a Chilcotin, Chief Klattasine, came to visit a friend, Chief Tellot, who was working for Waddington's company. As he encountered Smith at the ferry, he requested food and was refused; angered, he and his companions killed Smith and took the food.

Proceeding up to the main camp to meet Chief Tellot, the Indians persuaded the latter to join them in throwing out the intruders from their country. Until bedtime the visitors mingled with the construction men, talking, eating, and joking. When the camp was silent, except for the snores of the construction men, bedlam broke out. Visiting Indians joined by those who worked at the camp collapsed the tents on top of the sleeping men, shooting them as they lay. One man was knocked unconscious by a falling tent pole and was thought to be dead; at least one other escaped into the woods, making his way to the ferry. He linked up there with Smith's two assistants, who had not been around at the time of his killing, and the three set out for Bute Inlet to tell of the massacre. In the *Victoria Colonist* of May 12, 1864, appeared this account:

A survivor, Edwin Mosely, was awakened near dawn by two men who entered the tent yelling. As he arose startled, the Indians collapsed the tent on Mosely and two others. "While lying in this position I saw knives on each side of me come through the tent and pierce the bodies of my two companions." Seeing that the raiders were going on to other tents, Mosely jumped up, ran to the river and dived in. From the safety of the river he later saw the Indians—men, women, and children—hallooing where the cook's tent and provisions were.

Meanwhile, the Chilcotins jogged up the trail to the advance camp and killed all the men there, mutilating the leader Brewster. Realizing that retaliation would soon be forthcoming, the Indians traveled swiftly to their villages to encourage others to join the uprising. En route at Puntzi Lake they killed a settler and, on the Bella Coola trail, they encountered a pack train led by packer Alexander MacDonald (not Ranald's younger brother Alex, possibly related through clan Donald). The eight packers put up a vigorous defense, throwing up earthworks and hastily carving out trenches, and held off the Indians for several days until they gave up and left. Thinking the attack over, MacDonald and his crew packed up and moved on toward Waddington's camp. But Chief Tellot and his Indians were waiting in the brush and shot MacDonald and two of his men. The other five escaped to tell the lurid tales to the miners and settlers.

One of the survivors of the first attack blamed the attack on the amorous activities of construction party workers with the Chilcotin Indian women. According to Edgar Fawcett, a Canadian Pacific Railway surveyor of 1872, he found articles of women's clothing at the scene—eight years after the event— and in the *British Columbia Chronicle*, it is inferred that the manner of mutilation of some bodies might verify this assertion. However, if this were so, why would the event have begun with the murder of Timothy Smith . . .

Shocked settlers and military men in the area converged at Puntzi Lake to deal with the matter, enlisting the major chief, Alexis, to assist in rounding up the renegade Indians.

Meanwhile, Donald McLean, Ranald MacDonald's next door neighbor and operator of McLean's Restaurant, set out with his son Duncan and twenty-three other men to track the killers, even as William Cox, gold commissioner in the Cariboo, organized a party of forty to rendezvous with McLean. With a thick thatch of red hair, tall and muscular, the handsome and intelligent but hot-tempered McLean had a bad reputation with the Chilcotins. Back when he was a chief trader at Kamloops, an Indian identified as Tlhelh had shot a Hudson's Bay man without cause. McLean went to apprehend him and, not finding him at home, confronted the man's uncle. When the uncle denied knowing where Tlhelh was, McLean killed him, instead, and—in the somewhat wild fray—one of his party also wounded the uncle's stepdaughter, and killed the son-in-law, with their baby also killed accidentally by a stray bullet. Later, McLean threatened another Indian if he failed to bring in Tlhelh; so the frightened kinsman killed Tlhelh in cold blood, and scalped and cremated him. Other tribal members related to Tlhelh bided their time for an opportune moment for revenge.

An account by Brian Belton in *Bittersweet Oasis*, a history of Ashcroft, a town fourteen miles south of MacDonald's ranch, declares that the pack train involved was that of Ranald and Allan MacDonald, but, if so, Ranald himself was away on the Vancouver Island Exploring Expedition. As a friend of Ranald's and an experienced hunter, McLean supposedly went to the rescue. His brutal dealings with the Indians were to be his undoing. As he traveled north, tracking Chief Klattasine, an Indian called Anukatlk was following him; here was his chance for avenging Tlhelh's death. Near Tatla Lake the McLean party thought they sighted some Indians; with an Indian friend named Jack, Donald McLean went ahead to reconnoiter. Here was the chance Anukatlk was waiting for, and he shot McLean dead.

There are conflicting accounts of the pursuit and apprehension of the murderers of Waddington's men, MacDonald, and McLean. Through the intervention of Chief Alexis, eight men, including Klattasine and Chief Tellot, surrendered. In September, 1864, two men became government's witnesses, five were hung at Quesnel after a trial under Judge Begbie—the famed lawman of the Cariboo—and one imprisoned, later escaping.

Ten years later, during additional disturbances by the Chilcotins, Ranald wrote from Hat Creek to his brother Ben on January 14, 1874:

"By the arrival of a special messenger from Kamloops that the Indians were massing and making warlike preparations, coupled with former rumors of Indian raisings also with an urgent request from Clinton to Gov't for arms in anticipation of a raid on the settlers from the combined tribes of Chelicotin [sic] and Indians of the Frazer River, has caused quite an excitement in our peaceful community. But I must candidly state that I am an unbeliever that there will be a combined raising. I knew some time that there was discontent also a mystery about their present relations with the Dominion Government which they could not understand. There was nobody to explain it to them. Those who could, did not care to interfere. They had their grievances about their lands & pastureage to make but to whom, how, and where was the puzzler. To go to Victoria, you might as well refer them to Ottawa it is beyond their range. My personal belief is that persons have taken advantage of this state of affairs."

He went on to suggest that, since business was dull in the Cariboo, unscrupulous persons were stirring up rumors to encourage the government to send troops into the Cariboo, with a resultant increase in business. He felt the Indians around Kamloops were as peaceable as those in the Bonaparte Valley where he resided, who certainly were not planning anything.

In this same letter, Ranald's restless nature begins to reassert itself. He was interested in the new strikes around Dease's Lake or the Cassiar country, undecided as to whether or not he should go.

He was ever willing to see new lands. This had never been more obvious, when ten years earlier, in June, 1864, he had been tapped for an important exploring expedition on Vancouver Island—a party both for surveying and searching for minerals (see Chapter XXIII).

XXI
Moriyama Serves at USA-Japan Treaty Negotiations

All the while Ranald was blazing new trails in the gold rush country of the Cariboo, new political trails had been threshed out in Japan. Central to those important negotiating years in the opening of Japan for trade and interchange of knowledge were those men to whom Ranald taught English—especially Moriyama, Namura, and Hori.

After the signing of Perry's treaty, Japanese officials relaxed somewhat, feeling they had bought time to consider their entry into the international scene. However, the lull was brief.

Under the treaty of March 31, 1854, Article XI stated:

"There shall be appointed, by the Government of the United States, Consuls or Agents to reside in Shimoda, at any time after the expiration of eighteen months from the date of the signing of this treaty; provided that either of the two Governments deem such arrangement necessary."

The government of the United States deemed it necessary; for one thing, the clauses of the original treaty were sketchy, providing that supplies should be available to needy ships, shipwrecked sailors treated well, and other amenities, but no real outlines or agreement on mutual trade. An American official would need to be appointed to implement the "consul" clause and return to negotiate a sound trade treaty. On July 31, 1855, eight prominent citizens of New York recommended Townsend Harris to the President, whereupon President Pierce summoned Harris to Washington for personal interviews. On August 4, 1855, Harris was notified by letter of his appointment as consul to Japan.

According to knowledgeable men of the time, he was superbly qualified for the job. He had been President of the Board of Education of New York City before 1848. For the following six years he wandered the world, especially the South Pacific, on trading ventures. At the time of his appointment, the President also engaged him to negotiate a commercial treaty with Siam, which he would conclude on May 29, 1856, before sailing on the *San Jacinto* for Japan. Henry Heusken, subsequently his aide in Shimoda, worked with him on the Siamese treaty.

The two men boarded ship in Hong Kong and departed for Japan on August 12, 1856, encountering extremely stormy seas en route—so ferocious that the *San Jacinto* went to the aid of several stricken vessels. She arrived in Shimoda on August 21, watched from the heights ashore with apprehension by the villagers. The Japanese officials were expecting Harris, but—in keeping with the extraordinary climate of secrecy that constantly existed among governmental servants—the local Shimoda officials had been aware only that the Edo government was making mysterious and pointed inquiries locally about this matter and that. There had been great consternation ever since the Perry treaty among governmental bodies, which wondered how to handle the situation when and if the consul mentioned in Article XI should appear . . . And here he was, arriving in a warship.

On August 25, with some formality, a party including Captain Bell, Heusken and Harris went ashore to be received and greeted by Governor Okada, Vice Governor Miosaburo Wakana, and his staff (actually, most regions had two governors—one who stayed in the city, while his counterpart was in Edo; they switched locations periodically). At this social affair and during the subsequent dinner party, Einosuke Moriyama was introduced to Townsend Harris as a member of the governor's staff—appointed to be the coordinator between Harris and the Japanese. The Americans found him to be pleasant, dignified, and in command of the situation, unlike earlier interpreters who had been exceedingly nervous—probably certain that any mistake would bring dishonor or worse. In his diary, Harris declared Moriyama to be "a good interpreter, of most agreeable manners and a true courtier." Harris assumed that Moriyama was somehow attached to the Edo Ministry of Foreign Affairs, because he made occasional trips to and from Edo. Oliver Statler in his book, *Shimoda Story*, suggested that Harris apparently did not recognize who Moriyama was, even though Perry had mentioned him at some length in his writings. Therefore, Harris did not realize at first that Moriyama understood and spoke English (for the conversations were held in Dutch, with Heusken translating). One wonders if indiscreet remarks were absorbed soberly by an understanding Moriyama then.

At the time of Perry's treaty, diarist Williams noted that at a critical time Moriyama quietly took charge of negotiations and maneuvered both sides through to agreement. Now Harris, too, would see Moriyama every few days during the two years of treaty negotiations.

After tiresome sparring with local officials and those sent from Edo about where he should dwell—these men insisting that Harris could not live there at all—Harris was established in a temple at Kakizaki, a small fishing village across the bay from Shimoda town. Shimoda was in shambles, having incurred severe damage from an earthquake and tidal wave a few months earlier. Against Harris' vehement protests, guards were stationed at the temple. He was not able to rid himself of this close surveillance until early in 1857. Actually the Edo government was not as worried about the foreigners doing harm as having harm done to the foreigners by dissident samurai or *ronin*, who were roaming the countryside at this time. Sometime earlier, officials had decreed that, when foreigners arrived in Japan, special restrictions should be maintained; that, if suspicious persons did not submit to arrest, they could be killed by swords or beaten to death. A fledgling country feebly trying its wings in the international community, Japan wanted to avoid any international incident, at all costs.

During the ensuing days, Harris was frustrated by resistance to his demands for servants, workmen, and other assistance; the Japanese resisted providing quick decisions about what seemed to be the most minor requests. On September 4, with a considerable lump in his throat, Harris waved goodbye to the captain of the *San Jacinto* as the ship put to sea, knowing that he had gained merely a toehold on Japan.

During the initial stages of his stay, Harris dealt with local headman Yoheiji, Assistant Inspector Genzō Saito, and his superior, Inspector Isaburō Aihara, plus other minor officials, as he tried to settle in.

On September 6, interpreter Moriyama called on Harris, supposedly a social call, but in reality the interpreter was trying to determine what could be done about Harris' numerous (and sometimes belligerent) requests—for instance, asking where could he hire house servants? Moriyama pointed out that there were no servants in Shimoda, that they would have to come from elsewhere, that the Japanese did not decide on anything as fast as Westerners, etc. In an eloquent and silent plea for help, Harris showed Moriyama his blistered hands from doing unaccustomed labor. On September 15, Moriyama brought two teenage boys, one for Harris, one for Heusken, as general servants. Harris' earlier request for a cow as a source of milk was viewed with some horror, as cows were used to work the fields and Japanese did not drink milk. Months later Harris finally would obtain one.

There were additional visits with the governors, with Harris always forced to call on them. Moriyama had explained that it was against the law for the Imperial governor of any city to visit a foreigner's residence. It was a real breakthrough on October 30, when the two governors, Kiyonao

Inoue, Lord of Shinano, and Tadayoshi Okada, Lord of Bungo, plus the executive officer or governor, Miosaburo Wakana, and others came to call at Harris' residence. At this time, the governors expressed agitation and resentment about surveyors discovered working along the coast. Harris' assertion—that surveying waters and subsequently sharing information was an international custom—was accepted with apparent misgivings by the Japanese. Surveying, considered a sort of invasion of privacy by the Japanese, had been of so much concern that Moriyama later told Harris of his intense relief that the governors had accepted his explanation—that he had been worried lest he, Moriyama, might have to commit *seppuku* over the matter.

Behind the scenes in Edo, factions were parrying over the admission of foreigners to Japan, over the earlier Perry Treaty, and—unknown to Harris—whether he should be allowed to stay at all. Lord Masayoshi Hotta, Chief of the Great Council, finally sent word to the governors of Shimoda on September 22. Even though Japan did not want him there, he said, Harris WAS in residence and to expel him would cause unpleasant international consequences. From top to bottom, however, it was to be an official policy to contain the "invasion" and, to an extent, make life frustrating for the Americans. This surely was the case for some time to come, until a softening of attitudes seemingly took place.

A trusted governmental servant, Shuri Iwase, was sent by Hotta to Shimoda in late September, specifically to monitor Harris, and returned to Edo about three weeks later. While Harris was in Shimoda, a Russian corvette came to call, welcomed by Harris but adding still another thorn to the intense climate at Edo. The official, Iwase, was sent by Lord Hotta with the concurrence of another influential daimyo, Lord Masahiro Abe, to confer with Lord Nariaki Tokugawa, retired daimyo of Mito, a most highly placed adviser, and a member of the Shogun's family. Nariaki Tokugawa was adamantly opposed to foreign intrusions and was not comforted by the report of the boldness of Harris. He wrote an agitated letter to another powerful man, Lord Yoshinaga Matsudaira, nostalgically recalling that when Mongolia and Korea invaded in the 1200's, Japan's armies merely drove them away. Now the country was faced with pressures from Britain, the Netherlands, Russia, France, and others, and he worried about the Emperor's safety in tranquil Kyoto. Some said Tokugawa was more eager for an excuse to challenge an arch-rival, Lord Naosuke Ii, who was directly responsible for the Emperor's safety. As time progressed, this political turmoil roiled on ceaselessly, with Lord Hotta managing to maintain an uneasy control over all.

For the entire autumn, Harris had been dedicated to changing the currency rate, asking that the Japanese *bu* be exchanged, weight for weight, with the American dollar; if accepted, the exchange rate would improve almost three hundred percent (three *bu* for one dollar) in the Americans' favor. This discussion continued monotonously for more than a year, with Harris stubbornly refusing to budge from his own criteria for the rate.

Moriyama had his hands full with Harris. Through his diary and Japanese accounts, Harris appears an exceedingly stubborn man, although reasonably fair. His seeming unwillingness to attempt an understanding of Japanese customs in doing business or in making decisions appears highhanded. Yet historians, Japanese and American, credit the man with hammering out reasonable treaty terms that enabled Japanese officials—who were rather unsophisticated about international matters after two hundred years of isolation—to enter the world trade situation without disaster. The Japanese were able to tolerate Harris' immovability better than the informality they encountered, at times, from other foreigners.

Harris' intransigence and the intense strain of the negotiations took their toll on his physique; starting as early as December, 1856, and persisting throughout the rest of his stay, his stomach was in frequent disorder. At times he was seriously ill. Surrounded as he was by people often outwardly hostile, if not dangerous, and confronted with situations daily for which there were no precedents in international intercourse, it is not surprising that his body rebelled.

But the man made progress. On January 7, 1857, when he again protested the presence of guards at his residence, they were removed. Demanding answers to letters written to the government at Edo (and being told that, by law, Japanese did not write letters to foreigners), Harris received a letter on February 25, 1857—a sheet of paper five feet long and eighteen inches wide, answering some of his queries and signed by no less than five important Edo officials: Hotta, Bitchiu-no-Kami; Abe, Ise-no-Kami; Makino, Bizen-no-Kami; Kuze, Yamato-no-Kami; and Naito, Kii-no-Kami.

During most of 1857, Harris through interpreter and intermediary Moriyama was engrossed in the preliminaries to making a treaty. The Japanese, of course, were not interested in any further dealings with the "barbarians," and threw up opposition to most of the suggestions for trade. As time went by and Harris proved to be a formidably stubborn man—and not outwardly discouraged by the roadblocks thrown into his path—Edo officials reluctantly began to entertain the idea of some kind of treaty. They were always aware that any concessions made to the Americans probably would have to be extended to other countries.

Although Harris often misread their endless postponements as a lack of understanding of the terms, or as deliberate attempts to discourage him, in truth the Edo officials were far more knowledgeable about the consequences of the treaty than Harris was aware. Also, as stated above, the biggest problem that loomed for Edo's government was how to convince the anti-foreigner elements of Japan that it was time for a change, that Japan must open her doors to the world at last.

One by one, the terms were debated. In February, 1857, Harris opened the matter of obtaining supplies and coal in Nagasaki (as well as the two ports already agreed upon, Shimoda and Hakodate). After all, Russia had been given those rights in their treaty, he said. The Japanese agreed readily to this opening.

The next matter was the right of American citizens residing in or visiting Japan, who committed a crime, to be tried under American law by the consul and, if guilty, to be punished "according to Japanese laws." Of course, said the governors; but Townsend Harris had made an error in his phrasing—he meant to say "according to American laws." This unintentional agreement was to cause knotty problems for later administrators.

Next came the matter of owning or building property on Japanese soil; the Dutch had this right at Deshima, said Harris. The negotiators never heard of such a thing, they declared, even though Harris said he had seen the agreement with his own eyes when Captain Fabius of the Dutch Navy visited him at Shimoda. By March 2, the Japanese gave up the point. Moriyama arrived with copies of the Twelfth and Thirteenth Articles of the Dutch Convention, which verified Harris' statements. Harris learned that the Japanese had this copy all along and he thought they were feigning ignorance of the concessions given to the Dutch. According to Statler, the Dutch Convention had only been written, not officially ratified, and furthermore, a later version left out Articles 12 and 13. Nevertheless, the Japanese allowed Harris' request—after all, the Americans apparently were in Japan to stay, so what did it really matter.

During this visit, Moriyama—now on a friendly conversational basis with Harris—confided that he had been promoted one step when he last visited Edo and was appointed to the Revenue Board. Since a Japanese man adopted a new name each time he was promoted, his name was now Takichirō Moriyama.

The currency exchange rate still came up regularly for negotiation; in February the Japanese offered 4,670 *seni* per dollar, where the earliest offer was 1,600, nearly three hundred percent concession. Somewhat unreasonably, it seems to the author, Harris refused to concede because the Japanese stuck to a six percent recoinage request where Harris asked only five percent. The Japanese already had reduced their demands from twenty-five percent.

In some ways, the currency matter was counterproductive. When the ship *Messenger Bird* came into Shimoda to sell its wares and bring messages to Harris, the goods aboard were so high-priced for the Japanese that few sales were made.

In addition to Moriyama, who worked closely with Harris, during this period the interpreter Tsunenosuke (Gohachiro) Namura, as well as Tatsunosuke Hori, also were working for the governors in Shimoda. Hori studied English industriously from a copy of *Webster's Dictionary* left by Admiral Perry, which enabled him to translate directly if imperfectly for ship masters calling in Shimoda without any Dutch interpreter as intermediary.

Moriyama quietly and persistently tried to coach Harris, usually without success, on the finer nuances of Japanese dealings, apparently with a genuine interest in assisting both sides to make progress. However, his relationship with Harris enabled him to assess the consul's intentions and report them to the Edo government, too. In March, he reported to Edo that Harris' threats of war, if the treaty were not satisfactory, were to be disregarded; in this, Moriyama's opinion was scorned and the Edo government quaked at the very idea of a war.

Softening their stance, the Edo government sent an edict to Shimoda, relaxing their former regulations about travel in Japan and about purchase matters—specifically that the restriction of travel to seven *ri* from Shimoda should not apply and no taxes should be levied on Harris' commercial purchases.

While Governor Kiyanao Inoue (who, incidentally, was a brother of Iwase), Lord of Shinano, was in the area on March 30, a visit was arranged with Harris, mostly a social affair.

Throughout April, Moriyama periodically came to call on Harris, carrying decisions or proposals back and forth from government to government, but also explaining to Harris matters of Japanese custom. He corrected Harris' referral to the Shogun as the *Ziogoon*, saying that it was *Tycoon*. Different departments of government did not confer or report to each other about all matters; only the Tycoon and heads of departments were privy to information about each section. They talked about the protocol of gun salutes, of the history of firearms; Moriyama said that guns were introduced first at the island of Tanegashima, three hundred years earlier, and that pistols were still called "Tanegashima." He explained to Harris that, for Japanese, to say a thing is very different from writing it down. Moriyama also admonished Harris that he should not be so impatient, that, if he incurred too much resentment by his demands, things would not progress. He propounded the philosophy that, if a man, even a powerful one, is too forceful in getting his way, he will not be respected; further, he hoped that Harris' impetuous ways would not force the Edo government into difficulty. Their friendly conversations often ended with a drink or dinner.

Eventually, Moriyama on April 15 asked Harris—just suppose, like it was a dream, you did make a commercial treaty with us, how would you go about it? Harris replied that he would be glad to negotiate with the governors, if they were empowered officially to do so. The matter was dropped.

Moriyama never lost sight, however, of which side he was serving. In his reply to a letter from the Edo's governors of finance, he said "Every time we talk with the Americans his[Harris] attitude changes. His true intentions are beyond conjecture. But I will do my best to guide the negotiations in a direction favorable to Japan."

At the end of April Harris reviewed his accomplishments to date: (1) the currency question was now far more favorable, almost three to one compared with earlier ratios; (2) Nagasaki was open as a supply port to Americans; (3) Americans would be responsible only to American authority (note earlier reference to his error in penning the clause); and (4) American ships in distress without any money could pay for emergency supplies by barter.

From the beginning of his stay, Townsend Harris had asked for an audience with the Shogun at Edo, a request originally viewed with horror and absolute rejection by the officials. It is interesting, also, that Harris always had a misconception about where the ultimate authority of government lay. He viewed the Shogun as the head of Japan, whereas, under Japanese law, the Emperor in Kyoto truly was and always had been at the top. It is also true that the Shoguns over the past two hundred years were to all practical purposes the real authorities, having the worldly management skills and largely maneuvering the Kyoto religious leaders, including the Emperor himself, as they saw fit. Still, the Emperor and his immediate court DID have to be consulted by the Bakufu, the great council of lords.

Little progress had been made by Harris on arranging a visit to Edo, it seemed. The summer of 1857 was a lonely and difficult one for Harris, with a persistent stomach disorder—likely a case of bleeding ulcers. He mentioned in his diary that he had given up oils, vegetables except potatoes, and other foods, eating mostly rice, bread and meat; still he grew thinner and more strained, a condition that was eased, no doubt, by the addition of a woman as his personal servant. No significant progress loomed. He was not aware, of course, of the seething controversies between political factions that were hindering any firm decisions about trade or even the tolerance of barbarians on Japanese soil. Especially difficult was the standoff between Lord Hotta and Lord Nariaki Tokugawa, one reluctantly favoring trade, the other opposed. The officials also realized that their past dealings with the Netherlands through Deshima left the door open to new demands for trade by other Europeans and Americans. Lord Hotta sent a neutral commission to Nagasaki to study the situation, directing them to stop en route at Shimoda to meet with Harris and assess matters there. One lord, Iwase, was Hotta's best foreign affairs man, and the other was Mizuno, who leaned more toward the isolationist view. Mizuno, one of the two governors of Nagasaki, was currently in Edo (in accordance with the custom described earlier), and the two envoys were to work with the on-site Nagasaki governor in their investigation. Periodically, Moriyama, the headmen of the village, and other officials contacted Harris. In June (replacing Prince Shinano as governor) came Tameya Nakamura, Lord of Dewa, a man who impressed Harris favorably from the beginning.

In June, also, the points included as acceptable for a proposed treaty were: (1) the port of Nagasaki would be open to American ships; (2) the Americans could have permanent residences at Shimoda and Hakodate and could appoint a vice-consul at Hakodate; (3) the currency question was settled at roughly 3:1, dollar to *bu;* (4) Americans would be tried by "American law"; and (5) the Consul General could travel in Japan and use Japanese money to make purchases without intervention of Japanese officials. All of these matters, however, were merely hard-won details for ordinary living, not a trade treaty.

By September, Harris was truly distraught. It had been more than a year since he arrived in Shimoda, and still he had no inkling of receiving permission to travel to Edo. He was out of touch and hungered for news of the world outside of Japan. Fortuitously, on September 8, the United States sloop-of-war *Portsmouth* arrived under Captain Andrew Hull Foote, bringing supplies, money and—more important—news and familiar foods.

On September 22, the political impasse at Edo was resolved suddenly by the officials' alarm at Harris' threat (backed by Foote) that he would come by ship to Edo to deliver the American President's long-scorned letter. Although outraged by the council's decision to entertain the idea of a trade treaty, Nariaki Tokugawa's influence had faded and, on September 11, his resignation as advisor was accepted. Harris' diary for September 22 records the joyful news, "At the Goyosho this morning at eleven o'clock. The Governors informed me that they had received letters from Edo relating to the President's letter; that after many anxious consultations it was finally settled that I am to go to Edo, in the most honorable manner, and, after my arrival, I am to have an audience of the Shogun, and then present the letter of the President!"

By the end of the month, Moriyama and Prince Shinano returned to Edo to confer with officials about Harris' forthcoming visit, while the Commissionary (Harris' term) of Shimoda came to review travel details, manner of dress, etc., with Harris. He decided not to take his Chinese servants for, at this time, the Japanese disliked the Chinese intensely. His entourage would include Henry Heusken, their two Japanese servants, and about forty porters bearing baggage and supplies. Ever mindful of protocol and a proper display, so important to the Japanese, Harris listed his train— all of whom would bear the coat-of-arms of the United States on their garments:

20 norimon bearers	1 sword
12 guardsmen	2 swords
2 standard bearers	2 swords
2 shoe and fan bearers	2 swords
2 grooms	1 sword
2 quinine (Gokenin) or commanders of foregoing	

(Note: The author believes that one of the commanders was Yasuemon Matsura, grandfather of Frank "Sakae" Matsura, later a renowned photographer in Washington state between 1903-13.)

Escorting Harris would be: Executive Officer Wakana; Superintendent Usaburō Wakiya (Harris identified him as the Mayor of Kakizaki); Vice-Superintendent Sennojō Kikuna (the Commissary of Shimoda); and the private secretary of Governor Nakamura.

Turmoil reigned, meanwhile, among the important houses of Japan and the lords of the Great Council. Now leading the movement to open the country were Yoshinaga Matsudaira and Nariakira Shimazu, a number of highly respected outside daimyo, and several houses of the Tokugawa family other than Nariaki's House of Mito. Amidst the din of dissent and confusion, the arrangements for receiving Harris went forward—with the details of each move, the ceremony, and the dress all specified precisely.

On November 23, Harris' impressive train coiled over the rough hills, three hundred fifty persons strong. Before the convoy went three boys waving wands of bamboo with strips of paper attached to the tops, crying out periodically, "shita ni iro, shita ni iro," or "kneel down, kneel down," to the curious spectators that gathered silently at every hand. Thus, the common people would bow their foreheads to the ground in respect to the "American Ambassador," as officialdom chose to call Consul Harris.

The route lay through rugged but spectacularly scenic country near Mount Fuji—via Ohito, Mishima, and onto the Great Road *(Tokaido)* used by the Dutch when they traveled from Nagasaki to pay homage to the Shogun. Then over the mountains to Hakone, where its lake framed perfectly cone-shaped Mount Fuji, to Odowara, Oiso, Fujisawa, Kanagawa, Kawasaki, Shinagawa and into Edo. Here spectators five deep, many of them two-sworded samurai in ceremonial dress, watched the astonishing entrance of a foreign barbarian into their city. Harris remarked that the silence (proscribed by law) of such a multitude for the seven mile route from Shinagawa to his lodgings "had something appalling" or menacing about it. His lodgings fronted on the castle moat, not far from the Shimizu gate.

Throughout the trip Moriyama was nowhere to be seen—as far as can be determined. No doubt, he awaited with dignity in Edo for further duties. Possibly Namura, who had been mentioned as being in Shimoda during Harris' stay, was with the procession throughout the time, however. Heusken mentions him in his description of entering Edo, saying that Namura walked beside the door of his norimon. At Harris' lodgings, Moriyama and Inoue were there to greet him.

On December 1, the day after Harris' arrival, a special committee of eight commissioners paid him a social visit of welcome, the spokesman being Toke, Tamba-no-Kami. Three days later, in some splendor, his retinue traveled to visit Lord Hotta, where, after mutual courteous pleasantries, Harris handed Hotta a copy of his intended address to the Tycoon. Harris mentioned an interpreter for this event, unnamed, who was so nervous that he perspired in huge droplets.

On December 7, Harris was admitted to see the Shogun or Tycoon and, after several ceremonial greetings, he handed the letter to the great man. Harris' description of the event is vivid:

"At length, on a signal being made, the Prince of Shinano began to crawl along on his hands and knees; and when I half turned to the right and entered the audience chamber, a chamberlain called out in a loud voice, 'Embassador Merrican!' I halted about six feet from the door and bowed, then proceeded nearly to the middle of the room, where I again halted and bowed; again proceeding, I stopped about ten feet from the end of the room exactly opposite to the Prince of Bittsu [Lord Hotta] on my right hand, where he and the other five members of the Great Council were prostrate on their faces. On my left hand were three brothers of the Tykoon, prostrated in the same manner, and all of them being nearly 'end on' towards me. After a pause of a few seconds I addressed the Tykoon as follows:

"May it please Your Majesty:

"In presenting my letters of credence from the President of the United States, I am directed to express to Your Majesty the sincere wishes of the President for your health and happiness and for the prosperity of your dominions. I consider it a great honor that I have been selected to fill the high and important place of Plenipotentiary of the United States at the Court of Your Majesty; and, as my earnest wishes are to unite the two countries more closely in the ties of enduring friendship, my constant exertions shall be directed to the attainment of that happy end."

The Shogun, who must not have met many—if any—foreign barbarians before appears to have been nervous, jerking his head over his shoulder and stamping the floor with his foot. After a short silence he spoke firmly but pleasantly, saying:

"Pleased with the letter sent with the Ambassador from a far distant country, and likewise pleased with his discourse. Intercourse shall be continued forever."

Although Harris' records say nothing specific about the interpreter's identity, it is assumed that Moriyama served at this momentous occasion—the shattering of a two hundred year wall of isolation.

The audience essentially was over. Harris later recounted the scene. "The Tykoon was seated in a *chair* placed on a platform raised about two feet from the floor, and from the ceiling in front of him a grass curtain was hung . . . it was now rolled up . . . The dress of the Tykoon was made of silk, and the material had some little gold woven in with it. But it was as distant from anything like regal splendor as could be conceived. No rich jewels, no elaborate gold ornaments, no diamond hilted weapon."

The glass wall was shattered, but several months of further negotiations ensued. One historian relates that the Japanese noted that Harris liked to talk, to propound facts as if he were a teacher, and that their position was to encourage him to talk and talk, that he would thus feel flattered and be more amenable to making a treaty that could be more advantageous to them, the Japanese people.

By January 23, 1858, Harris' draft of a treaty was completed—the translations finished and rechecked. Then the negotiations started in earnest. The first point to be questioned by the Japanese was that they wished the minister and consuls to reside somewhere between Kanagawa and Kawasaki, coming to Edo only on business, and also to be restricted as to where they could travel. Among other reasons, the Japanese were deeply concerned about the physical safety of the Americans; Harris had not been fully aware of the depth of opposition to his treaty. The negotiators told him of a death threat by *ronin*, bands of samurai of low status, who—with little to do—sometimes (not always) were little better than armed thugs. Harris shrugged this revelation off as conjured up to frighten him; however, the death threats were all too real and were thwarted by the Japanese officials. In 1859 and 1860, several foreigners (including Henry Heusken himself) would be killed in isolated incidents. According to Statler in *Shimoda Story*, Lord Nariaki Tokugawa had declared that Lords Hotta and Tadakata Matsudaira should be ordered to commit *seppuku* and Townsend Harris' head cut off.

Behind the political arena, envoys had been sent to the Emperor in Kyoto, seeking approval, but this mission found progress very hard going indeed. At Kyoto, since the Shogunate had kept the religious leaders and Emperor away from worldly matters for two hundred years, the court was shocked, dismayed, and completely unready to make sweeping decisions. The Shogunate knew, however, that if the Emperor were to declare his consent, most of the other opposition from lesser lords and even Tokugawa family members must fall.

While Hotta was in Kyoto and the powerful, complex regime governing Japan met and conferred, Harris became severely ill and returned to Shimoda, so weak that he had to be carried to his norimono by Heusken. Later researchers have concluded that Harris had typhoid fever, but he recovered by the latter part of March—attended, in part, by a physician, Dr. Kansai Ito, sent by the Great Council itself.

On April 18, against the advice of his physicians and attendants, Harris traveled by steamer to Edo. This was the day Lord Hotta had agreed to sign the treaty. The small party was met by Moriyama—all smiles and bearing gifts—but Lord Hotta sent word that he could not sign yet.

On June 1, Hotta returned from Kyoto without obtaining the critical concurrence he sought. Upon arrival in Edo, he found, to his dismay, that—during his long absence—a coup had overthrown his supporters and appointed Naosuke Ii as Chief Councillor of the Great Council; the latter, however, was also in favor of signing the treaty, although further delays ensued.

In July an American warship, *Mississippi*, one of the ships from Perry's venture, arrived; and two days later came the *Powhatan*, with news that the Chinese had been defeated by French and English armies and were forced to accept their terms. Furthermore, Russian Admiral Putiatin had arrived in Nagasaki. Harris pressured a decision by suggesting that the reasonable treaty he proposed be signed without delay; that if the other Europeans, fresh from victories, came to seek treaties, they likely would seek much more stringent terms unfavorable to Japan. If the American treaty were signed, the others probably would seek only similar arrangements. Harris and his assistants boarded the *Powhatan* on July 27. Anchoring between Kanagawa and Yokohama, a messenger was sent to Lord Hotta. However, it was Naosuke Ii who led the move to sign; hastily assembling their advisors, the Great Council finally concurred and agreed upon the treaty, summoning Inoue and Iwase, accompanied by Moriyama, to meet with Harris.

On July 29, 1858, with surprisingly little fanfare, the treaty was signed, after which American and Japanese flags flew side by side from the mast while the *Powhatan's* guns thundered out a twenty-one gun salute heard in Edo—undoubtedly with mixed reactions from the populace.

Harris returned to Shimoda, later entertaining visitors such as Lord Elgin of England and Baron Gros of France. Both countries later signed treaties with the Japanese similar to that of the Americans. In April, 1859, Harris went on a vacation to China (he still suffered from stomach ailments and moods of despair), leaving Henry Heusken in charge of the consulate. Harris returned in late June, as Minister to Japan instead of Consul-General, to move his offices to Edo.

Basically the treaty provided for the following:

*A diplomatic agent to reside at Edo, and a consul or consular agents to reside at any or all opened ports.

*Free travel on discharge of official duties.

*The government of Japan would appoint similar diplomats with like privileges in the United States.

*Mutual assistance to ships and crews in trouble.

*Ports opened: Shimoda, Hakodate, Kanagawa, Nagasaki, Niigata on the west coast (or if unsuitable, another one), and Hyogo. Differing dates for openings.

*Certain duties on imports and exports.

*Foreign exchange established.

*Americans to be tried by Americans, Japanese by Japanese.

*Free exercise by Americans of their religion.

*The Japanese could purchase ships of war, merchant ships, munitions, and hire scientific or military men as advisers.

*Regulations governing the manner of trade were spelled out at length.

Thus, while Ranald MacDonald was laboring in the gold fields of Canada and exploring the region for practical supply routes, progress was being made leading to trade between Japan and the United States and Canada (still part of Great Britain). Undoubtedly, as he made contact with Governor Douglas in Victoria, Ranald learned the startling news and pondered his own role in this drama.

Much later, sometime during the last six years of his life as he wrote his memoirs (which were severely edited by Malcolm McLeod), he said:

"Here, in reference to this incident of my having been the first during their hermit seclusion, to be teacher of English to the Japanese, and in that was the first instructor—apostle in a sense—of English thought, influence, and power for good, to this people—then in darkness in such matter—the following questions suggest themselves. I give them as they present themselves to me; though with diffidence, from their seeming egotism:

"1. What moved the Japanese to thus, exceptionally, make me a teacher of English to them?

"2. Was there any pressure brought to bear upon them by Great Britain, or by the United States of America, or any other foreign power, for such action?

"3. Was there any special inducement, external, or internal, held out to them for it?

"4. If it was their own spontaneous act—as seems to have been the case—what enlightened or prompted them to it?

"In answer, from my knowledge of them, I would say:

"1. That their own self-enlightened appreciation of their position, in the family of nations so moved them.

"2. That there was no external pressure brought to bear on them in that direction; and that in receiving my teaching and its incidental advocacy of international relations on the general principles of comity of nations, they but followed their own spontaneous desire for that.

"3. To question 4, I would say, in all sincerity, but with all proper diffidence:

"That that enlightenment with its own inherent suggestions, probably prompted them to the course taken by the Conventions and Treaties referred to [with the United States and Britain].

"The Chinese and Dutch, with whom alone they held communication, were naturally, and in actual public polity, opposed to such opening of their ports. It took time—a little—for my humble teaching to mature; its inculcations had to reach the Imperial Executive itself, far off, high, on its Throne of State. Under Providence, in time, it did so. So at least, I flatter myself; and so, in generous concession, have intelligent Japanese themselves declared."

Ranald was referring to the report on the manuscript by a Reverend K.T. Takahashi, Presbyterian clergyman of Montreal, Quebec, who wrote in 1888 that Ranald's story was especially pertinent because it shed light on the inner current of thought which was gradually changing at the time Ranald was in Japan. Takahashi believed that the students of Ranald, in addition to learning English, were seeking information about other Western nations which Japanese authorities needed badly at the time. He went on to say that "it is not in vain that Mr. MacDonald should flatter himself the fact that he has been the first instructor and propagator of the English language in Japan, and much that was needed to enhance their notion of Western nations to the Japanese of the time."

XXII
Ranald's Interpreters Continue to Serve

Finally, Townsend Harris was ensconced at Edo at the Zempukuji Temple. It was an uneasy place to be, since renegade samurai still roamed the land opposed to the "hairy barbarians," and foreigners sometimes were depicted by artists as grotesque monsters. For those Japanese factions opposed to intercourse with the West, their worst fears were being realized as—in addition to the American treaty—on August 12, 1858, a British ship, *Furious*, anchored in Shimoda Harbor, bearing Lord James, Earl of Elgin, to seek a treaty. Elgin lost no time in handing Moriyama, again representing the Edo government, his draft of a treaty on August 16. He commented that Moriyama was a very acute and smooth-spoken person but, like Harris, Elgin was dubious of the dependability of the opinions put forth by the Japanese, saying that they objected to everything first and then eventually gave way—in Elgin's opinion, a bad plan. The six commissioners assigned to negotiate once more included Lord Inoue and Lord Iwase. Since Harris had already broken many barriers, Lord Elgin managed to conclude his treaty, giving Britain essentially the same rights as the Americans in just two weeks time—not the two years that it took Harris. The treaty was signed on August 26, 1858. Lord Elgin presented the Japanese with a lovely yacht and sailed away to new adventures. In the telling, the event seemed almost casual.

However, the important American trade treaty of July 29, 1858, had yet to be ratified by the governments of the United States and Japan (as did that of the British). In September, 1859, Chief Councillor Naosuke Ii proposed an embassy to the United States for exchanging ratifications (an event that took place on May 22, 1860, in Washington, D. C.—a historic event, for Japanese officials had not been abroad within memory). The councillor asked if Harris' government would be willing to transport a Japanese ambassador to Washington for the purpose.

The three men chosen to lead the embassy were: Masaoki Shinmi, Lord of Buzen, Chief Ambassador; Norimasa Muragaki, Lord of Awaji, as Vice-Ambassador; and Tadamasa Oguri, Lord of Bungo, acting as the *metsuke*, a special man often a part of any official Japanese group. He was more or less a censor or spy—one who made sure the others in the group behaved in accordance with proper Japanese rules or customs. The three officials would always act together in official matters. With considerable trepidation and excitement, the three assembled a party totaling seventy-seven men, who were to be transported to Washington on the U. S. ship *Powhatan*. Included among the party was Gohachiro Namura, Ranald MacDonald's former student and a descendant of the distinguished interpreter family of Nagasaki.

Muragaki believed that it would be demeaning for the embassy to be transported entirely on the United States ship and wanted to have a Japanese ship for the journey. However, after centuries where the Shogunate discouraged the building of ships large enough to cross the oceans, there were no suitable ships and few ocean-experienced sailors. A compromise was reached by preparing a Japanese corvette, the *Kanrin Maru*, used for training at the Naval College in Nagasaki, for the trip, and appointing Lieutenant John M. Brooke and a contingent of experienced American sailors to cooperate in manning the ship. Brooke happened to be in Edo at the time after losing his surveying ship during a fierce North Pacific storm.

The highest-ranking ambassadors and aides would sail on the *Powhatan*, lesser dignitaries on the *Kanrin Maru*. The latter set out on February 10 and the *Powhatan* departed February 13, 1860, both bound for San Francisco. How amused Ranald MacDonald, then venturing into new experiences in the gold fields of the Cariboo, would have been to witness the extraordinary voyages of both ships.

The *Powhatan*, sailed by experienced American seamen and commanded by Commodore Josiah Tattnall, had been outfitted within manageable limits to accommodate the tastes and living styles of the Japanese. Vast stores of baggage and Japanese foodstuffs—bean paste, pickles, dried fish, rice, etc.—were stowed, and cabins furnished with the thick quilt bedding favored by the Japanese. Never having been aboard a ship before, the Japanese had to be instructed firmly that open fires below decks and candle usage were to be controlled, lest fire break out. Suitably horrified at the very thought of fire at sea, the Japanese complied. In addition to dried stores, live animals complained bitterly from stinking pens—curried and fed until their slaughter as needed.

Most of the Japanese promptly became seasick as soon as the long rollers of the North Pacific began lifting the ship. Worse yet, on the 18th of February, just five days out to sea (eight days for the *Kanrin Maru*) a screaming storm arose. The animals were crying piteously, stores and cases broke loose and were smashed, and the terrified Japanese were convinced their days were at an end. The waves became so high that the *Powhatan* came into the wind and laid to; then the wind switched and conditions worsened. Eighty thousand Mexican silver dollars burst out of containers and piled up knee-deep in Kimura's cabin. (The Japanese were uninformed about the status of international credit, hence were carrying large stores of coins.) The commodore's barge was swept away, a sailor was battered against a mast, and a section of the ship was inundated by the towering waves after a fitting broke. Only the valiant response of the American sailors saved the lives of the Japanese passengers housed on the lower deck, who were brought to a safe location. About twenty-four hours later, the wind eased and the sea flattened somewhat, permitting the crew to set things in order.

Meanwhile, the smaller ship, the *Kanrin Maru*, faced not only the weather, but the strangest crew any American officer ever had to command. In addition, Lieutenant Brooke was supposed to be subordinate to Yoshitake Kimura and Rintarō Katsu. Neither Kimura, the administrator of the Naval Academy, nor Katsu, the captain of the *Kanrin Maru*, had much seagoing experience—their training exercises had been performed in calm coastal waters. Class distinctions among the Japanese outweighed the practical applications of seamanship. The samurai aboard saw themselves as givers of orders, not sailors. The Japanese commander was loathe to station an experienced sailor in charge of a crew, if he was of lower rank than those whom he directed—even if the latter were totally inexperienced. Neither the commanders nor their lower-class compatriots were experienced in the hoisting and lowering of sails under stormy conditions. Many were paralyzed with fear, having only sailed in calm waters during their naval careers. Among the crew was Manjiro Nakahama, the castaway rescued by an American whaler in 1841 and eventually repatriated through the Ryukyu Islands in 1851. At least he was an experienced sailor, as well as the chief means of communication between Lieutenant Brooke and the Japanese crew. It took a few tight situations, such as the storm of the 18th, to establish some order aboard ship, based on ability instead of class distinctions. Nevertheless, Brooke indicated later that he became very fond of the crew and learned to respect certain of their qualities.

However, after the severe storm that buffeted both ships ceased, the *Kanrin Maru* found itself blown far off course and out of contact with the larger ship. Brooke had no choice but to continue on course for San Francisco. A young Japanese, Yukichi Fukuzawa, kept a diary of his experiences, which is very enlightening regarding the impressions the Japanese had of the Western world and its ways. Fukuzawa went on to become one of the founders of prestigious Keio University in Japan.

In some respects, the *Powhatan* suffered more from the adverse weather. Since the stormy winds had made sailing impractical, the ship ran mostly under steam and used more coal than anticipated. It was necessary to ration water, too. On February 27, prudence dictated that the ship turn southward to Hawaii, where coal supplies could be restored and certain repairs made.

The Japanese ambassadors took this news with mixed reactions. Muragaki was thoroughly disturbed that they were visiting a country with which Japan had no formal relations. Still, it would be good to step on land once more, an opinion in which he was joined fervently by the rest of the party. It was with keen interest, then, that the Japanese watched the beautiful shores of Hawaii appear out of the mist, en route to an anchorage in Honolulu. After accommodations had been obtained for the official party at the French Hotel, the Japanese came ashore to the intense stares and comments of the local Hawaiians and European foreigners living there.

Little did Namura know that, more than a century later, his offspring would reside in Honolulu as *rokusei*, or sixth-generation Americans of Japanese descent.

Indeed, Hawaii was fascinating to the untraveled Japanese interpreters and ambassadors. After their first night at the French Hotel, the delegation was moved to the Dudoit House. Muragaki was invited to dine with King Kamehameha IV (Alexander Liholiho) and Queen Emma. Somewhat scornful of the "barbarians" in Hawaii—then the attitude of the Japanese for anyone not from Japan—Muragaki assumed that the king was a sort of tribal chief. According to Lewis Bush, who describes the entire 1860's voyage entertainingly in his book *77 Samurai*, Muragaki was quite astonished at the opulence and dignity of his hosts. (According to Muragaki's diary: "A dark-skinned man, he possessed a majestic dignity, worthy of a king. He wore a black, tight-sleeved jacket, white trousers, and a golden sash draped from the shoulder across his chest. Beside him stood an interpreter of the Dutch language and on either side about twelve military escorts, four with spears ornamented with large and gorgeous feathers from rare tropical birds; there were ambassadors, ministers, and attendants as well.")

The king welcomed them: "I am glad to have this fortunate opportunity to meet the Japanese delegates, and I hope you will make the best of your stay and not have too much inconvenience while your ship is at anchor."

Namura, the interpreter, and his senior ambassadors were both astonished and pleased with the meeting with a real king and queen:

"The Queen awaited us, a very beautiful, copper-colored woman with both her shoulders exposed and her breasts almost bare, covered only by a very thin material. Around her neck was a chain of jewels and a fine brocade skirt hung from her waist; indeed Queen Emma, for such is her name, resembled a veritable living Buddha."

According to Bush, Namura later told the executive officer, Lieutenant James D. Johnston, that the Japanese were especially interested to see the easy relationships between men and women but were disapproving: "how men could condescend to put themselves on an equality with women, much less pay court to them." They were even more shocked when Queen Emma and her female attendants came to visit them aboard ship, even though Lord Shinmi was still impressed by the Queen's beauty.

Seizing the opportunity to further Hawaii's own ends, the Hawaiian Minister of Foreign Affairs, Robert Crichton Wyllie, sought to gain access to the visitors. In a letter to King Kamehameha, he asked: "Would your Majesty permit me to request their Excellencies, when I see them, to give us (subject to the approval of their Emperor) the same treaty as that with the United States? As a small but growing Kingdom, and looking ahead to what *we ought to become*, I think it well to place Your Majesty's Foreign Relations, on *as wide a basis as possible*." The Japanese party was uneasy about these overtures by the Hawaiians. With no official instructions from above, the Japanese feared disapproval of any actions not first sanctioned by the Bakufu. An even more pressing problem was the necessity of continuing the voyage. Given nine months to complete their trip to and from Washington, D. C., the ambassadors feared that, if they were late in arriving home, they might have to pay for their tardiness with their lives or ceremonial suicide.

Accepting the fact that the delegation did not have the authority to conclude any treaties, Wyllie suggested merely a treaty for friendship, commerce, and navigation, which would be subject to ratification by the Emperor. The Japanese, however, declared that all treaty matters must wait until they returned to Japan. Wyllie then forwarded a request to Washington, D. C., asking if the Secretary of State, Lewis Cass, would use his influence to obtain such a treaty. Cass replied "NO" because the situation was too delicate regarding the American treaty, but if any opening arose he would at least mention the matter to the Japanese.

While the *Powhatan* had left Hawaii but was still at sea, the *Kanrin Maru* arrived at San Francisco to a tumultuous welcome. Admiral Kimura, as the ranking official, was given official acclaim and the entire group of Japanese were wined and dined—even though the main ambassadors had not yet arrived. Streets were lined with the curious, who marveled at the Japanese dress and odd hairdo of shaved forelock and bound topknot. The ordinary sailors reveled in their temporary fame and joined their counterparts in sometimes raucous celebrations ashore.

On March 28, the *Powhatan* steamed into San Francisco harbor. Muragaki wrote, "The land was covered with a beautiful green velvet carpet sloping softly from each side; the grazing sheep and cattle made an idyllic scene, refreshing and welcome after our long days at sea."

Lewis Bush recounts the observations of the *Daily Alta* on March 30th, sagely gazing into the future:

"It is a prophecy that many of those among us will live to see fulfilled—when we say that the day will come when the iron horse, lashed to the long train of railway carriages, shall take up the produce and manufactures of Japan from our docks and warehouses and set forth with the rich freight to the borders of the other great ocean."

The ambassadors stayed only a few days in San Francisco: days filled with entertainment on their behalf—navy bands, sightseeing, official receptions, etc. Much of the fanfare was unintelligible to the Japanese, who viewed the noise and commotion and the casual behavior of the populace with interest but considered American customs strange beyond belief. The official reception was particularly overwhelming, where vast numbers of foreigners mingled closely with them and, from the balconies above, were looking down on them—a situation repugnant to Japanese of the time. Bush notes:

"But the sight that followed was indeed a rare one, and Muragaki may perhaps be excused if he expressed some degree of wonder. First there came the extraordinary spectacle of champagne corks popping, then the Mayor rapped on the table, and then toasts began: to the Emperor and the President, to their respective armies and navies, to all the foreign consuls who were present, to the ambassadors themselves as well as to city officials, and finally to the press and to the Transcontinental Railway. All this was accompanied by periodic roars of 'Hear, hear!' and the singing of 'For he's a jolly good fellow' . . . Meanwhile the band played on, and Muragaki watched the hellish pandemonium with ever-growing shock—though he knew that it was all in honor of the ambassadors and the country that had sent them . . .

"Back on board the *Powhatan*, they laughed loud and long over their experience of the afternoon—laughter that would probably have surprised their American hosts, who were convinced that the Japanese taboo on any expression of surprise, amusement, or grief was a strict one. And indeed, official Japanese ceremonies always were marked by quiet formality, with much bowing and exchange of sake cups, but seldom by any real gaiety or laughter."

The Japanese admitted privately, though, that the Americans were a good-hearted, if strange people. Oguri, the *metsuke*, observed that, "It was noisy today, like a wild festival, but all the Americans seemed so happy that

I think we should imitate them and smile and laugh as they do lest we appear ungracious, for they are a warm-hearted generous people."

The extent of mercantilism in San Francisco alone impressed upon the visitors the necessity of learning English—that the Dutch language and ways, formerly considered by the Japanese to be the most important in the world, might not be so regarded internationally.

On April 6, the *Powhatan* with its colorful guests left San Francisco for Panama, where the official party and escorts boarded a train to cross the Isthmus of Panama, another novelty for the Japanese visitors. Facing the Caribbean Sea and Atlantic Ocean, the visitors felt very far from home, indeed. But there was little time to dwell on the matter, for they went aboard the steam frigate, *Roanoke*, for the trip to Hampton Roads, Virginia, over twelve thousand miles from distant Tokyo. There a small steamer, the *Philadelphia*, commanded by Captain Dupont conducted the ambassadors to Washington itself. A familiar face among the welcoming dignitaries was A. L. C. Portman, the Dutch interpreter who had been with Perry.

Once the party was ensconced at Willard's Hotel on Pennsylvania Avenue, seemingly endless and glittering functions ensued until the departure of the party on June 30, aboard the largest United States warship, *Niagara*. The bewildering behavior of the Americans, who pressed in upon the visitors with curiosity, albeit friendly for the most part, continued to astonish the ambassadors. Equally appalled at certain Japanese customs, but quietly noncommittal, the American hosts tried to make the strangers comfortable. An entire floor of the Willard Hotel was assigned to them, and the hotel management attempted to restrain uninvited guests from entering. The Japanese stoked their charcoal furnaces in the middle of the floor, lit them, and sat comfortably about smoking their pipes. A special kitchen was assigned for their own use, to cook in their own manner. Despite the proffering by the hotel (and previously by the ships' cooks) of the best American foods available, the Japanese were loathe to try any of it— indeed revolted by much except the fruits and fish. They seldom touched dairy products or meat (a Buddhist taboo for most at that time), adhering to a rather monotonous diet of rice, fish, bean paste, pickles, and sometimes poultry dishes. Although they admired the cleanliness and luxury of beds, they were accustomed to sleeping on the floor, using a wooden pillow. Being unaccustomed to gas lights, at first they blew out the light—a dangerous act, as an explosion could have occurred—until the lighting mechanism was explained. Strange to them but very acceptable were flush toilets.

Parties were a different matter; especially amazing to the visitors were the intermingling of beautifully gowned women with the men, the act of dancing, and the "hideous" sound of music, even martial band music. One Japanese officer talked of dancing in horrified tones, "The way men and women, both young and old, mixed in the dance, was simply insufferable to watch." Another referred to it as bouncing and leaping, and another, more kindly, as dazzling dancers like butterflies crazed by the sight of flowers.

The movements of all seventy-seven Japanese were governed by decisions made before ever leaving Japan. Behavior and even curfews and restrictions on how far away one could go were prescribed. It was not that the Japanese were afraid of Americans; rather, that they expected to behave in a foreign country exactly as they did at home. One diarist, an ambassador's servant, chafed at such restrictions, saying that, "Among the members of this Mission no one—from the Ambassadors down—is interested in the conditions and customs of the Americans. They [the Americans], on the other hand, are trying to show us everything without any intent of concealment. But no one on our side cares."

However, their apparent lack of interest in their surroundings stemmed from the cultural restrictions in which they had lived and the fear that any deviation from accepted JAPANESE behavior would earn censure after returning home.

Certainly the affairs held in their honor—in Washington, Baltimore, New York and Philadelphia—were spectacles no one would forget. The Japanese visitors were resplendent in their costumes, so barbaric and interesting to the Americans, who commented favorably on the dignity and stoicism of their guests. Interpreter Namura was complimented heartily on his excellent English.

Extremely nervous about the upcoming ceremonial meeting with President Buchanan, the ambassadors, through Namura, were full of questions as to exact procedures. Although all felt misgivings about the somewhat vague instructions as to how to proceed, Shinmi observed that, if they misunderstood something and did it wrongly, no one would be there to report back to Japan for them—that they would not have to atone for lapses in etiquette by ceremonial suicide or *seppuku*.

When the day came, all went well. From the book, *77 Samurai*, Muragaki's diary is quoted:

"Shinmi, myself, and Oguri wore the *Kariginu* court costume, while members of our suite were all in full dress in accordance with their rank. Our procession was long and imposing, headed by twenty men in gray uniforms, a band of thirty musicians, and mounted policemen. Then came some of our men bearing a dispatch box tied with silken cords of various colors, then more of our own men on foot preceding the ambassadors' carriages, all of which were drawn by four splendid horses. Shinmi was in the front carriage with Captain Dupont, I in the second with Commander Lee, and Oguri in the third with Mr. Ledyard. Those which followed carried our secretaries and interpreters. A spear-bearer preceded each carriage.

"I could not help smiling, as our party came in sight, to see the look of wonderment in the eyes of the crowd, beholding costumes they had never seen or even dreamed of. We must have seemed to them like people out of a fairy tale—as indeed Washington that day appeared to us. I could not help feeling proud of displaying the dignified costumes of our country before these people, who after all are barbarians, and of driving in such splendor through the streets as the first ambassadors ever sent abroad by Japan, and to such an enthusiastic welcome."

Although impressed by the splendor and dignity of the White House, the ambassadors must have been disappointed by the plainness of President Buchanan, as he welcomed them:

"We are all much gratified that the first Embassy which your great Empire has accredited to any foreign power has been sent to the United States. I trust that this will be the harbinger of perpetual peace and friendship between the two nations."

Muragaki recorded later, "President Buchanan is a genial, dignified man, over seventy years of age . . . he wore a plain black costume of coat and trousers in the same fashion as a merchant, and had no decoration or sword on him."

He went on to describe the greater grandeur of the military officers present and deplored the presence of women during the ceremonious occasion. Apparently he concluded that these lapses in behavior were due to the fact that,

"The President is only a governor voted in every four years. (There will be a changeover on October 1 this year. We heard them suggest a certain man, when we asked how they could tell before the 'auction,' they answered that this man would be the President, because he was related to the present one. Judging from such remarks, I don't believe that the fundamental laws of this country will last much longer.)"

The ambassadors were surprised to learn, too, that the President did not own a castle or palace. "The house he lives in is not his own but the property of the State, which he occupied only while he is in office."

Lewis Bush adds that, "To Muragaki it seemed ridiculous for the ambassadors to have gone to the trouble of wearing their grandest court costumes for people who did not even bother to prepare appropriate clothes for so momentous an occasion—and who received them, moreover, in only a large house rather than in the palace or castle in which they had expected to find the ruler of the United States."

Truly the cultural and economic chasm betweem Japan and the United States yawned large, but, from a practical standpoint, the visitors admired much that they saw in manufactured products, armaments, and also the apparent classless society of America. The latter was of particular interest to the younger visitors of the party, and of great appeal to some. It would be several decades before people of the two countries would begin to understand each other.

Waiting somberly for the ambassadors on their return to Edo was not a welcoming committee but a huddle of friends, warning the ambassadors to slip quietly into their old roles. Minister Ii had been assassinated during the ambassadors' absence by those who opposed social or economic intercourse with the hairy barbarians; the very lives of the ambassadors could be in jeopardy. The grand presents sent to the Shogun by President Buchanan were "carted off to a swamp some ten miles off, where no preparation had been made for their reception, and all the cannon, machinery, clothing, and valuables were dumped down promiscuously, like so much dirt and with no ceremony whatever. The minister had not been near, and had never seen what the *Niagara* had brought." (From the *San Francisco Bulletin.*)

When Townsend Harris went to a reception at Edo Castle given by the Chief Minister, he found the ambassadors in a degrading situation; and rumor had it that they would be sent to a post on a distant island, so their knowledge of the Western world, newly discovered, could not contaminate or enlighten the people. For the time being, it seemed that nothing had changed—no doors had been opened, no friendliness acknowledged. But in Japan of that time, ominous forces and restless rebels were at work in the land—and the tumultuous 1860's would culminate in the return to power of the Emperor's supporters who supplanted the Tokugawa family, ushering in a period of rapprochement finally with the West.

It was said, though, that—when Muragaki went home to relate his marvelous adventures to his wife—he exclaimed to her, "From what I have seen, we must no longer refer to them as barbarians."

Because only a handful of men had knowledge of foreign languages in Japan, Ranald's students continued to figure prominently in foreign affairs until the 1880's and beyond—after which time more English schools in Japan turned out bilingual statesmen and businessmen. The accomplishments and experiences of these interpreters were many:

Moriyama collaborated in the compilation of an English-Dutch dictionary into an English-Japanese dictionary entitled *Engelsch en Japansch*

Woordenboek (still in Dutch, though, as per the title), the first of the seven volumes having been published in 1851 (before Perry arrived). The compilation was never completed, however. Later he worked as an interpreter in Tokyo (as Edo became known after the Meiji Restoration) and was said to be promoted to a cabinet-level position. In 1861, he accompanied Ambassador Takeuchi as he visited England, France, and other European countries. During his later life he established a private school for English in Koishikawa.

Shozaemon Motoki was the fifth generation of the Motoki family to work as an interpreter, commencing his career in 1814. He had assisted in the negotiations for the release of Ranald MacDonald from prison in Nagasaki, working with Commander Glynn.

Sakuschichiro Uemura had assisted Hendrik Doeff, the Dutch scholar, in translating and preparing a Dutch-Japanese dictionary in 1812, but little is known of his later life.

Keitaro Nishi and Tanesaburo Shioya began studies of physical science and engineering in the late 1850's under the auspices of Dr. Van den Broek.

Hyoma Nakayama, Tatsuichiro Shizuki, and Yoshiro Iwase all had worked with Moriyama on the seven-volume dictionary.

After his return to Japan, Gohachiro Namura married Kame Machino and adopted a daughter, Shizu, who married Tsurukichi Tanaka in 1887. As a lad, Tsurukichi had heard about the opportunities in the United States from a family friend, an (unidentified) interpreter for Townsend Harris. At age eighteen he hired onto a ship as a cabin boy and went to San Francisco. The ship's captain liked Tsurukichi and, when the ship landed in San Francisco, he assisted the youth in finding a job as a part-time domestic helper in the home of the president of a shoe manufacturing company. Tsurukichi stayed there for thirteen years, eventually leaving the domestic job and working in the shoe factory.

In 1872, thirty-seven Japanese living in the San Francisco area were asked to meet the visiting ambassador from Japan. He told them that any with Western skills or knowledge would be welcomed back to Japan. Interested in returning, Tsurukichi went to work at the South Alameda, California, Salt Works to learn the production of salt by solar evaporation. In 1881, he returned to Japan to establish a salt works on an island seven hundred miles southeast of Tokyo, but unfavorable weather conditions caused the project to fail.

Although penniless, Tsurukichi Tanaka returned to Tokyo, where he met and married Shizu Namura. With two friends—but leaving his new wife behind until he could earn passage for her—Tsurukichi Tanaka now returned to California in 1887, going to work in a Livermore winery and vineyard as the cook. Later he worked at the Orpheum Theater as a janitor, then headed a crew maintaining two theaters. Finally he had enough money to bring his wife and her mother to California. He prospered, became an assistant treasurer of the western division of the Orpheum circuit (theaters), and became a naturalized citizen in 1899, changing his first name to Thomas.

The Tanakas continued to be staunch Japanese-Americans, sending their three daughters to business college. Their second girl, Chiyo, and her daughter eventually went into the florist business, helping her husband, Chomatsu Izumi, to send their sons to college: both became physicians, Ernest a pathologist in Connecticut and Homer a physician (now retired) in Honolulu. His family members, many also involved in medicine, still live in Hawaii—the land that seemed so wonderfully strange to their ancestor, Gohachiro Namura, so many years earlier.

As far as Ichiro Hori is concerned—the "eleventh man or eleventh scholar"—modern Japanese historians believe that MacDonald incorrectly listed him as a student. Ichiro Hori was the eight-year-old son of Tatsunosuke Hori at the time Ranald was in Nagasaki. On the other hand, Tatsunosuke was an interpreter who, according to his official record in Japan, studied under interpreter Nishi. From the accounts of Perry's expedition, clearly Tatsunosuke was an interpreter and he appeared to be known to Namura and Moriyama. At an undefined time, Tatsunosuke also published an English-Japanese dictionary, listing himself as the editor. The distinguished professor, Seiichi Hasegawa, in a research paper for the Japan-English Studies History Society, suggests that the interpreter's name was Jujiro Hori, who later changed his name to Denzo Hori, and who definitely was in Hakodate for some time as an interpreter and later in Nagasaki. He also acknowledged that the same man had been reported as "Tatsnoskay Hori." Undoubtedly, Tatsunosuke Hori was the mysterious "eleventh student," with the frequent name changes then practiced by Japanese persons creating an identity problem in modern years. This author has referred to Hori, thus, as Tatsunosuke Hori.

(Note: Some of the information about the above scholars was furnished by Dr. Torao Tomita of Rikkyu University, Japan. The update on Namura came from the author's visit in Hawaii with Namura's descendants and an account in the *Honolulu Star-Bulletin*.)

XXIII
Ranald Continues His Explorations

Ranald's students were exploring the world; he, their teacher, roamed only the rugged lands of British Columbia. Although it had not come to fruition, his explorations to Bentinck Arm had commanded respect, and he was a veteran of the formerly trackless country of the Cariboo mining areas. Therefore, it was not surprising that MacDonald was asked to be a part of the Vancouver Island Exploring Expedition in 1864.

Ever since the settlement of Vancouver Island, especially concentrated at Victoria, the government knew it was necessary to investigate the resources of the rest of the island. Sir James Douglas, when he was governor, offered a prize of fifty pounds for an essay setting forth the capabilities, resources and advantages of Vancouver Island as a colony for settlement, and the prize was awarded in 1861 to Charles Forbes, M. D. and Surgeon of the Royal Navy. Unfortunately, no significant measures were taken to organize and utilize the data. A subsequent award of one thousand pounds offered by governmental proclamation for the discovery of paying gold fields went unclaimed. Finally the new governor, Arthur Edward Kennedy (Douglas had retired that spring), came up with an offer to match two-for-one any funds furnished by the people to underwrite such an exploration.

On April 29, 1864, a governing committee was chosen: Selim Franklin, chairman; George Cruickshank, secretary; and twelve others. The exploring party included: Dr. Robert Brown, the leader and government agent; Lieutenant Peter John Leech, astronomer; Frederick Whymper, artist; John Buttle, naturalist; and Alexander S. Barnston, John Meade, Ranald MacDonald, John M. Foley (dismissed July 26), Thomas Henry Lewis, Richard Drew, and William Hooper (joined August 6)—all pioneers or miners with practical experience. Added were Tomo Anthony and Lazare Le Buscay as hunters and sometimes guides, as it turned out. Brown described his crew as a queer-looking lot, "wondrously motley."

Brown himself came into this assignment in a rather peculiar manner. Only twenty-three years old, he was already on an assignment from the British Columbia Association of Edinburgh—a Botanical Expedition to Oregon, having begun his work on February 23, 1863. During the summer of 1863 he traveled through the southern limits of Vancouver Island—Alberni, Ucluelet, Nootka—on a plant- and seed-gathering search. Then he moved on to explore the Olympic Peninsula and Whidbey Island, and went to Snoqualmie Falls for a visit. That winter he stayed in Victoria after a trip to Lillooet, writing to his sponsors that his stipend was far too low, that even an Indian packer would not work for such wages. Due to the slow mail service, the Edinburgh group did not receive the missive until after Brown had taken on the job of leading the Vancouver Island Exploring Expedition, which he figured would combine nicely with his seed-gathering mission. Brown did have a scientific education from the University of Edinburgh that qualified him for the post, at least in theory.

Of all the men, Ranald MacDonald was the oldest at forty years of age, but Brown later said that his persistent high spirits made him a popular member of the group. Several of the men, including Brown himself as the leader, kept journals. Ranald's journal reflected his own scholarly background and keen insight, acknowledged later by Brown, who noted on the frontispiece of the 45-page report, "Mr. McDonald's [*sic*] journal may be generally relied upon. His opinion on some points were however rather accounted singular—probably dogmatic."

In 1859 and 1860, Commander R. C. Mayne had examined, for the British government, the peripheral areas of southern and eastern Vancouver Island, and trekked across to Alberni Inlet. However, the area between Comox and Cowichan, the outer coast, and the lands adjacent to the Strait of Juan de Fuca were so heavily forested and broken up with mountain ranges, lakes and swamps that the Victoria government really did not know what was there. Interest was sparked particularly by the significant coal deposits already being mined at Nanaimo and other indications near Cowichan. A geologist with the Boundary Expedition (marking the international boundary between the Northwest United States and British Columbia) said "the two seams of coal near Nanaimo were a soft black lignite, of a dull earthy fracture . . . [resembling] some of the duller varieties of coal produced in the South Derbyshire and other central coalfields in England . . . For economic purposes these beds are very valuable. The coal burns freely, and yields a light pulverescent ash, giving a very small amount of slag and clinker." Perhaps there were more such deposits. Geologists theorized, too, that since gold was being found everywhere in the West, it seemed it might exist in this wilderness as well. Victoria residents were eager for an influx of prospectors (who would leave behind their gold dust in the shops and stores), such as occurred in the Cariboo.

Hence, at the direction of their leader, Robert Brown, the men were to search for minerals and, in the process, map, explore, and assess the feasibility of a road to the rugged western coast.

On June 7, 1864, accompanied by friends, the company was addressed by Governor Kennedy before boarding the gun boat, H. M. S. *Grappler*, commanded by Lieutenant Verney. The explorers were transported to Cowichan Bay, sixty miles north of Victoria on the eastern shore, where a few settlers were farming near a mission. Here they anchored for the night.

The following day, at the party's first camp, Ranald described the fertility of their host's ranch (John Compagnon): "The ranch is counted the best in the valley, the soil is good, labour and care appear to be bestowed on the grounds adjoining the house. Vegetables grow large—but more particularly the Oregon grape trees some measure nearly 6 inches in diameter." Compagnon furnished the men with fresh trout and vegetables—welcomed, indeed.

The next day the explorers started up the Cowichan River. At camp that night Tomo Anthony arrived to join the party, a man whom Ranald had known as a youth at Fort Langley and had not seen but once in thirty years. Tomo, Tomo, or Tomah Anthony from the Shuswap Lake area near Kamloops was of pure Iroquois blood, and had been in the Cariboo with Long Baptiste, an Indian credited with showing the miner Dunleavy gold nuggets from the Horsefly River. Tomo claimed to know the island country well and spoke the local Indian language fluently—in fact, virtually every dialect of the area, as well as good English—an asset, indeed, since one of the expedition's tasks was to record the population and conditions of the Indian tribes along the way. Brown was a bit reluctant at first to employ him, having heard that Tomo had been accused (but cleared) of killing his wife.

Ranald mentions talking with Ka-ka-latsa, "chief and constable of the Sa-me-na [Someno] tribe," telling him that the manner in which the Indians treated the party would be recorded and sent to England. The chief had been engaged to guide the party for part of their forthcoming trip. He was a picturesque fellow with a small tufted beard and wore a stovepipe hat when he dressed for special occasions.

A few of the explorers struggled along a faint trail upstream, while others—usually Foley and Barnston, the best canoeists, plus Chief Ka-ka-latsa and an Indian boy, Johnny Limon, traveled along more easily, bringing supplies by water. Toward the end of the second day of travel, Tomo—who had foraged widely and successfully to kill a deer—reported that deposits of coal were evident about a mile from the river. Tomo was proving to be a stalwart guide and mentor. It was he who brought in food, chopped through obstacles to permit the canoe's passage, guided the land party, and generally made himself useful.

No discernible settlements existed in the heavily wooded wilderness until near the great falls—a series of falls, really, twelve to eighteen feet high. There was a small settlement, and another across the river, neglected and overgrown with weeds. These two lodges or ranches were used in winter for hunting. Wet and miserable in a heavy downpour, the explorers occupied one of the lodges for the night.

The next morning, still moving in a depressing rain, the advance party skirted the rapids of the canyon, traveling along a rim some two-hundred-feet high above the falls, and found a spot to launch the canoe in smoother water. It took the combined efforts of the main party to drag the canoe up and over the rough portage. That night, the canoeists, Barnston, Foley, Ka-ka-latsa and Limon, did not show up at the rendezvous; worried and in a pouring rain, the land party including Ranald spent a restless and miserable night without supplies and under makeshift shelter.

It was a hungry and distraught group that greeted the tardy canoeists at ten o'clock the next morning. Tomo had been sent to look for them, finding them in no difficulty, just slowed down by upstream paddling. The river had been swift and the canoe, momentarily out of control, slammed into a rock and had to be repaired. After breakfast, the Indian chief and boy moved on into Lake Cowichan to pitch camp on the southeast side.

Moving along on foot through incredible torrents of rain and hail, Brown encouraged MacDonald to cheer them up. In a 1989 publication of Robert Brown's diary, John Hayman relates that MacDonald was a happy-go-lucky fellow that the party dubbed "Mark Tapley." Tapley was a character from Charles Dickens' story, *Martin Chuzzlewit*, noted for his persistent exuberance and cheeriness.

Brown mentioned traveling through magnificent Douglas Fir forests, admiring and assessing them with a speculative eye for commercial purposes. Ranald also recorded passing through magnificent groves of cedar, hemlock and maple during the previous two days.

Not far below the entrance to the lake, the party came to signs on a cedar tree recording the passage of "Harris and Durham," whereupon Brown added the names of the expedition members. Samuel Harris had made three explorations up the Cowichan River in 1860, and, on the second trip with Langley and Durham, reported finding gold.

On June 17, the two Indians went up the lakeshore to establish a camp on the stream they called Quoitquot, meaning "rushing stream," where good prospects of gold were said to exist. The other men explored the area before coming into camp. At the new campsite, one used by others before them, a paper with four names was tacked to a tree. One of the names was that of Joseph Lowry, a man who had traveled with Ranald MacDonald from the Fraser River to the Chilcotin country, and later on the Bentinck Arm expeditions in 1862. Naturally he wondered what the man was doing there but assumed he was hunting.

While Foley and Barnston trekked upstream to prospect the stream, which they now called Foley's Creek, Leech and Meade surveyed the lake, Lewis and Tomo went hunting, and Ranald guarded the camp. With nonchalance, as far as Ranald's diary shows, Foley and Barnston returned to report finding good color in their gold pans.

Charged with the duty of discovering gold, but not to pursue mining, several members of the party nevertheless subsequently inspected a reported copper mine in the area, returning with good samples of copper and iron ore. Foley reported a deposit of quartz that was supposed to contain gold.

On June 22, the party split up. Leech, Meade, Foley and Tomo Anthony were detailed to explore west from the Cowichan River to Port San Juan (near today's Port Renfrew), where the VIEE Committee had arranged to deposit supplies. With MacDonald in command, Whymper, Buttle, Barnston, and Brown continued to the head of Lake Cowichan and across country to Nitinat. The two Indian guides were dispatched to Victoria with messages and reports for local newspapers.

Ranald described the trek to the Nitinat River (about ten miles) as alternately skirting swamps, following a stream, and walking through pleasant, wooded valleys. On either side, snowcapped mountains were accented against the sky. At the Nitinat River, some traces of copper were found, among very large trees in the vicinity of rushing rapids. Below the rapids, the men launched a raft 20 feet by 8 feet, shoving off for a leisurely float downriver. However, only three to four miles downstream they heard the ominous roar of a great rapids ahead. Here, Ranald says, they had a narrow escape:

"The circumstances of the case were these: immediately above the rapids we were in a large poole [sic] the bottom of which we could not reach with our poles so were fast drifting to the edge of the rapids and would have been drawn in were it not for Mr. Buttle & Barnston. The one with great presence of mind jumping ashore while the other giving him his pole to hold on by till they were assisted by the rest—The line was got out & the raft drawn to smooth water. What the result of our being drawn into the rapids would have been I could not pretend to tell."

They abandoned the raft and shouldered their "swags" again on foot. From the path the canyon ahead looked formidable, but from the heights the men could see two canoes drawn up on the bank below the rapids. These proved to be damaged and abandoned, and left beside an old Indian encampment site. After repairing one of them with flour and resin melted together and—with the assistance of nearby Indians—building another raft, MacDonald and Whymper rode the wild waters while Buttle, Lewis and Brown walked the shore toward Nitinat Lake. A lively diarist, Ranald described the twenty-mile ride as hair-raising. At first, "we jumped riffle after riffle without any accident. But on one or two occasions came near being drawn under large trees lying across dangerous parts of the river which if it did would have been disasterous [*sic*] to us. On another time came near being snagged. The whole river is one succession of rapids, riffles and salmon weir with small lakes or properly speaking large water holes, very deep, we not being able to reach bottom with our poles, also very winding. I believed that we headed every point of the compass [but generally south]."

Along the way they spotted ten Indian villages, all seemingly deserted, probably occupied only during certain hunting or fishing seasons. Near the entry of the river to the lake, they picked up specimens of iron ore and also saw indications of gold and copper. Some of the best timber on the island grew in this area; Buttle and Lewis measured one tree which was forty-eight feet in circumference.

Nitinat Lake was estimated to be about twenty or twenty-two miles long, one to two miles wide, and seemed to be a natural wind tunnel for fierce afternoon breezes. Having paddled part way down the lake and rigged a makeshift sail, the party had to seek shelter in the lee of an island. Eventually they came to the main Nitinat village, where the lake emptied into the sea, and were welcomed excitedly by the Indians, spending the night and trading with them for a small supply of beans, flour, dried meat and halibut. They were a fierce-looking lot; some had faces smeared with blood, others blackened, and most had pieces of shell in their ears and nostrils. The Indians called their village Y-ack and the inlet Et-low and said their principal chief was Mo-quan-la.

Following some friendly but spirited negotiations as to payment, three Indians skillfully manhandled a large canoe to transport the party to the ocean and on to Pachena Bay, deftly passing through high breakers. Ranald wrote that Pachena Bay, "is large but exposed to southerly winds. Port San Juan is situated in the mouth of the River of that name emptying into Cooper's Inlet—here is shelter for very small crafts. Messrs. Spring & Laughton have commenced to build a jetty."

The explorers were met by this Mr. Laughton, a trader for the past fifteen years, and were invited to pitch tents nearby. By July 2, Ranald's group expected Foley, Leech and party, who had gone overland to explore from Lake Cowichan westward. On schedule, Foley alone turned up, cut, scratched, tired and bedraggled from bushwhacking his way westward after losing touch with his main party. He reported crossing three mountain ranges, discovering signs of copper, silver and iron, having an encounter with an aggressive panther, and finally meeting an Indian and his wife—the Indian man almost shooting him, thinking Foley to be a deer as he crashed through the brush.

Foley now remained with the Indians and the next day—armed with ample ammunition—Foley and the Indians paddled upriver, shooting into the air periodically to attract the attention of the missing men. The entire party was thus reunited at the campsite by noon.

The trader Laughton mentioned the extensive trade in dogfish oil, about 15,000 gallons annually prepared by the Indians for trade. They caught the fish, boiled it and skimmed off the oil.

The party was happy to receive a sloop from Victoria with their supplies, the captain reporting that an earlier boat had been forced back by high seas. Later, traveling south through a rough ocean in two canoes, the men could see a major seam of coal in the cliffs, but it was impossible to land; in fact, the party was forced to seek shelter after a dismasting, but eventually made it into the Sooke River to camp across the river from a settler named Brule. Robert Brown and Alexander Barnston started for Victoria to transact business concerning the expedition, while the rest of the party under the leadership of Mr. Leech continued to the headwaters of the Sooke River. Thereafter they were to split into two parties, one headed for Qualis, the other to Somenos.

On July 14, after a long climb over a mountain range called by the Indians Se-na-to, Ranald and his party came to a high point they called "Buttle's Peak," raising a small flag atop a pole with rocks piled around its base to mark it as the summit of that ridge. The Indians with the party said that from the next range eastward one could look down on Victoria.

As they skirted the Sooke River, Foley panned for gold, gleaning as much as twenty cents to the pan. The stream entered a deep canyon called Who-ton-gas, meaning "the jumping-off place," and joined a larger river. Ranald wondered if this larger river was the real Sooke and the one they had been following merely a tributary, but they continued up the original stream, with good panning all the way. On July 18, Mr. Leech sent Foley, Meade, Tomo (who usually was the provider of game and fowl), and Ranald back to the forks to explore the larger river, which they named Leech River.

During the next few days Ranald became more and more excited about the growing color in the gold pans, sometimes as much as a dollar a pan. He noted that there was plenty of timber to build flumes and speculated that the area might support five thousand miners. In his diary, he hoped his party would be able to claim a finder's benefit, saying "We are sanguine about the success of this exploring party from the fact that we expect to derive the full benefit of the Gover't Proclamation." Ever the philosopher, he laughed at himself verbally the following day: "I believe that I am not mercenary nor yet avaricious—but I could not help thinking when I found myself kneeling and delving with all my might to disembowel a nugget—and, at the same time, offering up my prayers to the Committee Chairman and Commander for the neglect of the pick [the supplier of the expedition had included other mining gear but no pick]—that I looked like one."

Quartz reefs appeared, indicating the probability of actual veins of the yellow stuff. The party made explorations still farther up the Leech River, discovering other streams or branches, and more rugged canyons. Ranald described the area as "wild and rocky with some very large boulders in its bed" and mountains soaring on either hand. Eventually, the canyon grew tame and a plain began to open out; Ranald commented that here began the slate, quartz and gold range of the Island. "How far it will extend will be determined by future Explorations."

When Ranald's party returned to Leech's camp, a note pinned to a tree directed them to proceed up the Sooke and rejoin their companions. However, as they approached Sooke Lake, the eerie glow of a forest fire alarmed them and they subsequently found that Leech's group had narrowly escaped death as they fled onto an island in the lake. Even so, Leech's haversack with bank bills and coins was burned and Leech burned his foot. (Sooke Lake, of course, today is central to Victoria's water supply area). Intermittent prospecting of small streams here proved fruitless, and the party moved on to Shawnigan Lake to join Brown and Barnston at the home of the Indian boy, Johnny Limon, in Cowichan.

From some point, Lieutenant Leech sent notice to Victoria on July 14, 1864: "A discovery which I have to communicate is the finding of gold on one of the forks of the Sooke River about 10 miles from the sea in a straight line . . . The whole value of the diggings cannot be easily over-estimated. The gold will speak for itself." The *Colonist* of August 1, 1864, under a restrained headline reported: "A messenger arrived last evening from Cowichan, with another dispatch from Dr. Brown, dated the 29th July, enclosing the individual reports of Corporal Leech [he was a Lieutenant], Sergeant Meade and Ronald

McDonald [*sic*], respecting the recent discoveries at Sooke, together with a map framed by Sergt. Meade, of the Sooke and Leech Rivers." Another tidbit noted that, "Some excitement was caused in town on Saturday, arising out of intelligence brought to town by Mr. Michael Muir, of Sooke, that a man in his employ had exhibited two nuggets of the value of $6 and $8, said to have been taken out at the new diggings . . . The man after replenishing his commisariat left again for the same locality."

The gold reports from the Sooke River sent Victoria into a paroxysm of gold fever. Today the site is little more than an hour's drive from downtown Victoria, but then it was a treacherous trip over the mountains on foot or on horseback. During the first days, hundreds of would-be prospectors eager for news hung around the docks to monitor the arrival of every ship and pass rumors far and wide. It was said that even the patients at hospitals leaped from their beds and joined the stampede to the mines, especially when a nugget worth $72 was exhibited by a returning prospector. A tent city dubbed Leechtown sprang up on the shore of the river, and soon crude shacks followed. The expedition members at Nanaimo learned that "the Sooke mines were paying $10.00 per day," but their duties were not completed.

On August 2, having left Barnston, Whymper, Meade and Tomo with Leech, who was nursing his burned foot, Ranald MacDonald and the balance of the explorers set out northward, crossing the Chemainus River toward Nanaimo and points north—partly on the Government Trail. Probably at today's Ladysmith, for he talks of a visit with a settler (Mr. Smith), Brown was able to hire an Indian canoe to transport them to Nanaimo. Ranald mentions traveling opposite Valdes Island, "the headquarters of the renowned Chief Jo-se-ia who I recalled seeing at Fort Langley, purchasing materials for a Fort he was building."

At Nanaimo, Ranald talked with J. P. Franklin, formerly of the firm Franklin and MacDonald and a member of the VIEE Committee, who "recognised me—congratulated the Expedition in a flattering manner in the successful discovery of gold at Sooke as benefactors etc.etc. of the country."

The party lingered at Nanaimo for more than a week, preparing for the next stage of exploration, hiring packers and locating canoes. Of course, several men straggled in and out of the taverns, too.

Here a long-festering dissatisfaction with Foley came to Brown's attention, because a furious Leech refused to stay under the same roof with the man. It seems Foley had cursed every man of the expedition at one time or another, and, as the capstone, he pulled a knife one evening on Ranald MacDonald—who proceeded to knock him down. Brown told a friend in a private letter that he always had thought Foley was interested only in gold prospecting. He hired William Hooper as a replacement, and gave Foley his walking papers. True to predictions, Foley turned up at the gold diggings at Leechtown. He is quoted as an experienced miner in a story about ghost towns, *Vancouver Island*, saying at one point, "I have seen many [would-be miners] laboring up Leech River, asking those they met where the gold was. These men, if they had a claim, would know as much what to do with it as if they were made a present of a wild lion or an elephant!" Foley believed the real strikes would be made in the banks and benches of the river, not in the streambed.

On the 15th, Leech, Barnston, Lewis, Hooper, and Lazare Le Buscay left overland with four Indian packers. Ranald left in Brown's party on the 16th by canoe, owned by an Indian, E-yees, northbound along the coast toward Comox. As they went, they noted the shoreline terrain, explored the mouths of rivers, and blazed some markers on trees "V.I.Ex.Ex." The foot trail, they noted, was in almost impassible condition.

Many meetings with Indians—some of dubious reputation—were recorded. The expedition's Indian compatriots were particularly alarmed by the appearance of a party of Fort Rupert or Coguels Indians (Kwawkewlth). This tribe had been known to smash and pillage canoes and kill or enslave their Indian owners.

Safely reaching Comox, the party stopped overnight. Comox had two stores, about thirty white settlers, and seventy Indian "warriors" (so one may assume perhaps a village of two hundred total). On August 23, Meade, Tomo and Ranald set off inland on a five-day exploration trip which took them up Brown's River—named by the party in honor of the expedition's leader. Some distance upriver, they were rewarded by the discovery of significant coal seams, easily visible in the cliffs—one five or six feet thick and one hundred feet long. The location was in a canyon of two-hundred-foot vertical walls in places, but only about fifty-feet high at the coal site. An exuberant Ranald declared, "If the quantity of coal exposed is any richness, then I certainly endorse Tomo [Tomo was the discoverer, while out hunting]. That there is nothing on the Pacific Coast to equal it." At this point, the party returned with their good news to Comox and reported to Robert Brown. Indeed, these finds brought lasting prosperity, as it was in the Comox Valley that the truly significant mines were developed—both northeast and southwest of Comox Lake.

Their next project was to check out Alberni Inlet. Unable to hire a canoe and paddler from the Indians, the party bought a large and sturdy canoe for the forthcoming foray. Laughingly, some expedition members suggested its name should be "The Twelve Spies," after the twelve men sent out by Moses to spy out the promised land, since the Vancouver Expedition now numbered twelve men.

The party set out on September 1st to further explore Brown's River and to attempt a trip overland and by water to Alberni. From a camp near the forks of that stream and the Puntledge River, the coal seams were reexamined and the Puntledge explored upstream. Several falls and rapids barred the way, often necessitating portages over rough terrain or the dragging of the canoe through shallow, rocky waters. Finally the men entered the source of the river, a lake that one man proposed be called MacDonald's Lake. Flattered but modest, Ranald said the river and lake should bear the same name, Puntledge. Ranald wrote that no white men had ever been known to go upstream into that lake, and that very few Indians made the difficult trip either, although they had hunted near there.

Triumphantly, the expedition paddled around the lake for two days, now Comox Lake, where they saw strong indications of coal. Before leaving the lake, "Mr. Whymper nailed a piece of ceader [sic] across a tree and as usual marked the number of the camp and our names . . . while thus engaged some of us erected a flag staff first nailing a crosspiece tieing a piece of deer hide on the end of the staff and inserted a ____ [undecipherable] bottle bottom up." At the end of the lake, which they considered to be about ten miles long and in a reverse "S" shape, they searched unsuccessfully for some navigable stream. What they did see all during this wilderness exploration were scores of deer, elk, bear, wolves, and beaver.

On September 10, a significant river was discovered, the size of the Puntledge—which MacDonald, Meade, Drew and Whymper, with MacDonald in command, were ordered to ascend, explore and prospect. This stream, which Brown named the Cruickshank River, came from today's spectacular Strathcona Provincial Park. It was deeper and more navigable than the rocky Puntledge, at first. Eventually it ran through a rugged canyon strewn with boulders, at the mouth of which panning produced good color. Ranald was very anxious to get above the canyon, with his old prospecting fever telling him that upstream might be the mother lode, but— since time was running out for the three-day expedition (the limit set by Robert Brown)—it was impossible to proceed.

En route back to the lake and floating swiftly along with the current, MacDonald slammed the canoe against a fallen tree while he was steering, splitting the canoe wide open. In relatively shallow water, the men narrowly escaped and were able to grab the canoe and drag it ashore; some of their supplies were damaged but saved from sinking entirely. With some ingenuity, the men repaired the canoe and made it back to the lake. On the 16th, the expedition hauled out the canoe and struck off on foot southward toward Alberni Inlet—difficult traveling through underbrush and timber, frequently crossing streams and sloughs, to enter another small lake, and fording it by a makeshift raft. On the morrow they hoped to cross a formidable divide and reach the Great Central Lake—or so they thought. Actually it took them four days to attain the large body of water, encountering several sizeable lakes and detouring across low mountains in between. When they finally could see the lake, they were somewhat to the northeast.

On familiar ground now but proceeding with difficulty because of lakes and swamps, the men made their way around Sproat Lake to a small logging camp on Alberni Inlet. When reunited with Leech's party, some of whom had split up and suffered from a lack of provisions, the men had their first good dinner in days and enjoyed a bottle with the mill manager, Mr. Leedgate.

From there the party walked into Alberni, first paying a call at the company store to get more warm clothing, then following with a good dinner and a room. Alberni was a larger settlement than expected, dominated by a mill employing one hundred and fifty men. The Indians fished extensively, too, mostly with torches at night. There were many houses, a store, boarding house, church, reading room and other buildings. However, here they learned that there was an Indian uprising in this very vicinity, particularly toward Nootka Sound, where the expedition planned to go next. Additionally, some belligerent Indians had threatened to burn down the Alberni mill.

Nevertheless, the expedition left by canoe on October 3rd for a comfortable paddle down Alberni Inlet, prospecting occasionally where streams entered. Again the party split up, with Leech leading a group on an unrecorded side exploration and with Ranald remaining along the inlet. Members of the latter group ascended streams to view Nahmint Lake and Henderson Lake, and to look for signs of minerals, despite warnings from an Indian chief who quietly but firmly said, "this is my country." The chief called coal "to-mase," copper "kle-kle-na-sum."

After surveying and exploring the environs of the inlet for almost two weeks, Ranald and his party returned to Alberni and from thence went overland to Qualicum Beach, returning to Nanaimo on the *Grappler*. Why the party did not pursue a course to Nootka was not explained, but was possibly due to the Indian unrest.

The group landed, to be hailed as heroes, and touted, for awhile, with flattering comments. Brown's 27-page report was published in April, 1865.

He always stressed that this was not a gold prospecting trip, but a fact-finding expedition, and always wanted to publish a more colorful commercial version of his diary. Ranald MacDonald's 45-page journal also has lain, unpublished, for one hundred thirty-three years, most recently in the British Columbia Provincial Archives.

Thus, for over four months Ranald MacDonald had pursued yet another quest for mineral wealth. Considering his life of wandering, however, one must believe that—for him—just exploring itself, seeing new places and marking out trails, was the main magnet.

Perhaps—when the expedition disbanded—he might have spent some time at Leechtown. There, a makeshift town had been developing, complete with roadside inns and hotels. But by 1865, the gold was already losing its sheen, even though a reported $100,000 had been taken out. Gold was there, but the area was so fractured and the streams so strewn with large boulders that getting to the gold—whether in a bank or under a stream, or, indeed, in the stream—cost more in time and supplies than the results were worth. The town soon disintegrated into a tangle of fallen logs and the green jungle that covers everything left derelict in the Pacific Northwest.

Ranald probably returned to his ranch before long to find out the unfortunate details of the death of his neighbor—Donald McLean—at the hands of a vengeful Indian (see Chapter XX). Sophie McLean ran the roadhouse for a period thereafter, eventually selling out to George Dunne.

In June, 1865, Ranald was dispatched once more on a government exploration. In fact, two groups were sent out from an undetermined point in the Cariboo—James Orr with fifteen men to prospect the range of mountains running from the bend of the Columbia River toward the Cariboo country, and Ranald MacDonald with five men to commence work in the Horsefly Valley. An editor for the *Cariboo Sentinel*, in Barkerville, June 12, 1865, castigated the government, charging that Orr would be remunerated at fixed rates while MacDonald's party only received provisions as a return (probably with the proviso of a finder's fee or right to claim, such as MacDonald wistfully wished for during the Vancouver Island exploration). The reporter said he did not disparage Orr as a man of honor, but that "in this part of the country very little confidence is felt in his qualifications for directing and superintending such an expedition as that which the Government has entrusted to him. For such labors, not only the head, but every member of the company, should have been selected from the bold pioneers to whom the colony and empire is indebted for the discovery of Cariboo." (Do we read here a tacit resentment by the writer, perhaps, that the local man, MacDonald, did not receive the larger plum?)

The writer went on to say that the men should have been selected and sent out from Williams Creek to explore. "In the opinion of all experienced miners we have met the Government has made a grand mistake in the course it has pursued, and the country will have to pay for it, and probably suffer immensely by the large expedition turning out a huge failure. It is much to be regretted that the Government did not appoint the right men . . . The system of paying men monthly salaries is also universally condemned, inasmuch as the great stimulus to exertion—hope of reward—is wanting."

An earlier squib in the *Sentinel* on June 3, 1865, prior to the above editorial, noted that MacDonald's exploring party had arrived at Summer's House, forty-six miles from Blair's, "today after many detentions on the way up from the want of feed. The party seem to be all good explorers; they will start tomorrow morning up the Horse Fly, keep south of the range on their prospecting expedition, and will not get back here for a month at least. I have every confidence in their succeeding in their enterprise. Macdonald is one of the discoverers of Leech River." This note, signed merely "Prospector," continued on with other news, but this is the only notice the author has seen officially crediting MacDonald with the Sooke gold discovery at Leech River.

XXIV

MacDonald and the "Mile Houses"

As early as there were prospectors hiking up the trails or trudging along on horseback, there were crude roadhouses where a man could obtain supplies and a hot meal. The Cariboo Road spawned a series of such hostelries known as "Mile Houses." While the contractors were building the Cariboo Wagon Road, they put down mile markers first indicating mileage from Lillooet, and then from Yale when the later routing bypassed Lillooet from Lytton north.

One of the very first hotels was McLean's, adjacent to MacDonald's ranch, later known as Hat Creek House (mentioned earlier). Others went by the names of their mile markers—70 Mile, 100 Mile, 108 Mile, 122 Mile and 150 Mile (both favorites), some of them still standing in good condition. Generally speaking, they were located at the junctions of trails leading into the Cariboo Road or where there was good grazing for teams. Like hotels everywhere, facilities and the cuisine varied widely, the good ones starving out those that did not measure up to the miners' few standards—mostly, dry and warm sleeping places, usually several men comfortably housed together, and hearty, basic, tasty food. Art Downs in his first edition of *Wagon Road North* relates the story of a miner visiting the hotel at Beaver Lake between Williams Lake and Quesnel in 1863: "When the supper bell rang I went in with the crowd. At the head of the table was a large roast of beef and scattered over the table were dishes containing all kinds of vegetables. The milk and cream placed on the table were not only plentiful but of the very best. Sellars [co-owner of the place] pointed to a large huckleberry pie, supported by a dish of fresh cream, and said to me, 'This is your supper.'"

Sometimes at other mile houses, travelers had to deal with drunken bedfellows, noisy companions who played cards all night, or cold houses with no beds, and sleeping where one could—but at least they were sheltered from the elements. In the later days of the Cariboo Road, after stage service was established, it was not uncommon for French chefs to be hired—their superb cuisine attracting patrons to one mile house instead of another.

At Deep Creek Ranch, a Harry Jones of the Hudson's Bay Company was recorded to be traveling with a Mr. MacDonald in 1863; with Ranald's Hudson's Bay connections, one cannot help but wonder if it was he. The two men were noted as arriving at Soda Creek, as well, where Peter Dunleavy had established a popular hotel.

With the good education provided him at the Red River settlement and experience in banking at St. Thomas, Ontario, it was natural that Ranald would gravitate to the roadhouse business. It is likely that he abandoned packing in 1866 after he returned from the Vancouver Island Expedition and the later assignment into the Horsefly country. His first venture as a hotelier was at Hat Creek House, purchased that year by George Dunne from Sophie McLean. Dunne started out smartly by adding a second story to the roadhouse, capitalizing on his good location at a changing point for the stage from Lillooet as it joined the Cariboo route. Ranald was hired as the manager or accountant. Unfortunately, Dunne was forced to mortgage the property for $2,000 to Jerome Harper in 1873, subsequently defaulting.

In the 1870's, Ranald worked for the Bonaparte House, owned by Semlin and Parke, at the junction of the Big Bend trail and Cariboo Road and at the extreme south end of today's town of Cache Creek. This was a busy location handling traffic to and from Kamloops from the main Cariboo Road. Either as part of his managerial duties or as a separate concession, Ranald handled freight matters for the F. J. Barnard Company. The Cariboo freight service, taken over in 1879 by ex-driver and part owner Steve Tingley, became popularly known as the BX Express—an enterprise that thrived until replaced in the 1900's by motorized vehicles.

The founder of the BX Express, F. J. Barnard, was a man of vision. From Quebec but of American parentage, he joined the gold rush in 1859, arriving at Yale with five dollars in his pocket. He cut and hauled wood and became a policeman, handcuffing prisoners to tree stumps since there was no jailhouse. Soon he saw there was more promise in freighting than in working his way north to prospect. With only one competitor of note, a Billy Ballou, Barnard first carried mail and small packages on foot, then by horse. When the government awarded Barnard the mail contract to Barkerville in 1862, Ballou was forced to quit and Barnard had a virtual monopoly on anything that moved. His service, the F. J. Barnard Company, became to the Cariboo what Wells Fargo was to the American West.

Barnard's business grew to include a manager—Steve Tingley, mentioned above. Raising capital from local businessmen, Barnard sent Tingley to purchase two hundred horses in Oregon and several stages from San Francisco. In the spring of 1864, driver Charles G. Major on the first 14-passenger stage traveled from Yale to Soda Creek near old Fort Alexandria, changing horses every thirteen miles. The first passengers included Robert Stevenson, who had been instrumental in the Cameron claim at Barkerville. Out of necessity, roadhouses or mile houses grew at the stopping points, some of them numbered now from Yale instead of Lillooet.

At Soda Creek, passengers transferred to the new steamers for a trip to Quesnel on the Fraser River, which was relatively placid in this area, then it was back to a stagecoach once more into Barkerville.

The stages carried gold—$600,000 of the stuff on one trip. Another stage carried a gold ingot cast in the form of an artillery shell, weighing 650 pounds and worth $178,000. By the end of the first twelve months, the express had carried $4.6 million of gold and 1,500 passengers.

The horses, well fed and brushed, sometimes with their hooves blackened and shined, had been selected and trained for one thing only—pulling stagecoaches. Accounts tell of the procedure in leaving a stage station. First the mail, express and passengers were loaded onto the stage, and the driver climbed onto his seat. Only then were the horses led out, harnessed to the stage and the lines passed to the driver. The brakes were released and the horses lunged forward; some horses would rear and behave so wildly that one would fear a complete wreck. However, they careered along for only a short way, then settled down into a ground-covering trot.

The Concord stages purchased from California were strengthened to meet the rigors of the Cariboo Road, which often was just a pair of ruts sprinkled liberally with rocks. It was a thrilling trip for passengers. At Yale, after a breakfast of ham, eggs and flapjacks known as "Rocky Mountain deadshot," the stage was boarded. The best seats in nice weather were outside with the driver and the guards, where a passenger could vicariously share in Cariboo life through the hair-raising stories told by the driver. The Cariboo Road through the Fraser Canyon, hanging sometimes literally along the cliff, afforded an all-too-clear view of the raging waters below. There were tunnels along the way and sections of the road were hewn from the rock itself. Although the stages had a surprisingly good safety record, on March 3, 1881, veteran driver Alexander Tingley went over a cliff below Spuzzum in the Fraser Canyon. Two passengers received broken legs, two horses were killed, but Tingley was unhurt. Two months later, on May 26, Tingley tried to work his way past a rockfall but caught a front wheel of his four-horse coach on a rock and toppled the stage. A passenger tried to stop the coach from going over the edge of the cliff by putting his shoulder against it and was flung over the bank, fetching up against a tree which prevented him from falling the rest of the way down the cliff. But a disaster for the stage was averted. At times the stage would travel through violent mountain storms, raise clouds of alkali dust, or struggle through deep snow in below-zero temperatures.

In 1871, Barnard tried to use huge steam-operated cars on the Cariboo Road, ordering six big tractors and six engines from England. The investment was a disaster; the first one could not make it over Jackass Mountain in the Fraser Canyon. The rest were scrapped; one remained to become the first logging tractor in the British Columbia logging camps, hauling downed trees near Vancouver at Little Mountain, Capilano and Shaughnessy.

At the roadhouses, payment would be made in gold dust carried in leather bags, although English sovereigns were plentiful and, later, small gold dollars were coined. There were few robberies, partly because the British Columbia police placed guards on the stages during times of large shipments; furthermore, with such rugged country and few trails, a criminal simply had difficulty in escaping. When captured, the trial was swift and punishment sudden.

But the days of the stages were numbered. The railroad was coming—or at least there was fevered speculation about when it would come, if it would come, and where it would go.

Those were halcyon years for the Cariboo. Even as America reeled from the bloody Civil War of 1861-1865, and the eastern Canadian provinces simply believed there was no civilization west of Winnipeg (and barely there), the British Columbia colony bumbled along comfortably, growing steadily. Because of the lack of practical overland transcontinental transportation, anyone traveling to British Columbia from eastern North America either went via the Isthmus of Panama, or later, by railroad to San Francisco and north by steamship. No wonder the lovely lands, temperate and rich in resources, went largely unnoticed by the British and French of eastern "Canada."

Cariboo residents, now connected by The Road, thought nothing of traveling for days to attend a good party, dancing well into the night, or, indeed, all night. Dances in winter might continue for two or three days, with visitors sleeping on the floor rolled in blankets. A courtly, well-mannered, and handsome man, Ranald was well-liked, especially by the ladies, who were charmed by his manners learned so well in the days of St. Thomas, Ontario, and before. He danced and—on at least one occasion—fought with the best of them. A tough named McCune challenged Ranald, for some pretext, to a fight and—with bare fists—did knock down the equally proficient fighter Ranald. Undaunted, Ranald challenged him to a rematch naming any weapons he chose, suggesting single sticks. McCune agreed and, with a three-foot club, Ranald outmaneuvered McCune deftly and administered a thorough drubbing. Not a good loser, McCune spread the word that he could lose to his equal but hated to lose to a "Siwash." It was a new and hurtful experience for Ranald—educated as a Scotsman though equally proud of his Indian heritage—to be spoken of in derogatory fashion. The name stuck, and for years he was referred to as "Siwash" MacDonald. Used by cohorts, it was a friendly and good-natured term with no overtones of discrimination; there were so many MacDonalds in the Cariboo, some related, some not, that it seemed a handy distinguishing term. After all, the majority of the Hudson's Bay men had taken Indian wives and properly educated their children, and mixed blood was exceedingly common in British Columbia.

Changes in fortune during these Cariboo years seemed to little change Ranald's operations; he was known as a "good sport," a man always ready to help out a friend, entertain the ladies, or engage in the gambling and comaraderie in the saloons that formed the mainstay of recreational life of the mining and ranching communities.

The Cariboo was and is a gentle and beautiful place, far superior in climate to the extremes of the East, although there could be severe blizzards in winter or breathless heat in summer. The rolling hills interspersed with trees supported rich grasses, where deer, bear, and small game thrived to provide food for the shooting. The rivers teemed with fish, the marshes with birds of every description. Who could want for more?

For ten years or more, Ranald MacDonald lived a rather ordinary life in the towns and valleys of central British Columbia as a part of the mining and transportation community—not particularly influencing it, but moving through it and mingling at times with old Hudson's Bay friends, some in high places.

Ranald's adventures of a quarter century ago largely went unnoticed, except in the telling around a snapping fire on a Cariboo night—until Malcolm McLeod, the family barrister, launched his own private campaign through the Canadian press to encourage the building of a railroad across the nation. Suddenly, in 1869, the grand adventures of Ranald MacDonald were spread through Eastern newspapers as grist for McLeod's contentions under the assumed name of "Britannicus." From special data and personal knowledge, McLeod was advocating the building of a transcontinental railroad.

Difficult as it is to conceive, it appears that Ranald himself knew nothing about this until 1889, when he wrote to McLeod noting that "he had not contacted him for a quarter century" (i. e., since his comradeship with McLeod after returning from Australia). From McLeod's files in the British Columbia Provincial Archives, it seems that he, at least, had written to MacDonald during that period; but perhaps Ranald never received the letter.

XXV

Ranald's Adventures and the Canadian Pacific Railroad

With communication tenuous at best, the family barrister, Malcolm McLeod, lost track of Ranald MacDonald for at least two decades after the return of the MacDonald brothers to St. Andrews. Until about 1889, McLeod believed Ranald to be dead or lost, in one case indicating that he thought Ranald had returned to Australia. By 1889, however, Ranald and McLeod reestablished contact at long last.

Meanwhile, like most Canadians in the East, McLeod had for decades keenly followed the machinations of the politicians that led to the decision to build a railway across the nation. The matter of a railroad was all caught up in the stirrings of nationalism as, one by one, individual provinces joined the Confederation of Canada. It must be remembered that until 1871 British Columbia still was *British*, not Canadian; the move for a Dominion of Canada was a gradual affair, and railroads were a part of the inducement for provinces to join.

It all began, really, at both extremes, east and west. In the Maritimes, the provinces of New Brunswick and Nova Scotia were promised an Intercolonial Railway to link Halifax with Montreal, if they were to join the Confederation called Canada. These two provinces joined on July 1, 1867, followed by Manitoba in 1870. For British Columbia, it was essential to end the isolation due to the rugged Rocky Mountains and the vast plains if the Pacific coastal colony were to join the Confederation. Fearing that the colony would align itself with the United States, which was a more natural north/south commercial connection, the Dominion of Canada promised British Columbia it would begin constructing a railway within two years of union with the Confederation and complete it within ten years. Thus, British Columbia became a province in 1871. This event reestablished, in a sense, a venerable commercial link that had been partially severed during the decline of the Hudson's Bay Company's fur traffic—that of a shipping path from the British West over and through the mountains to Hudson's Bay and thereafter by ship to Europe.

Canada did try mightily to keep its promise, immediately holding a conference as to the solution of three main problems: (1) where to build the railway, (2) how to raise the capital, and (3) how to maintain control of the venture while soliciting assistance from American firms for capital and railroad-building. A lightly populated country, Canada simply did not have a well of construction experience nor sufficient financiers.

Years before the admission of British Columbia into the Confederation, talk of a transcontinental line was popular drawing-room speculation around the trading post stove. As a native son of the Northwest reflecting on earlier days, Ranald MacDonald said in 1889 that he had attempted to impress upon the Japanese, among other things, that the advancements made by Western nations in improvements in commerce and knowledge would soon be extended to Asia and bring advantages to them. "For at that early date," he continued in a letter to a recontacted Malcolm McLeod, "I had heard of the possibility of having a Rail-Road across the continent—the Pacific slope was then a wilderness." San Francisco would be the terminus, he had thought in the early 1840's, but when he visited there, he saw only a handful of adobe shacks. Then he considered the mouth of the Columbia River at Astoria the logical terminus. Later he explored today's western British Columbia with an eye for potential routes. When liberated from Nagasaki, Ranald stated that he suggested to Commodore Glynn of the *Preble* that, if the Americans ever returned to Japan for friendly conversations, they should bring with them models of inventions— proof of Western ingenuity.

It is likely that he discussed with Malcolm McLeod his deep interest in commercial contacts when he visited St. Andrews upon his return from Australia in 1853. The two men had become fast friends, since McLeod was responsible for introducing Ranald to Masonic Lodge No. 516 of St. Andrews, where he subsequently became a Master Mason.

Looking back, Malcolm McLeod was a somewhat enigmatic figure. To some, he was merely a rabble-rouser, quick to speak and write his views; to others, he was a largely unrecognized visionary, never credited with the influence he had in developing the western lands. He was born in 1830, and raised in the primitive lands around Fort McLeod north of Fort George toward the Peace River, where his father John was a Chief Factor. After the coalition of the Hudson's Bay Company and the North West Company, John McLeod was the first official from the Hudson's Bay Company to cross the Rocky Mountains and accept "delivery of the country" from the North West Company. Like Ranald and many other early Hudson's Bay offspring, McLeod's mother was of partially native blood. When he was a mere nine years of age, McLeod was sent to England to study under Dr. Boyd of Edinburg, returning to Montreal to be admitted to the bar of Quebec in 1845. Although he was a district magistrate between 1871 and 1879 for the District of Ottawa (resigning because there was insufficient salary) and a Queen's Counsel in 1887, McLeod's legal career was quite ordinary. A friend, T.P. Foran, of Hull, Quebec, said of him:

"He was a tall, spare-looking man, but, in conversation, is one of the liveliest and most interesting men I ever met. His knowledge of the North-west dated, as he was fond of telling, from the time when he moved along the banks of the McKenzie River on his mother's back."

Foran credited McLeod's early experiences for his adamant belief that a railway could be built through the Peace River Valley. McLeod had an extensive legal knowledge, according to Foran, but sometimes had difficulty in applying those legal principles properly to actual cases. But, "he never did an unkindness to anyone. As far as this world's worldly goods were concerned, he could not keep them and, when a wave of prosperity would come to him, he was as reckless as any Indian in squandering his money. Vices he had none."

McLeod was more a political writer than a brilliant lawyer. As such, the actual influence of his writings on Canadian events is impossible to assess; however, the ongoing publication of his articles in the *Montreal Gazette* and *Toronto Times*, major newspapers of the day, is significant.

In 1862, McLeod first came to the "podium" preparing a formal memorial, as essays or appeals then were termed, before Parliament concerning the need for annexation of the Red River settlement. He stated that the area (now Winnipeg) was in a state of anarchy, that the Hudson's Bay Company was not doing a proper job, and local residents wanted a government of some kind. The appeal by McLeod and others fell on deaf ears, because at the time the government was opposed to any western extension of Canada.

Undefeated, McLeod addressed the Colonial Secretary from Britain, the Duke of Newcastle, on the subject, enclosing petitions that immediate action of some kind should be taken by the Imperial government to establish a government there other than an HBC colony. Such papers were taken seriously. Shortly thereafter, in July, 1862, the duke brought the matter before the House of Lords, condemning the Hudson's Bay Company for improper management of the Red River settlement. Cohorts agreed and suggested withdrawal of the company's charter. Such censure certainly caused company officials to review and correct its practices for the better. Had they not done so, the company itself might have fallen into the hands of an eagerly awaiting syndicate of American fur traders headed by Sir Lampson Miranda Curtis.

One of the chief problems in connecting the West to the entrenched settlements of Ontario and Quebec was the yawning wilderness—not necessarily between Winnipeg and British Columbia, broad as that might be—but between Winnipeg and Toronto, a treacherous, swampy area more water than land, it seemed. Few could conceive of any road or railroad across this morass, where—making matters worse—any solid ground was rock. Travelers customarily detoured around the mosquito-ridden, half-unexplored, spongy terrain. They travelled via today's Detroit, Michigan, thence through the Great Lakes to Lake Superior, and overland to the Red River trail that was well established north and south from Minneapolis and St. Paul into Winnipeg. When railroads eventually accommodated this route, it served travelers all the better.

Politically, railway building was conceived as a way for government officials to stay in business. Between 1854 and 1857, a variety of railway building schemes sopped as much as a hundred million dollars of foreign capital, most of it uselessly and much finding its way into the coffers of promoters. According to an entertaining book largely about the political aspects of the transcontinental railway of Canada, *The National Dream*, the usual scheme was to form a company, keep control of it, float as much stock as possible and then award lush construction contracts to men on the inside. Would-be railway contractors dispensed champagne as freely as if it were water.

In a letter to the Honorable J. S. McDonald, Premier of Ontario, dated December 13, 1867, Malcolm McLeod pointed to the information he recalled from his father and other traders as a Factor's child—he remembered cowboys driving cattle into the Cariboo via a practicable Leather Pass (Yellowhead Pass) in the Rocky Mountains. He discussed the prospective western boundary of Canada vs. British territory, saying that, if it were established as suggested (due north from the source of the Mississippi, Lake Itasca, in Minnesota), the boundary would leave Rainy Lake and other parts of the Red River settlement's (Winnipeg's) watershed in Ontario.

By 1869, numerous schemes sifted out into more solid conjectures and plans as to where to build. It is this aspect to which Malcolm McLeod addressed himself, commencing a series of essays and letters published in the *Gazette* and *Times* intensively in 1869, and extending intermittently until 1875. His works were signed under the pseudonym "Britannicus." In a flowery, somewhat rambling style typical of nineteenth-century newspaper journalism, McLeod's first letter of May 27, 1869, began by quoting an early railroad seer, Major Robert Carmichael Smyth, a member of the Royal Engineers. After travel in Canada, Smyth said in 1849 that England should begin to unite "this wondrous empire on which the solar orb never sets," by building a railway across it. Never mind that this was a time when railroads were effective only on relatively level ground, and that no engines and rails had yet tried the leap over large mountains. Smyth conjectured that constructing a railway would give "remunerative employment to the population, to the wealth and to the inventive genius of England," would hold Oregon against the Americans and thereby secure a Pacific port, and could be a means for removing citizens from overcrowded places such as London to the wide open spaces. He thought that the government would receive a return on its investment sufficient to repay construction costs.

McLeod (on June 27, 1869) went on to describe a practical route for a railroad from Montreal to Bella Coola (the western terminus which Ranald had explored), visualizing a line more or less on the fifty-third parallel—figuratively a direct line from Liverpool to the British Columbia Cariboo country and the port of Bella Coola, sailing on in his imagination over the ocean to "Nankin (mid-China) and Jeddo [Tokyo] (mid-Japan)." He touted the abundance of coal along this route, whereas the American line (the Union Pacific/Central Pacific completed in 1869) had little; and the similarity of climate all along the line, "that on the Northern route one could travel from Pekin to London in the same garments." Before closing, he took a further swing at the American line, saying that it was authentically reported to be of cheap and hurried construction and scarcely safe—where the one across Canada would be a "thorough English road; substantial, well appointed and offering every security and efficiency." From the beginning and without wavering, McLeod's writings preached fervently against any involvement with Americans, fearing being swallowed by them as Jonah was by the whale. Some felt that the transcontinental line should connect partially through American rail lines, or utilize ships on the Great Lakes. Not McLeod. His preferred routes would be all-Canadian—no detours through the United States.

On December 19, 1869, McLeod closed a letter with the ringing declaration, "Commerce is power. Yes! and by it, and it alone can the seas, and in the seas, the isles, and other teeming shores be ruled. Give to the United States, with their immense material resources and wondrous vitality and enterprise, the monopoly, practically, of the transit trade between the two oceans, and they in a trice, will cover the seas. Then, the Great Republic will 'march the deep' . . . hold and use as her own the ocean-link which her Canadian sons propose to forge her, and her flag may for another thousand years safely brave all battle and the breeze."

Profoundly influenced by his earlier conversations with Ranald MacDonald, McLeod continued to promote the connection through a

Pacific port with a shipping line bound for the Orient—which actually did take place within a few years and operated in lively fashion for decades until airlines forced retrenchment of the steamship lines.

McLeod made few friends among the railway promoters with his adamant opposition to the giving of land grants. Most schemes involved donating large blocks of Canada's public lands to the Canadian Pacific Railway as part of the payment tendered. One proposal involved alternate blocks extending twenty miles from the rails; in others, extravagant awards of lands were to be picked from the best in the area—if those adjacent to the rails were not favorable for settlement. Of course, the local Indian tribes were startled to learn of such dispositions . . .

McLeod's view was that the "Mother Earth" is for cultivation and settlement. He wanted England or the "young fiduciary, the Dominion of Canada," to people the West with freehold husbandmen—free land grants or homesteads to such people—asserting that subsequent revenues for shipping and passengers would soon pay for construction costs. He grew expansive:

"But we may, for the second or third years of function double that item, and ever afterwards more than treble it; for the Mandarin of China, the Taja of Japan, rich, intelligent, and, at last, new awakened as from a long, long sleep, eager to see, and realize their dreams of the world and the hitherto hidden wonders thereof; yea, the essentially commercial masses of the Chinese and Japanese proper—the latter, to a man, all readers and writers, and of a most sprightly intelligence and social disposition. Yea, half the globe itself, and that the most active part, will seek travel." He went on to call attention to the organization of the new Pacific Steamship Line aimed at the China and Japan trade, capitalized for ten million dollars, mostly by Californians.

In his stand on land grants, his own editors vied hotly with him; from 1869 to 1873, readers were entertained by the spectacle of the editor of the *Montreal Gazette* arguing in print with his Britannicus "columnist" McLeod, with the editor finally saying, in essence, this is the last of the argument; we do not want to hear any more on this subject.

Earlier, the highly respected Sandford Fleming, who laid out the Northern Railroad from Toronto to Collingwood, had presented his own plan to the government for a route across the country. This was no guesswork, but an orderly analysis—as far as could be achieved since the precise route was undecided. Well acquainted with Malcolm McLeod, Sandford Fleming consulted with him as to recommended routes—a meeting forming McLeod's later abortive and prolonged effort at compensation for his part in the creation of the Canadian Pacific Railway.

Once the decision was made at high levels to maintain an all-Canadian route, engineers heaved an apprehensive sigh but knew they could manage to muck across the uncertain ground between Ontario and Manitoba. The main decision yet to be made was where to breach the Rocky Mountains. McLeod favored a northerly skirting of the highest of them, south of the Peace River and southwesterly through Pine Pass. He was influenced in this regard by the place of his birth being near that area. Also considered were Yellowhead (later used for the Canadian National Railway), Athabasca, and Kicking Horse. The latter, the most southerly pass, was selected, with secondary Rogers Pass farther southwest to wind toward the Cariboo country through an ingenious tunnel that swept downhill as it made a 360-degree turn. The tunnel is still in use today.

As indicated in a previous chapter, railway survey parties were a boon to the trading posts at Kamloops, including that of Christina MacDonald, aided by her cousin Ranald. Indeed, in later years and to the present time, Kamloops has been an important point on the Canadian Pacific Railway.

The first group to arrive in Kamloops was an official survey party under Dr. A. R. C. Selwyn, including engineer Walter Moberly, on August 9, 1871. The post was the marshaling point for explorations of the North Thompson, Tete Jaune Cache, Shuswap, and Eagle Pass. In 1872 and later, further exploration and construction parties came. These included the famous, such as George M. Grant, who later published his journals of the explorations, and Marcus Smith, who became Chief Engineer of the Pacific Section after Moberly.

The Canadian Pacific Railway established a large commissary in Kamloops to feed, house and equip their workers, with John McLennan in charge; in 1872, the Hudson's Bay Company billed McLennan for $2,000 worth of supplies. This boon was to change rapidly, as the firm of Mara and Wilson (the former a political figure) muscled in on the trade. But the independent trader, Christina MacDonald, held her own nicely.

Of equal steamy discussion throughout Canada was the site for the Pacific terminus. In earlier surveys, Waddington touted a route to Bute Inlet, and MacDonald's Bentinck Arm expedition (originally made for a road but kept active for a rail route) would have it end at the port of Bella Coola. McLeod in a "Britannicus" letter in January, 1874, continued to plug for his Peace River/Pine Pass routing, with Bella Coola as a Pacific port. In a laborious analysis, McLeod gave figures on Pacific Rim immigration prospects and trade returns from different countries—comparing them to the United States' trade returns with those same countries. He said, "The most marked feature in the above tables is the exhibit of enormous balance of trade, in products and manufactures, against both Britain and the United States, and yet it is much less than it used to be. Both pay largely, most largely, in coin (principally silver, I believe) for their imports from China and Japan. This balance must, I humbly consider, naturally diminish." Such imbalances still existed late in the twentieth century, however.

As part of McLeod's Britannicus letter was his story of Ranald MacDonald giving an "on-the-spot" sort of report regarding the Orient. McLeod indicated that he had written a manuscript for publication twenty-one years earlier, including a glossary of over five-hundred Japanese words and phrases, from material given him by Ranald in about 1853 and edited considerably by McLeod. McLeod maintained that the rejection for publication of the manuscript was because the United States government printed details of the "Commodore Preble expedition" (actually the *Preble* expedition commanded by Commodore Glynn).

McLeod explained, "In writing up the work I had to look into all available works on Japan, and the trade—and general foreign policy of that country, and also of its neighbour China. I was drawn to the little (a leisure) task, by the story, with a few notes, and a well told narration from an old native born British Columbian, Mr. Ranald McDonald [*sic*]... Let me give his story, briefly, as I gave it once before in my Britannicus letter No. 7, giving an account of his exploration and charter right for a waggon road with tollage from Bellacoola (Pacific tide water) to Cariboo, in 1862." He proceeded then to summarize Ranald's Japanese travels, concluding with, "I give this episode, to show that my humble authority [as to the Bella Coola route vs. the Bute Inlet road of Waddington] is not quite a nonentity... They [the Japanese], in fact, in heart and mind, are the British of the East. They require but the *iron link* to bind them in cognate bonds."

At this time, the first American Pacific Steamship line to the Orient had completed its initial year with a return of three million dollars in freight, plus an estimated two more million in passenger revenue. McLeod mentioned that tea was one of the biggest potential items for trade. His further assertion was that, should the railway be built, a million settlers would live along its rails by the time it was finished.

McLeod praised the Bella Coola idea as a site for a railway terminal, and criticized ports being considered further south. As far as Burrard Inlet was concerned or any other lower mainland port such as Victoria or New Westminster, McLeod—somewhat paranoid, it seems, about the intentions of the Americans in Puget Sound—asserted that it was unsafe to use a harbor on Georgia Strait because "the San Juan channel [from the Pacific Ocean through the Strait of Juan de Fuca and northward into then British waters] leads only to

British waters, British shores, British ports, and a British Province—the American is erecting forts on that impregnable fortress rock-isle [San Juan Island], with its thousand feet hill top, all ready for batteries of Rodmans, fit to sink, in one short day, all the navies in the world. A fearful fact!" If the terminus were in Bute, Burrard's or anywhere else on Georgian Gulf, he said, American guns would command its western terminus. There were, of course, small American and British garrisons at each end of San Juan Island. They spent lazy days exchanging social visits more than producing hostilities—almost coming to blows only briefly over the uprooting of a settler's potatoes by an errant pig. Through peaceful mediation by Kaiser Wilhelm, the boundary channel through the San Juans was delineated in 1872.

In his zeal and enthusiasm for a transcontinental railway, Malcolm McLeod combined his Britannicus letters into a pamphlet and gave away many copies to influential people. To amplify his campaign for the Peace River area, or Pine Pass, only eighteen hundred feet in altitude (actually 935 meters, or around three thousand feet), he published—apparently at his own expense—the entire narrative of Archibald McDonald's trip with Sir George Simpson in 1828, *Peace River. A Canoe Voyage from Hudson's Bay to Pacific* . . . , distributing copies broadly. Prefacing the account, he asserts—quite accurately and with considerable foresight, considering later economic developments—that instead of limited fertility in the North-west, there was an area of over three hundred million acres of potential croplands, forests, coal and gold fields adjacent to the Peace, Athabasca and McKenzie Rivers. Indeed, late in the twentieth century, the vast northeast coal fields south of the Peace River on Tumbler Ridge were being mined.

"The Widow and legal representatives of my lamented friend the late Chief Factor A. McDonald have, with a public spirit which commends itself, allowed me the use of his 'Notes,' as he calls them."

McLeod added other commentary on Sandford Fleming's survey report, of which he had received a copy. He was delighted to learn that a surveyor, R. McLennan, had penetrated the North Thompson River Valley, heretofore un-explored, and points out that the suggested route is essentially that of his Britannicus letter #7. He praised the surveyors, saying, "What the Americans took about *ten years* to do, we, with really greater difficulties to cope with, have done—and well done, so far—in ten *months*, or less!" He went on to dream of a cart road as well as a railroad to open up the verdant land for immigrant wagons. "At every halting place, at every step, in that truly golden way—a stretch of almost continuously level sward fifteen hundred miles in length—nature, all bountiful, has, in a manner, strewed her manna, and abundance is *there, all along*, for man, and for the animals that serve him."

In a renewed series of Britannicus letters during 1875, McLeod tackled, with considerable smoke and brimstone, the matter of "The MacDonald Contract" (Sir John MacDonald, Premier of Canada) vs. "The Mackenzie Scheme." Both involved land grant ideas, but he favored the MacDonald plans, while castigating MacKenzie's. Then, too, he continued his oratory about an *all-Canadian* line, ocean to ocean, assailing part of the MacKenzie idea of building a railroad to Lake Superior and then to Winnipeg, and also a line to Pembina on the international border from Winnipeg—which McLeod believed to be selling out to the Americans. His contention was that a railroad farther north was about a thousand miles shorter ocean to ocean than anywhere else on the North American continent, excepting Mexico, and that a straight line route should come out—more or less— near the northern tip of Vancouver Island. He related in letter #6 of his series, "looking at the work in its bearing as an Inter-Oceanic Highway . . . between the great 'sailing arc,' as laid down by Naury and others, across the North Atlantic and Pacific Oceans, our line from Halifax to some port near the northwestern end of Vancouver's Island, would be that of nearest connection . . . should command a fair share of the vast traffic of the Pacific." The Winnipeg-Pembina line, he growled, was of no use to anyone except the Americans, where it would provide a dandy ingress for military aggression.

Impartially praising and condemning railway entrepreneurs, promoters and politicians, McLeod printed another pamphlet in 1876: "Pacific Railway, Extra Tax for It, Not Necessary," the title itself being explanatory. And in 1880 came, "The Problem of Canada," a compilation of data on diverse matters, and largely a summary of railway matters already covered in other works.

Whether demagogue or patriot, McLeod must be judged by his Canadian and British brothers and sisters. To his credit, he seems to have been one of the chief voices calling for a Canadian transcontinental railway for at least a crucial ten-year period, and his writings certainly were influenced by his conversations in St. Andrews after Ranald MacDonald returned from Japan. Since he also seemed familiar with Ranald's explorations in the Cariboo, he probably learned the details from Allan or Ben MacDonald after they returned east.

As early as 1883, McLeod initiated requests to the Canadian government for remuneration. In his opinion, he had aided significantly in the efforts to secure a feasible route through the mountains and had shared his knowledge with Sandford Fleming and others.

His repeated pleas for some form of recompense, both privately and publicly, were politely discussed but tabled. In a printed "Memorial to the Government and Parliament of Canada" (1889), McLeod asked for indemnity—among other reasons—on the basis that on May 19, 1871, Sandford Fleming asked him for help, "expenses to be paid," per a telegram enclosed as evidence. In response, McLeod turned over to Fleming masses of information from personal knowledge and from private journals, including papers of his father and of Archibald McDonald, about parts of British Columbia never before surveyed. McLeod claimed that this data enabled Fleming to give sensible instructions to his survey parties. Signed certificates from Fleming were enclosed to support the argument. McLeod maintained that Fleming had suggested to him that it would be a good idea to publish information about the Peace River, which he did, including a map—and that he published pamphlets at his own expense and distributed them in England, Australia and Canada.

He had staunch support for his position. According to Fleming's certificate, "But for you, I may say, it is just possible that we might have known very little about the Peace River Region at the present day and—although the region may not be opened up by railways for some time it certainly weighed very heavily in the scales when the question of the route of the Pacific Railway was under consideration a few years ago . . . I FEEL THE PUBLIC IS DEEPLY IN YOUR DEBT." Ex-Governor Sir James Douglas said, "Your notes and tables of distance must have been of immense service to Fleming," and mentioned the extreme importance of his literary contributions. Ex-Lieutenant Governor Alexander Morris said, "I regarded you . . . as rendering very important service to the country."

Despite such powerful allies, it appears that McLeod's claims were to no avail. In one instance, there seemed to be no record of any such telegram from Fleming, since papers and books of the Canadian Pacific Railway were burned in 1873. (Perhaps, the purported telegram, attached as evidence, was McLeod's own copy.) With no signed contract encouraging him to write and campaign for the Canadian Pacific Railway, McLeod was in the position of a merely interested writer on the subject. His only lasting satisfaction was a personal one: that he (and certainly Ranald MacDonald, too) had played a part in welding Canada into one nation, and in spurring the establishment of commerce with Japan and China through the completion of the Canadian Pacific Railway—the last spike driven by Honorable Donald Alexander Smith at Craigellachie on November 7, 1885. Appointed by the Canadian Pacific Railway in 1882 to build the railway across Canada, a task many thought downright ludicrous, William Cornelius Van Horne then made a fifteen-word speech: "All I can say is that the work has been well done in every way."

XXVI
Ranching at Fort Colvile

In 1877, Ranald moved to Kamloops to help his cousin with her accounts. The adventurer who had scorned an accountant's post at Ermatinger's bank in St. Thomas so many years ago continued to use his talents at record-keeping.

As one of British Columbia's earliest female entrepreneurs, Christina MacDonald took over the trading post of her husband, James McKenzie, after his death in 1873, continuing successfully to run the business for a few years. It was a busy time for supply posts, since the railroad fever was at a high pitch. As indicated in the prior chapter, McLennan, Moberly, Tupper, and other railroad figures were supplied at Kamloops.

Christina, Ranald's cousin, was a daughter of Angus McDonald, Chief Trader at Fort Colvile for two separate periods until its closing in 1871-2. Her mother was Catherine Baptiste, daughter of a Frenchman employed by the Hudson's Bay Company and his high-born Nez Perce wife. Obviously a favorite of her father and of lively intellect, she often traveled with Angus as he went about his business or was present when he entertained important guests—such as Washington Territorial Governor Isaac Stevens, Captain George B. McClellan, or Chief Kamiakin of the Yakimas. Angus was very much the "Scotch laird," according to Christina, entertaining with grace and style and insisting on the best manners from his children.

As she grew older, she often acted as interpreter for him and helped him in his business dealings. In her memoirs, Christina laughed about Angus' penchant for bagpipe music because, when the Indians first heard the skirl of pipes played by Angus' friend, they ran away in fright—thinking there was a big fight going on.

There in the wilderness of northeast Washington, her companions were her brothers, Indian children and adults. Christina grew up—like her cousin Ranald—to be wild, free and independent. She was a superb horsewoman and loved to race against soldiers (from Fort Colville, the army post located south of the HBC's Fort Colvile), persons at the Hudson's Bay post, and with the children of other settlers. Among the racing stock were fine horses, including

imported French roan horses called "sandrien" by the French employees—
tough, hardy, trotting horses that could clock a three-minute mile.

In the 1860's, Christina accompanied her father to Portland to discuss with the Americans the settlement of the Hudson's Bay Company
claims under the treaty of 1846. They travelled across eastern Washington
by hack pulled by one of Angus' finest teams. At the Snake River, the two
embarked on the steamer *Idaho*, transferring to other steamers and hacks
until they reached Astoria.

There she and her father met with a Mr. Johnson of the United States
party, as well as Dr. William Tolmie of the Hudson's Bay Company. On a
sightseeing trip around the area, Dr. Tolmie pointed out the site of Fort
George, then little more than rubble, saying this was the place of her cousin
Ranald's birth. Later she stayed for almost a month at Fort Vancouver—a
splendid place, well furnished and with excellent table service. After Angus
had completed all his business, he and his daughter returned upriver only
to find that the fine team they had left near the steamboat landing on the
Snake River had been stolen.

On another occasion, Christina was traveling with her father across a
lake, when the raft on which the party was riding disintegrated, throwing
everyone into the water. A good swimmer, Christina calmly grabbed records
and books belonging to the company and took them ashore. A grateful
Hudson's Bay employee named the lake after her, Christina Lake, now
north of the international border in British Columbia.

Around 1869, Christina married James McKenzie, the last clerk at Fort
Colvile before its abandonment in 1871-2. It was at Fort Colvile where the
accounts for the Columbia and New Caledonia operations were retained before shipment to HBC headquarters. When Fort Colvile officially closed, the
young couple traveled with the precious records plus considerable gold dust to
Victoria, where they deposited the valuables at the company's offices. Thereafter the pair was posted to Kamloops, McKenzie being designated as Chief
Trader. With Christina's past knowledge of the company's dealings, she
was of considerable help to him, although she spent an equal amount of
time with her father, who was alone at Fort Colvile pending his move to
Montana. Angus' wife and other children had gone ahead in 1870. Turning the post over to Christina's brother, Donald, as a residence and as the
potential site for a new town, Angus retired to become a rancher.

Meanwhile, Christina's husband died in 1873, leaving her as administrator of his estate. To the surprise of most everyone, she elected to run
McKenzie's private trading post (opened after he left the company), giving
the rival Hudson's Bay post stiff competition. During a purchasing trip to

Victoria, she met retired Governor James Douglas, who expressed the wish that his own daughter would be as competent.

Competent and canny, indeed, was Christina. In the spring of 1873-4, when little remained on the posts' shelves and a resupply trip was urgently needed, the Hudson's Bay Company hired all available teams to acquire its supplies. Undaunted, Christina contacted her Indian friends from her days along the Washington-British Columbia border. Moving lightly and more swiftly than the heavy freight teams of the Hudson's Bay Company, Christina and her friends transported furs to Victoria and bought freight that was shipped to Yale on the Fraser, and from there by light packs to Kamloops. Instead of the Hudson's Bay Company shutting off her supplies, she received hers first and smartly turned the tables on her competitors.

It was 1874 when Christina met Ranald at Clinton, encountering him at the Bonaparte House where he was then working for the BX Express. Kindred spirits, the two cousins quickly became fast friends. Christina observed, "He was a very jolly companionable man—a great ladies man and his special business seemed to be to entertain and look after the company's lady passengers. He was a true sport, treating and drinking with the men, dancing all night with the ladies and showing them the little courtesies and polished attentions noticeable for their absence among the rougher elements of the west."

Cut from the same cloth, Ranald and Christina were a lively pair in the Cariboo and at the Kamloops post until Christina sold her business and moved to a ranch on the Thompson River, where she lived until 1888. Meanwhile, Ranald moved on to other tasks, prospecting for a time in the Peace River country. Since the CPR surveyors were probing the Peace River route (propounded by Malcolm McLeod and considered seriously by Sandford Fleming) as a way around the impassable sections of the Rocky Mountains, it is just possible that he worked with them. From time to time, Ranald visited his beloved cousin Christina at the ranch, where she was raising her three children—Alexander born in 1870, Katherine in 1872, and Mary Christina in 1876. These children (and later those of Donald at Fort Colvile) were dear to him. On that rough frontier, he spent much time teaching the girls manners, how to properly mount a horse side-saddle, and dancing—ah, yes, Ranald loved to dance. Christina remembered that her now aging cousin always was quiet, good-natured and mannerly himself.

Fond of children as he was, it must have been a shock for Ranald to witness what happened to the tots that grew up near him in the McLean household. Without a father to guide them, the younger McLean sons grew undisciplined and wild. By 1880, they bedeviled their neighbors, broke in and wrecked the interiors of cabins, then expanded to stealing

whiskey and horses, and threatening people. With the three McLeans—
the youngest only fifteen—ran a sullen friend, Alex Hare. The Kamloops
constable, John Ussher, rather liked the McLean boys despite the fact that
he frequently had to lock them up in his jail; Alex Hare was another case.
So it was when William Palmer, a local rancher, reported the theft of his
great stallion by the gang, that Ussher felt obliged to track them down in
the bush. With him were Palmer, Shumway, McLeod and Roxborough.
When the constable rode into the McLeans' camp and, in a weary but
friendly manner, said he would have to take them in, Archie McLean fired
at Ussher, killing him, and others injured Palmer and McLeod.

Later it was said by the McLean boys that they lost faith in their
neighbors, because a Kamloops merchant had seduced their sister and made
her pregnant . . . Or so they said. The three McLeans and Hare were hanged
in New Westminster on January 31, 1881. Since Ranald lived in Kamloops
at that time, the scene of the depredations and capture, and where the boys
were held for a time, one can imagine him with tears running down his
cheeks as he remembered those children, whose hair he had ruffled as babies, and who now were swinging from the gallows.

Around 1882, nearing sixty years of age, Ranald went to live at Fort
Colvile near Christina's brother, Donald, becoming a part of that lively and
teeming household. Donald and his large family had a prosperous ranch on
the broad, fertile plains, using the old Hudson's Bay Company buildings. Nearby
in September, 1885, Ranald also took up pre-emption rights on one hundred
and fifty-three acres of property adjoining the fort and constructed his own
small cabin, although he spent most of his time with Donald's family in the old
factor's house. MacDonald received patent to his lands on October 13, 1891,
but sold six acres of right of way to D. C. Corbin's Spokane Falls and Northern
Railway, one of the branches aiming to connect to the Canadian Pacific Railway. The railroad entered Marcus, north of Ranald's holdings, on May 20,
1890; then the Dalles in August, a point fifteen miles below the Canadian
border. There, a sternwheeler connected from the Dalles to Revelstoke, British
Columbia, where the new Canadian Pacific Railway chuffed along on its mission of making a nation out of eastern and western Canada.

In 1891, speculating that the railroad might bring settlers, Donald
platted the land around the old fort as a town, complete with easements
for streetcar, telegraph and telephone lines, but it never came to fruition,
and there is no record of any lots ever being sold.

Even though Fort Colvile was no longer a Hudson's Bay post or even a
fort, travelers frequently came through to renew old acquaintance with Donald
and Ranald. For many previous decades, virtually all cross-country travelers

had stopped at Colvile. It had been a key part of the great system of forts and trading posts operated by the Hudson's Bay Company, and ruled from London itself. In its heyday, the fort was the largest post between the Rocky Mountains and the Cascade Range. Fort Colvile was established in 1824, upon the advice of George Simpson and an earlier recommendation by Alexander Kennedy, a chief factor of the Columbia Department. It replaced Spokane (originally spelled Spokan) House, which was too far from the Columbia River and not well-suited for agriculture. Located on a plain above the Kettle Falls portage in a splendid valley protected from the worst wintry winds by low mountains, the fort began to take shape in 1825, and was named for Andrew Colvile, Governor of the Hudson's Bay Company, and a mentor of a younger Simpson. The task was assigned to John Work, a tough, capable man, who—with a crew of less than ten—managed to complete enough structures sufficiently so that the post replaced Spokane House by 1826.

The trading post was enclosed with high pickets, such as were used at Fort Vancouver. At one corner stood a blockhouse or bastion, complete with a small cannon that probably would have done little damage to anyone, and fortunately never was used in anger—the piece had seen service at the Battle of Waterloo, though, when the combined armies of Europe defeated the legions of France. The bastion had a four-sided roof with three portholes for rifles and another to accommodate the mouth of the cannon.

Within the stockade eventually stood several log buildings, including the trader or factor's home, a relatively substantial place compared to the other structures. It included a large living room warmed by an adobe fireplace so narrow that one could only insert logs vertically. In the commodious dining room, the famous would dine— including George Simpson, as he made his inspection tours of the Hudson's Bay Company's domains. From a richly stocked cellar of liquors and a groaning pantry of meats and vegetables, the chief factor or trader set a table worthy of a civilized world. Ranald remembered from his childhood the festive atmosphere that prevailed when the supply boats came from Fort Vancouver or Astoria—his father at the head of the table and the rest seated in order of their importance, even the women and children. Here were trappers, hunters, non-company travelers, Indian chiefs, and Hudson's Bay inspectors. To the colorful assembly, Archibald read aloud from newspapers and letters received from the outside world—many were hungry for any contacts with distant family or friends, or, indeed, for information about the world itself.

Inside the stockade stood the offices, the storage areas for furs, a flour storage area, powder magazine, meat in an icehouse, salmon storage, milkroom, saddlery, a grain storage area, blacksmith shop, and carpenter's shop. Also, there were two houses for visitors, an Indian hall sheltering those Indians who came to trade and stayed overnight, barracks, a gentlemen's mess, a kitchen building, and an apartment to the factor's home for family or close friends. The homes were not log cabins of the old style, but rather an architecture developed in Canada where houses were framed with heavy timbers, then walled with squared-off logs mortised together. A roof often was covered with earth or sod. Outside the stockade stood servants' houses, bakehouses and ovens, barns for pigs, cows, poultry and pigeons, corrals for horses, a boathouse, schoolhouse, etc. It was a veritable town.

Beyond spread tilled fields between the river and the chalky bluffs. On the fertile plain grew bumper crops of wheat, barley, oats, Indian corn, Irish potatoes, peas and other garden vegetables. Three calves and three pigs brought to the fort by Ermatinger, McLeod and Douglas in 1826, by 1837 had multiplied to fifty-five cattle and more than one hundred and fifty pigs under the husbandry of Archibald McDonald's crews. A mile away, the company maintained a grist mill to grind flour and other grains, a task later assumed in 1863 by a settler, L. W. Meyers, at Meyers Falls on the nearby Colville River. There, Mrs. Meyers opened a private school for both white and mixed blood children. Parents or guardians paid to have their children attend. The Indians industriously trapped for furs, bringing them to the post to trade for European goods. But equally important to the success of the Hudson's Bay Company's enterprises here were the crops and other foods grown or prepared for the support of almost all the company's employees throughout the interior of the Old Oregon Country, as well as today's Kamloops and north central British Columbia.

Less than a mile below the fort, the Columbia River quickened as it entered a canyon, cascading in two great and several lesser waterfalls and rapids. This site was important to the Indians as a key salmon fishery. Indeed, the local Indian chief had granted the fort site to the Hudson's Bay Company with the proviso that the British would not interfere with his people at their Kettle Falls fishery. There the Indians used spears, weirs, and wicker baskets, mostly the latter, to catch migrating salmon; in fact, the Indian word for the falls translates as "Basket Falls." The baskets were of stout hazel or birch and hung at the lower edges of the falls by ropes braided from supple branches. Fish that failed to surmount the falls on their leaps fell backward, some scooped up by the waiting baskets. Indian spearman also stood poised on the edge of the maelstrom, thrusting their sharp projectiles through salmon as they jumped and wriggled up the face of the falls—inevitably to fall backwards several times in attempting to defeat the obstacle. Spearing of the backwards-falling fish was deliberate, for, if the spearman engaged a strong, active fish *in* the water, it might drag him into the rushing torrent. A great Northwest salmon could exceed one hundred pounds. Salted down in barrels or dried in the sun and wind, the fish kept indefinitely.

River brigades coming from Fort Vancouver had to portage around the falls to the east, and since a boat could carry as much as two tons of cargo, portaging was a significant task. Along this very road rose St. Paul's Mission, founded by Fathers Peter DeSmet and Ravalli in 1845 to serve local children and their parents, both Indian and white. It was here that Jenny Lynch, daughter of Ranald's youngest brother Benjamin, was schooled.

For the most part, northeast Washington did not experience lasting hostilities between Indians and white miners or settlers. Nevertheless, in June, 1859, three miles northeast of today's town of Colville, the U. S. Army established a post under orders from Brigadier General William S. Harney—the primary duty of the contingent being the providing of protection and assistance for the Americans involved in the survey of the international boundary at the 49th parallel. A few miles to the northwest, a British Boundary Commission likewise was housed for a time at the old Hudson's Bay post, Fort Colvile. Later, the British commission erected some cabins north of the post; in 1862 after the Boundary Commission had moved on, a storekeeper named Marcus Oppenheimer purchased the British-built structures and opened a store at the site of today's hamlet of Marcus. It often is confusing for modern historians to sift out the difference between Fort Colvi"l"e, the Hudson's Bay post, and Fort Colvi"ll"e, the U. S. Army post named after the Colville Indian Tribe that used two "l's" in their name. The Army post was closer to today's Colville, Washington, whereas the town of Kettle Falls stood adjacent to the Hudson's Bay Fort Colvile on the banks of the Columbia just below the falls. (Kettle Falls was moved to higher ground before the waters of Grand Coulee Dam's Lake Roosevelt engulfed the site around 1940.)

During the years that American troops were stationed at Fort Colville, the post had a checkered history. The first dragoons were orderly and professional but, when the regulars were dispatched east to participate in the Civil War, volunteer units replaced them and proved to be undisciplined and rowdy, harassing nearby Chinese miners and other settlers. In 1879, when the fort was no longer needed, the troops (again Army regulars after the Civil War) were moved to Lake Chelan and the fort closed.

When General William T. Sherman arrived to inspect the closed-down post in 1883, he had with him eighty military and civilian personnel, including Associate Justice Horace Gray of the U. S. Supreme Court. Participating as a leader in this portion of Sherman's great inspection tour of western Army posts was a young lieutenant, George W. Goethals, who later became the guiding force for the construction of the Panama Canal. A MacDonald relative, Nellie Stanton, told the author that Ranald had entertained Sherman.

The general was hosted at St. Paul's Mission. Jenny MacDonald, then around twelve years old, was chosen to make the official welcoming speech. Later Jenny said all the children stood in a row to greet the well-known Civil War general. She made a bow and gave her speech. The children then sang a song and, when the general requested that some child sing a solo, Jenny sang "My Southern Sunny Home." Thereafter he kissed Jenny on the cheek. During an interview in her last years, Jenny said, "He had a fine personality, tall and with grizzly hair, but rough in appearance. Everybody thought it was a fine honor when he kissed me, but all I could think about was how rough his beard was." It is probable that her Uncle Ranald was present at this affair, since Jenny was a favorite of his, especially since her father had long since left the area. (Descendants assert that Jenny MacDonald's father was Benjamin, who might not have known that his Indian consort was pregnant at the time he left the West for Quebec in 1870 or 1871. Jenny married George Nelson, who died after fathering four children. Jenny then married James Lynch and had one daughter, Nellie Lynch Stanton, with him.)

With the establishment of the international boundary at the forty-ninth parallel in 1846, the Hudson's Bay Company had been forced to consider another location north of the new border, since eventual abandonment of Fort Colvile to the Americans was certain. The customs collector of Washington Territory already had demanded a significant duty from the Hudson's Bay Company for importing goods from Fort Langley to Fort Colvile. Hence, Fort Shepherd was established in 1854 on the Columbia River, only a few hundred yards north of the border, on a bend opposite to the junction of the Pend d'Oreille River with the Columbia. The job of supervising the construction of seven buildings fell to Angus McDonald. In 1856, prospectors in that area discovered an excellent quality of gold dust at the confluence of the rivers by panning or placer mining—apparently a gold find that predated that of the Fraser River. Despite the increase in trade, the post proved unsuccessful, especially in comparison with Fort Colvile, import duties or not. Its activities were curtailed as early as 1860 in favor of building a post farther west at Similkameen. By 1862, Fort Shepherd had only an Indian caretaker, who did such a fine job that the fort was reoccupied in 1864 as a depot for goods intended for Canadian trade. That year at Fort Shepherd, Ranald's young brother John died at the age of twenty-seven. Benjamin traveled to the fort to bring his body to Fort Colvile for burial.

During the brief but exciting gold rush in the area, Fort Shepherd was manned again, but, in 1870, it was finally closed due to declining business. It burned in 1872.

Even though Fort Colvile had been "demoted" in importance, requiring only a chief trader instead of a chief factor, Angus McDonald contentedly occupied the post until June 1, 1872, when he moved all the company goods and properties to Kamloops. The buildings were to be abandoned or sold. William Park Winans, a local farmer who was promoting the idea of a new Indian reservation, suggested unsuccessfully that the site be designated as a new Indian Agency office. Angus' claim to ranch property in the vicinity was denied on the basis that title to the land was not clear, due to Indian claims. Throwing up his hands in frustration, Angus simply left for Montana to ranch there among relatives, leaving the fort in charge of his son Donald.

Donald had the land surveyed in 1884, as indicated earlier, possibly in an effort to authenticate his claim to the property. That claim was based on an old deed belonging to Angus of one square mile granted by the "Chief of the place," as the grantor had been identified. He was successful in patenting his claim, receiving title on March 31, 1890, under the provisions of the Homestead Act of 1862. Ranald's claim was recognized a year and a half later.

Inevitably the old fort's numerous buildings began to collapse; so many structures were not required for a ranch. Yet the lively family of Donald McDonald and his benign cousin, Ranald MacDonald, enjoyed life in this peaceful community.

When Ranald came to live near Donald, the younger cousin had been married only five years. In 1877, he had married Maggie Stensgar, daughter of Angus' lifelong friend, Thomas Stensgar, who lived south of Fort Colvile at Addy with his wife Julia Plant, daughter of Antoine Plant. Julia's mother had been a guide to Governor Isaac Stevens in 1855 on his trip to the coast. At age nineteen, Donald had kept the company store at Fort Colvile. He then worked at Fort Shepherd and as a customs collector under Judge Haynes, but returned to take over the Fort Colvile property when his father Angus moved to Montana. The young couple enlivened the ranch with four children: Emma, Julia, Christie and Thomas A. At holiday times there were parties attended by local settlers, who danced from Christmas until one week after New Year's Day. During the long summer there were picnics and horse races. At such events, housewives competed with each other as to who was the best cook. The tables groaned with food—cakes, deer, fish, chicken, puddings, roast pig. There was little excessive drinking. For Ranald and his extended family, life was sweet in the verdant valley.

XXVII
Ranald MacDonald's Last Days

Slightly deaf and suffering the intermittent pains of arthritis, Ranald maintained his graciousness and clung to memories of his heritage, sometimes dreaming of his days as the son of a chief factor, of the arrivals of the voyageurs by canoe, of splendid dinner parties where gleaming silver and white linen graced feasting tables at the wilderness forts of his youth. Surrounded by the deteriorating buildings of Fort Colvile, a mute indication of the changing times, Ranald sought to influence his nieces and nephews for the better, to teach them the finer points of etiquette as he had endeavored to teach Christina's children. Nearby settlers had heard the entrancing story of his adventures in Japan and sagas of whaling days and gold diggings, and he was something of a local celebrity. Often when he went out on a social call, he carried a handsome, ivory-headed cane given to him by Tokyo newspaperman Murayama of the *Asahi Shimbun* (*Rising Sun News*), through Malcolm McLeod.

As mentioned earlier, Ranald and Malcolm McLeod had lost touch with each other for many years. It was only by chance in late 1888 or 1889 that Ranald learned through a news item in the *Colville Miner* that McLeod, of St. Andrews, had received a distinguished guest from Japan.

The chain of events leading to the arrival of the Japanese guest began earlier when McLeod had happened upon the name of Murayama, editor of the *Asahi Shimbun* in Tokyo. Thinking that he might be related to Ranald's interpreter friend, Moriyama, McLeod wrote to Murayama and enclosed a copy of his Canadian Pacific Railway pamphlet that contained an abbreviated account of Ranald's adventures in Japan. In this letter, McLeod added that he believed Ranald to be dead somewhere in the West. When Murayama received the letter and pamphlet, he turned the material over to a co-editor, Junichiro Oda, who had studied law in Edinburgh, Scotland, and was perfectly adept at English translation.

Intrigued by the MacDonald story, Oda proceeded to track down the descendants of the fourteen interpreters who had been taught English decades earlier by Ranald. Oda discovered, however, that the descendants knew nothing of Ranald or his teaching, but they were fascinated to learn about the story. Convinced that the tale was true, Oda and Murayama published the account translated directly from McLeod's CPR pamphlet, in the *Asahi Shimbun*.

Meanwhile in February, 1888, Munemitsu Mutsu, later a Japanese count, was appointed minister to Washington, D. C. (and later served as Japanese Minister of Foreign Affairs in his own country). On his first appointment to Washington, Mutsu requested that Murayama accompany him. Meanwhile, Oda, who remained curious about the intriguing revelations sent by McLeod, detoured to Ottawa during a trip to North America in the summer of 1888, staying with McLeod for a few days.

Even though Murayama actually was not related to the interpreter Moriyama (according to research done by Lewis and Murakami in the 1920's), Oda nevertheless brought with him a testimonial from Murayama as an honor to Ranald MacDonald. Receiving it later, after having re-established contact with McLeod, Ranald described it in his memoirs:

"The testimonial—carefully packed in two boxes, one within the other— was an ancient despatch [*sic*] or letter (in roll) box; in form, peculiarly double; in that one open box fitted in, or over another; dimensions, about twelve inches in length, five in depth, and four in width; of *papier-mache*, with a mixture of gold dust—composition technically called, in Japanese, *Kahamashee*.

"The sides, inside and out inlaid with plates of gold, in different arabesque forms; the top having a specially deep rich moulding, all in gold, in different and appropriate hues, of a perfectly natural scene, of lake (or sea), river, land, trees, herbage, flowers, and foliage in most minute and exquisite detail. Mr. Oda said it was the work of a Lost Art—lost for two hundred fifty years back. Yet it looked, in its bright sheen, as fresh from the artist's hands, save, (a little) in its time shaded silk cords with tassels. A princely testimonial truly!—Princely! not only in its intrinsic value; but, more still, in the motive of its giving."

At the time of his visit, McLeod gave Oda all of Ranald MacDonald's papers—the ones Ranald had left during his 1850's visit to St. Andrews. Among them were scraps of paper on which Ranald had practiced writing different Japanese words with a crow's quill, while compiling a limited glossary of English/Japanese words and terms. Also included were less than a dozen pages of Ranald's original journal. (Most of the journal had been lost during the shipwreck in the Indian Ocean, when Ranald had to swim for his life.) It was during this visit that McLeod learned that his illustrious visitor (Oda) was the co-editor of three volumes of national law called the Codes of Japan.

Oda promised a return visit with McLeod while en route home from Europe, but he became ill in London. His physicians advised him to return to Japan via the warmer route through the Suez Canal. Oda arrived in Japan, but died shortly thereafter at Kyoto. Ranald's original papers, it is assumed, passed into the care of Oda's relatives and probably are long lost. However, some fragments remain in the British Columbia Provincial Archives.

In his letter addressed to Malcolm McLeod (no date given), when attempting to re-establish contact after so many years had passed, Ranald expressed his astonishment at learning that a Mr. Oda had been visiting McLeod, saying that the news appeared in the *Colville Miner*, which also included a short account of Ranald's adventures. Uncertain of McLeod's address, Ranald wrote only a short note, while also requesting the addresses of his brothers, Allan and Sam, saying that he did not know where Allan was, and that he had written to Ben at Camas, Bingham County, Idaho, but received no answer.

McLeod promptly replied on May 1, 1889, but his letter addressed to the state of Washington first went astray to Washington, D. C., before reaching Ranald on May 28. In the letter, McLeod told Ranald that there was a possibility he still might be eligible as the heir of Chief Comcomly for some indemnity under the Oregon Treaty of 1846. Ranald replied, in astonishment, that he knew very little about what McLeod was talking about. "I faintly remember that about I think 1844 my father and Mr. Duncan Finlayson followed me to New York with the object of catching me, I suppose, & bring me home, but also there were certain claims pending the Oregon dispute connected with it." He added that he did not even remember where he heard this, maybe from his mother (stepmother Jane Klyne). Thus, it was in McLeod's letter that Ranald for the first time heard that the United States government had recognized such a claim. He urged McLeod to investigate further.

Obviously, McLeod now also had told Ranald that he had been compiling and attempting to sell the account of Ranald's adventures in Japan, entitled "A Columbian in Japan." In a letter to A. McKinlay on June 2, Ranald mentioned that McLeod was going to publish the story.

In his preface to Ranald's adventures, McLeod had prepared a lengthy dissertation on the people, customs, politics, etc., of Japan—a rather ponderous tome. Undoubtedly, McLeod's desire to publish Ranald's adventures was a spin-off of his earlier promotional efforts for a transcontinental railway, partially for the purpose of developing trade with Japan and China. Several publishers in the United States and Canada rejected the work. One reviewer to which it was sent was K. T. Takahashi, a clergyman of Japanese descent, who praised Ranald MacDonald's achievements, but was dismayed by other inaccuracies (in McLeod's section) about his people.

Takahashi said of Ranald, his "disposition seems to have quite won the confidence and love of our countrymen from whom, 40 years ago, I frankly admit, a foreigner could have expected nothing . . . It will be seen from his narratives that though a prisoner, he was a teacher, much beloved and respected, [of] over fourteen scholars, quick and intelligent, ever zealous of gathering information of western nations. Such information the country needed at this time very badly . . . In all probability, it was these 14 scholars of McDonald [*sic*] and their scholars in turn who made themselves invaluable when, later on, Japan had become involved in foreign intercourses. Moreover, it was no doubt through these fourteen that the foremost intellects of the country had gathered better knowledge of foreign countries and better prepared themselves to formulate the future plan of their national course . . . It is not in vain that Mr. McDonald [*sic*] should flatter himself with the fact that he has been the first instructor and propagator of the English language and much that was needed to enhance their notion of western nations to the Japanese at that time."

Takahashi went on to report, though, that the book contained so many inaccuracies, largely regarding religion, origins, and such, that he could not recommend it for publication as it stood. William Drysdale & Co., Montreal publishers, returned the manuscript enclosed with the critique to McLeod, stating that—unless the Canadian Pacific Railway or the Canadian government underwrote costs by subscribing for a certain number of advance copies (but there was no hope of this, they added)—they could not publish the book. Subsequently, Ranald received a ten-page letter from McLeod with many questions, which Ranald attempted to answer from memory. Rewriting, taking new directions from his original manuscripts (the first of which was written in 1857), McLeod continued attempts to publish the account, but without success.

Though honored by Oda and Murayama, Ranald received a different reaction from another Fort Colvile visitor in the summer of 1890—Elizabeth Custer, the widow of General George Custer. During a leisurely trip through the West, and later writing an article for the July 18, 1891, issue of *Harper's Weekly*, Elizabeth Custer was both fascinated by, and supercilious to, Ranald MacDonald during her surprise visit to Fort Colvile. Unfamiliar with Ranald's background, she was taken aback to be received by a "coarsely dressed antiquarian" with excellent manners. She said, "We felt that if our descent [from the carriage] was in keeping with the suave reception and the bared head, we ought properly to be picking our way, in brocaded gown and ruffed stomacher, down the old-time steps that were unrolled from the chariots of the time of the Louises."

As Custer and her party were shown around by MacDonald, she was more and more amazed by the anomalies in Ranald's cultured, somewhat flowery language and his rough appearance, calling him the "prince of paupers" in the article. Learning a little from a brief aside with one of her company, she said later during an interview for the *Kettle Falls Pioneer*, "I can scarcely think of anything more incongruous than this aristocratic old man with his high-flown expression, of which we knew nothing except in the literature of the style of Sir Charles Grandison, and the tumbled down, dilapidated, untidy old buildings around him. And yet the two clothes he wore and the straggling, gray hair and beard looked to me far more interesting than the dressed-up and commonplace looking man who occupied a panel of the family album, and represented Ranald when he was in the outside world."

As the tour of the old fort progressed, Ranald's eyes danced as he described the old days at the fort, when it was the center of activity in the region. When Donald's wife and children appeared, Ranald waved his hand possessively and said, "They are all MacDonald," naturally leading Mrs. Custer to believe they were his own. As she questioned him about his life, he told her that he flattered himself that he was the instigator of Commodore Perry's expedition to Japan.

She said in her interview, "I confess myself astonished at this, as it was hard for me to connect that distant world with this peaceful, old man."

Ranald continued to regale his visitors with stories of life at Fort Colvile, as well as his Japanese experience, and through his eyes, Custer said, "I saw the bustle of traffic, the industry of the little community, the military discipline and precision with which everything was conducted; for, though the governor of the company was not an officer, he was an autocrat, such as can scarcely be conceived."

Ranald explained that it was difficult to persuade Scottish women to come to the frontier, but some were induced to do so, he said, by the promise of all the tea they wanted. He explained that the favorite was Labrador or Muskage tea, growing about thirty inches above the ground, with leaves one-eighth inch in width, the outside hard, and the inside yellow and downy. He said the aroma was delicious and that missionaries paid five dollars a pound for the flowers to use as medicine.

A thoroughly captivated Mrs. Custer thought how her Eastern friends would enjoy MacDonald, and, in jest, said, "Oh, Mr. MacDonald, how I should like to take you home with me!"

MacDonald's reply was swift, as he bowed deeply and graciously, "Oh, madam, take possession of me. I am yours."

When time came for the party to leave, MacDonald said to Mrs. Custer, "I wish, madam, you would speak of [in her writings about the West] one man who loved this life and his duties here so well he did not want to return to England, even when offered knighthood for having attained by his exertions the furtherest point north then known, and he was Peter Warren Dease." (Dease was prominent in the Franklin Expedition of 1825-7, and between 1825 and 1830 served intermittently as the manager of Fort Colvile.)

In her article for *Harper's Weekly*, however, Mrs. Custer later spoke disparagingly of MacDonald's dress and suggested his story was a fabrication. Deeply hurt, Ranald replied in a letter to the *Kettle Falls Pioneer*, September 3, 1891. The newspaper's editor prefaced the letter, saying, "Why this lady should have so turned against and so sneeringly commented on the dress and even doubted the veracity of Mr. MacDonald is a mystery, unless, since her brave and fearless husband was so foully butchered by the Indians, she has an abhorrence for anyone with Indian blood coursing through their veins. We think the lady must have certainly known better. Then again she may have thought it funny and that class of literature would suit the readers of Harper's Weekly; but in our minds the dubbing of Mr. MacDonald as the 'Prince of Paupers' was uncalled for." In his letter, Ranald humbly declared his purpose for responding: "But it is not to assume any pretention [*sic*] of social eminence in that regard [that he was the oldest living pioneer in that wilderness] . . . but solely to rectify two or three little mistakes affecting myself and family associates which by inadvertence evidently, have been made by Mrs. Custer."

Ranald went on to deny ever being a pauper in any sense of the word, and that, "by the sweat of our brows and enterprises, [we the first pioneers] filled or at least covered every valley and plain with the fruits of our industry in herds and flocks and bands of horses for hundreds of miles in every direction."

As to his "only two articles of apparel," he replied, "she forgot the moccasins and clean underclothing, all I have to say is that I was at work at the time. I am always at work and consequently not always prepared nor warned to receive such honoured company . . . Clothes I had in abundance and of the finest quality." He went on to strenuously object to disparaging remarks made about Mrs. Donald MacDonald, pointing out her heritage as the daughter of Thomas Stensgar, a worthy officer of the Hudson's Bay Company, and his wife. Custer also had said Ranald's adventures took place in China, instead of Japan, a statement he corrected.

In St. Andrews, McLeod remained unsuccessful in marketing Ranald's story. As he answered questions sent from McLeod, Ranald also wrote or rewrote portions of the story, with encouragement from his cousin Christina and niece Jenny. In fact, Ranald may have begun writing his memoirs from memory even before his contact with McLeod. In 1891, Ranald wrote that he remembered Moriyama fondly: "his countenance when in repose was a mild dignity observable in our clergymen, when in deep thought he had that peculiar habit of nibbling his finger nails whatever may be thought of such characteristics to me, my Friend appeared to derive inspiration after mature reflection, suddenly his countenance would beam with animation."

Ranald reiterated his earlier assertion of not knowing the facts of his birth until thirty years later, after he had returned from Australia. "Why my family ever kept it dark was always a puzzel [*sic*] to me. Edward Ermatinger of St. Thomas called me Kum-Kumly & so did Peter W. Dease." Ranald claimed these terms, and even that of "an old King who called me Qua-ame, or grandchild" failed to have meaning for him.

Ranald said he had read about the Japanese's impertinent treatment of Commodore Biddle during his first effort to penetrate Japan, and how the press had commended Biddle's policy of moderation. It was the Biddle affair, Ranald claimed, that "was one of my reasons for adopting the plan I did, going all alone."

McLeod's efforts at finding a publisher continued to fail. Publishers suggested he raise money for self-publication. Likely because he was short of funds, McLeod appealed to friends for assistance, including railroad-promoter Sandford Fleming, still friendly and supportive, and now the head of a newly formed Institute of Learning for Canada. In a letter to McLeod dated July 16, 1891, Fleming said he had read the Japanese manuscript and, "It is quite obvious to me that year by year we Canadians will come to be more & more interested in the Japanese whom we must consider as our neighbours for all future time. The ocean is, as it has been in the early days of the human family, a means of intercourse, a bond of union."

Urged by Fleming to read the manuscript, publisher W. Foster Brown of Montreal finally expressed interest in the project. In a letter to Ranald dated April 1, 1892, McLeod indicated that he offered Brown a subsidy of $100 cash in advance, plus $100 and certain costs on delivery, for a mere 100 copies of the book, tentatively titled "A Columbian in Japan." Later, up to 1,000 copies were to be delivered and paid for, when sold to the public. McLeod added, however, that Brown had yet to reply: "As a cause of delay on his part I thought that probably he was waiting for Mr. Sandford Fleming who first spoke to him on the subject; & who, I supposed from his personal interest in the matter; had in some way, assumed some contingent responsibility to him in the venture. Mr. Fleming was then absent in Europe traveling about throughout it from London to Bordeaux thence to

St. Petersburg; thence to Norway, in the course of which any letters to him remained long unanswered. Then when he did return to Canada he (Mr. F) again showed such an earnest & urgent interest in the thing—in connection; as I understood with C. P. R. & his own Pacific Cable scheme—that I thought he would confer with Mr. Brown & himself supplement what further cash current payments Mr. Brown might require. He did not however. I could not ask him bluntly to do so; and moreover his inquiries to me, from time to time; about the thing or—its issue;, led me to suppose, naturally, and reasonably, that he would assist by something more than a mere subscription for ten copies."

McLeod went on to say that Fleming had suggested that Sir Donald A. Smith, governor of the Hudson's Bay Company, indirectly said he was interested in such a work. McLeod's efforts to contact Smith, however, were unsuccessful. McLeod added that Putnam & Sons estimated publishing costs of over $1,000, and suggested an unidentified publisher, or "Japanese Department," in Chicago. However, McLeod said, in order to publish there, the manuscript "will require to be wholly rewritten—recomposed by me excluding all *Canadian* argument & matter & adapting it alone to your special audience."

Fragments of other letters discovered in the files of local historian Judge William Brown of Okanogan, Washington, and donated to the Washington State University archives, indicate efforts were ongoing after April 1, 1893, and through November, 1893. Comments by two readers, David Douglas (not the botanist) and a Reverend Fletcher, both praised the project, but suggested the writing was too florid, that it was unfortunate that the book was not published immediately after Commodore Perry's expedition, and etc. McLeod told Ranald he might try English magazines, and that he had no faith in American ones, or—again—that he might try self-publication.

On November 8, 1893, McLeod indicated, "for the Canadian work I have expunged all that [some references to Mrs. Custer] & other passages," and that he had prepared a version of the story for publication in the *Kettle Falls Pioneer*, where the first chapters of Ranald's story appeared in installments between November 16, 1893, and January 4, 1894. During 1894, Ranald also corresponded with A. D. Burnett of the Spokane *Spokesman-Review* about publication possibilities.

Meanwhile, the national economy was deteriorating. Cash became scarce, culminating in the severe depression of 1893, affecting Canada and the United States. McLeod was in dire financial straits; in fact, MacDonald was shocked to receive a letter in August, 1891, in which McLeod admitted he was starving and would be buried in the hard cold earth this winter!

Ranald replied, "I imagined that you were desponding on account of the obsticals [*sic*] in the way of publishing the Book & were foreboding—but if really the actual want experienced by the hungry, then I wished I were near you that I might share of our abundance."

McLeod's ongoing efforts at obtaining funds included a demand for a portion of the "Oregon Indemnity" for descendants of those chief factors active at the time of the Treaty of 1846, when the American government paid the Hudson's Bay Company $650,000 in 1869 for certain properties below the forty-ninth parallel. He had filed claims on behalf of himself as the son of John McLeod, for the offspring of Archibald McDonald (including Allan, Ranald, etc.), and others of his acquaintance. Indeed, he prepared a printed memorial, or appeal, presented it to the Canadian Parliament, and pursued the matter diligently, but apparently fruitlessly.

McLeod also requested that Ranald attempt to locate financing for the publishing of Ranald's story. MacDonald did try mightily to raise funds to contribute to the effort—even attempting to take out loans with his farm as collateral. The letters from MacDonald to McLeod give insight into his kindly concern and warm nature. While reminiscing, he spoke of the bond between Hudson's Bay Company families: "perhaps there is no bond more sympathetic . . . that web of sympathy is interwoven in the lives of each member of the different families . . . I cannot explain, individuals we have for the first time seen belonging to that Corporation whether a French Canadian or Iroquoi[s], that feeling comes. He is one of us . . . he knows and understands the long years of suffering and privation, endured and shared in the earliest days of the dawn of our civilization in the wilderness. You and I have seen it, have been with Nature face to face. Mountains, prairies, Forests, Lakes & Rivers, in its primitive state, even the human, the child of Nature."

In February, 1891, Ranald's humble log cabin burned to the ground. He constructed a new one with the help of Donald's family and James Hayes, a friend connected with the new Spokane Falls and Northern Railway, to which Ranald had sold six acres of land for a right-of-way.

In early 1892, Ranald sold his ranch to Donald for $1,500, and recorded the deed. However, Donald had yet to come up with the money. Donald did not want to mortgage his own homestead, and the cattle that he owned in Montana were not ready for market, and etc. Apparently the delay incurred no rancor from Ranald.

Ranald wrote to Allan, from whom he had received one letter during the past thirty years. Ranald reminded Allan that he never received the $400 designated for him by his mother from Archibald's estate, and that was all right, but now he would like to borrow $255—to cover the costs of

preparing certain maps and sketches for the book, plus 200 advance subscription copies. Individual subscriptions from the Kettle Falls area and
the East were coming in at this time.

Unsuccessful in extracting $255 from Allan, Ranald appealed to a
reasonably wealthy cousin, Duncan McDonald, a Montana rancher, who
generously did lend him the money with the promise of more later, when
needed. The $255 was sent to McLeod. Despite the subscriptions and the
donation from Ranald, McLeod seemed no closer to publication in late 1893.

Months earlier, on New Year's Day, 1893, Ranald had approached a local
writer, Mrs. L. C. P. Haskins, to enlist her aid in the publication effort. Her
daughter, Eleanor Haskins Holly, remembered the encounter with delight:

"My maid, a German girl who spoke but little English, came to call
me, saying: 'There is a "gross Mann" wants to see you.' . . . I saw that the
description was not amiss, for he was a 'gross' man. The height of his figure
did not impress you at first glance, on account of comparison with the
breadth of his shoulders and general proportions, but as he seemed to tower
up beside his companion . . . I realized how imposing a figure he really was.
He wore a light-blue, army overcoat, made with capes and brass buttons,
such as, I believe, was used during the Civil War . . . it certainly added to
his size and dignity. He carried a wide-brimmed hat of black felt, with
which he made a sweeping bow—then crossing the room he clasped my
hand and lifted it to his lips with a courtly obeisance . . . At that time Mr.
MacDonald was about 69 years of age, but from his erect bearing and
strong vigorous appearance you would not have thought him more than
60. His hair, worn rather long, was gray, thick and *curling;* he wore a full
beard cut rather short, but not close, which was quite gray and also very
curly. His features were rather rough-hewn, but the high cheekbones and rather
large and flat nose (with peculiarly wide nostrils) were the only features which
would appear to show his Indian ancestry. His complexion, while dark, was
not more so than that of many men who have spent much of the time in the
open. His rather small and deep-set eyes were *gray,* and peculiar in that the gray
iris was encircled at the outer edge by a distinct line of hazel-brown.

"I have seen eyes with that peculiar combination of colors a few times
since, but it appealed to me then as being very odd, and I used to think of
it as showing the two races to which he belonged, which in him met and
harmonized, but did not blend."

Holly's insightful description of Ranald beautifully summarizes the
appearance of the man.

Ranald, however, would not have the pleasure of seeing his memoirs published in his lifetime—of sharing with the public the wondrous adventures he

had enjoyed. He was a product of his times, and his life reflected the strength of the Scottish traders and their fierce forebears, as well as the versatility and courage of his Indian ancestors of the coast. MacDonald was proud of both heritages, although essentially he lived in the manner of a Scotsman. Spanning the time when Pacific Northwest lands changed ownership from Indian, to British, to American and the new Canadian, he walked through history as a participant, not a spectator. In an extraordinary way, he perceived the effects of events swirling around him. The kind treatment afforded him by the Japanese, and his contribution to their early knowledge of the British and Americans, formed an initial tenuous bond across the sea, a bond today strengthening as time goes on. In his narrative, written only three or four years before his death, he said, "In my old age; while living out, still in sweat of brow, the fast falling evening shades of life, in my native homeland of the Columbia, after having, in my wanderings, girded—I may say—the Globe itself, and come across people many, civilized and uncivilized, there are none to whom I feel more kindly—more grateful—than my old hosts of Japan; none whom I esteem more highly."

In midsummer 1894, Jenny Lynch, while at her home in Ferry County, Washington, was informed that her beloved uncle Ranald was seriously ill. She hitched up a buggy and traveled fifty miles of rough road across Sherman Pass to Fort Colvile. She gently attended Ranald, severely ill with flu, and conveyed him back west to her home to nurse him there. In his niece's modest log cabin, and far from his brothers and sisters in eastern Canada, Ranald gasped his last breath on August 5, saying to Jenny, "Sayonara, my dear, Sayonara." His earthly quest was over; he began the last great adventure of us all.

Almost a century passed before Ranald MacDonald again came to the attention of the world. He had not been totally forgotten, to be sure. His diary was published in 1923, followed by two books and occasional articles about him in scholarly journals. In 1974, the Astoria Public Library sponsored a local observance of their native son's 150th birthday. In 1979, respected Japanese professor Tarao Tomita of Tokyo published MacDonald's memoirs of Japan.

Meanwhile, the Committee on Historical Sites (of Washington's State Parks and Recreation Commission) erected a new granite marker on MacDonald's gravesite at Toroda on the Kettle River, Ferry County, Washington. The text reads: "RANALD MacDONALD, 1824-1894, Son of Princess Raven and Archibald MacDonald. His was a life of adventure sailing the seven seas, wandering in far countries, but returning at last to rest in his home-land. 'Sayonara'—Farewell." Listed on the marker are the significant places of his life: Astoria, Japan, Australia, Europe, the Cariboo, Ft. Colville.

Renewed interest likewise was sparked by the Japanese. On July 4, 1987, the Rishiri Rotary Club dedicated a monument to MacDonald on the rocky, black lava cape of Notsuka on Rishiri Island, Hokkaido—where MacDonald had come ashore 143 years before. The memorial was made from a rough log of Ezo-matsu (spruce), native to the small island. It was about ten feet high and fourteen inches in diameter with a text describing MacDonald's landing. Another sign nearby explained: "The memorial stands facing the Pacific Ocean, looking out toward Oregon in North America." The wooden memorial was unfortunately destroyed by a hurri-cane, but was replaced with a stone marker in 1996.

With funds provided by the Rotary Club under the supervision of Professor Jukichi Suzuki, the project was described as "the first spontane-ous cultural exchange between Japan and North America." Stephen Kohl, a professor at the University of Oregon, was director of an educational exchange program at Tokyo at the time and conferred with Professor Suzuki about the memorial's wording.

A year later, in 1988, a newly organized group, Friends of MacDonald, erected a two-sided monument on the site of old Fort Astoria, Oregon. The text is in English on one side and Japanese on the other. It tells MacDonald's story and lists the organizations and individuals in Or-egon and Japan whose gifts made the monument a possibility. The author was invited to the unveiling and became a member of the Friends of MacDonald. Annually on February 3 the Friends place a flower on the MacDonald monument and gather for an informal lunch later.

The Friends of MacDonald have attracted a colorful membership of 200-300 people from Oregon, Washington, Montana, British Colum-bia, Alberta, Japan, Scotland, and elsewhere. A newsletter and annual meet-ing keep members appraised of new books, articles, or bits of pertinent history pertaining to MacDonald. After republication of the 1923 version of MacDonald's memoirs (with additional notes) by the Oregon Histori-cal Society in 1990, the Friends donated copies to 110 Canadian and American universities and colleges with study programs about Japan, as well as to 30 Japanese scholars, universities, and organizations, 33 Oregon high schools that offer Japanese language courses, 23 Japan-America soci-eties in the United States, and a handful of state officials and libraries.

In 1988, Nagasaki scholar Kenji Sonoda used MacDonald's pa-pers in the Provincial Archives, Victoria, B.C. to compile a list, or small dictionary, of Japanese words that had been copied phonetically by MacDonald. Sonoda furnished the correct spellings of the 1850's Japanese words and Mas Tomita of Hillsboro, Oregon, added modern words for the objects or expressions written down by MacDonald. The three-way dictionary was published as a pamphlet by the Friends.

In 1994, with the continuing keen interest in MacDonald as the first teacher of English in Japan and the first American to reach across the seas, a monument was erected in Nagasaki to his memory. At the same time, KTN-TV Nagasaki produced and aired a documentary—filmed in Oregon, Washington, Hawaii, and Canada—celebrating Ranald's life.

International interest also spurred renewed attention to the three Japanese sailors shipwrecked in 1834 at Cape Alava on Washington's coast—long believed to have especially fascinated Ranald MacDonald and initiated his desire to enter Japan. A descendant of one of the sailors came to the cape in 1993 to lay to rest the spirit of his ancestor in a private ceremony.

The events of MacDonald's life must be placed in the perspective of his times in order to truly understand the importance of his daring intrusion into a Japan closed to the outside world. In recognition of this fact, the author spent two years researching the background history of his movements, visiting Japan, Australia, and Canada, and gleaning obscure facts from museums in those countries, as well as in Oregon, Washington, and Hawaii. For some portions of Ranald's own daily life, exact accounts cannot be found. To recreate the pertinent settings, the author often used books and documents recorded by others at a closely similar time, e.g., life on a whaling ship. The author also interviewed many members of Ranald's family, including distant cousins. Like a jigsaw puzzle, the pieces gradually began to fit, creating the mosaic of this remarkable man's adventurous life.

(Note: At the time of Ranald's death, the latest versions of Ranald's memoirs, partly written by Malcolm McLeod, were in the hands of A.D. Burnett, then of the Spokane *Spokesman-Review.* Ten years later, in 1904, Donald McDonald, still living in Marcus, wrote to ask Burnett to return the manuscript. He divulged the fact that Ranald had endorsed a note for a D.T. Stuart; the note was not repaid, and the lender was turning to Ranald's estate [i.e., Donald] for settlement. Donald wrote to Burnett that he had written to Ben MacDonald, asking him to relinquish his claim to the manuscript as Ranald's brother. Donald could then attempt to publish the memoirs and earn money to pay the debt. He went on to indicate that the "Historical Publishing Company" was trying to acquire the manuscript, but he did not plan to give it to them. Whether Burnett ever returned the papers and journals, we do not know. Their whereabouts are unknown.)

Bibliography:
Acknowledgments and Sources

In writing about a historical figure who lived more than a century ago, one obviously must rely on research that has gone before, gleaning information that makes the tale come to life and placing that person in a time frame where he seems real. Thus, the story of Ranald MacDonald's life has evolved not only from his written reminiscences but also from countless bits and pieces of letters, manuscripts, newspaper articles, books, and personal observations—a phrase here, a paragraph there. When no direct information could be gleaned from Ranald's notes, I used the experiences of others paralleling in time and place those of MacDonald. To many researchers and writers, some nameless, I express my deep appreciation. Listed below are some of the dozens of books and other materials I scanned, those most important to the narrative and which were heavily used, and those of most interest.

I acknowledge with particular gratitude the use of the outstanding collection of books and materials on Japan, Canada, and the Pacific Northwest in the Wilson Library at Western Washington University, Bellingham. The personnel at the British Columbia Provincial Archives, Victoria, in which I did extensive research, were extremely gracious and helpful. Other sources for information were the Bishop Museum of Honolulu, the Eastern Washington State Historical Society Library (Cheney Cowles Museum) in Spokane, the Stevens County Museum in Colville, the Suzzallo Library of the University of Washington, the Northwest Collection of the University of British Columbia, the Hilo Public Library, the Astoria Public Library (and Bruce Berney), the Oregon State Historical Society, the Bellingham Public Library, the Washington State University Library, the Kamloops Museum and Archives (Ken Favrholdt), the Hat Creek Ranch (Gordon Everett), and the National Park Service at Kettle Falls and the Grand Coulee Dam headquarters. Conversations with members of the Friends of MacDonald, including Torao Tomita, also proved fruitful.

My thanks go to Dr. Ulrich Mammitsch of Western Washington University for examining the chapters on Japan; and to Professor Torao Tomita, translator of Lewis' and Murakami's *Ranald MacDonald* into a

Japanese language version published in Japan in 1979. Tomita shared his research about the later lives of the fourteen Japanese interpreters. I have had absorbing conversations with Jean Murray Cole (author of the Archibald McDonald biography, *Exile in the Wilderness)* about MacDonald family matters and Japanese castaways. Thanks go to George Thurman of St. Thomas, Ontario, who furnished materials about fur trader Ermatinger and old Ontario. Gordon Yusko, formerly of Fort Langley, searched diligently for material on Port Douglas. I appreciate the assistance rendered by Teruko Kyūma-Chin of the University of Washington's East Asia Library in deciphering the phonetic spellings of Japanese words written down by Americans in the mid 19th century. Also appreciated were talks with David H. Wallace of Annacis Terminals, New Westminster; Ed Druxman, a board member of the Stevens County Historical Society; and the keen interest exhibited by my husband, Ernie Burkhart, now deceased, throughout the five years that I was absorbed in this subject.

In the process of investigating Ranald's life and placing him in the context of his time and place, I personally have visited Nagasaki, Japan, and the Island of Hokkaido (but not Rishiri or Matsumae); Ballarat, Australia; St. Thomas, Ontario; and Astoria, Fort Vancouver, Fort Colvile (HBC site), Fort Colville (U.S. Army site), Fort Langley, Kamloops, Barkerville, Ashcroft, Cache Creek, Soda Creek, Lillooet, Port Douglas (it still remains), and points in between. I am familiar with the Okanagan valley of Canada and the Cariboo country, and with Vancouver Island and the lower mainland of Canada.

I am the author of another biography, published in 1981, about Frank "Sakae" Matsura, an early-20th-century Japanese-American photographer of the north-central Washington frontier. A different text of the Matsursa story became a book published in the Japanese language in 1983. In 1984, TV Asahi made a movie from the book. Through these contacts and other activities with Sister Cities International, I have gained considerable understanding of contemporary Japan and the historical roots of the Japanese people. I also have found that the well-known modern travel guidebooks, *Fodor's Japan,* as well as *Fodor's Hong Kong,* have proven useful in my historical travels.

Historical Sources

Ranald MacDonald's journals and his other writings have been key to my research and the preparation of this book. Several versions of the MacDonald journals (most of which actually were edited or re-edited by Malcolm McLeod), as well as numerous letters and other pertinent items, are preserved in the

Malcolm McLeod Collection, 1249, Box 1-10, at the British Columbia Provincial Archives, Victoria.

In the early 1920's, a version of the MacDonald account was edited and annotated by William S. Lewis and Naojiro Murakami, appearing as *Ranald MacDonald, The Narrative of His Early Life on the Columbia under the Hudson's Bay Company's Regime; of His Experiences in the Pacific Whale Fishery; and of His Great Adventure to Japan; with a Sketch of His Later Life on the Western Frontier, 1824-1894* (Spokane: Eastern Washington State Historical Society, 1923). The Lewis and Murakami book remains today as the primary "published" version of MacDonald's (and McLeod's) account. In 1990, the Oregon Historical Society Press reprinted the book, while adding a new foreword and afterword.

The MacDonald/McLeod writings, of course, are the central documentary basis for the Ranald MacDonald story, but numerous additional sources contain essential information about MacDonald's life and times. These references are listed here as they specifically pertain to each chapter in *Ranald MacDonald: Pacific Rim Adventurer.*

Chapter I. "Columbia River Beginnings," pp. 1-4.
Curtis, Edward S. *The North American Indian . . . ,* 20 vols. New York: Johnson Reprint, 1974. [Originally published 1907-30; the most pertinent volume regarding Pacific Northwest Indians appeared in 1911.]
Drucker, Philip. *Cultures of the North Pacific Coast.* New York: Chandler, 1965.
Gunther, Erna. *Indian Life on the Northwest Coast of North America . . .* Chicago: University of Chicago Press, 1972.
Hazeltine, Jean. *The Historical and Regional Geography of the Willapa Bay Area, Washington.* South Bend, WA: South Bend Journal, 1956.
Ruby, Robert H., and John A. Brown. *The Chinook Indians: Traders of the Lower Columbia River.* Norman: University of Oklahoma Press, 1976.

Chapter II. "At Fort Vancouver," pp. 5-14.
Bain, Read. "Educational Plans and Efforts by Methodists in Oregon to 1860." *Oregon Historical Quarterly* XXI.
Ball, John. *Autobiography of John Ball, 1798-1884.* Grand Rapids, MI: Dean-Hicks, 1925.
_____. Letters to Dr. Brinsmade of Troy, N.Y., printed in *Zion's Herald,* February 22 and December 18, 1833, and January 15, 1834. [Oregon Historical Society, Portland]
Barker, Burt Brown, ed. *Letters of Dr. John McLoughlin, Written at Fort Vancouver, 1829-1832.* Portland: Binfords and Mort, 1948.
Campbell, Marjorie Wilkins. *The North West Company.* New York: St. Martin's, 1957.
Cole, Jean Murray. *Exile in the Wilderness: The Biography of Chief Factor Archibald McDonald, 1790-1853.* Seattle: University of Washington Press, 1979.
Cox, Ross. *The Columbia River . . . ,* ed. by Edgar I. and Jane R. Stewart. Norman: University of Oklahoma Press, 1957. [Cox's account originally appeared in 1831.]
Evans, Elwood, et al. *History of the Pacific Northwest . . . ,* 2 vols. Portland: North Pacific History Company of Portland, Oregon, 1889.

"Fort Vancouver." Handbook 113, Division of Publications of the National Park Service, U.S. Department of the Interior, Washington, D.C., 1981.

Innis, Harold A. *The Fur Trade in Canada: An Introduction to Canadian Economic History.* New Haven, CT: Yale University Press, 1930.

Lent, D. Geneva. *West of the Mountains: James Sinclair and the Hudson's Bay Company.* Seattle: University of Washington Press, 1963.

Lockley, Fred. "Early Education in the Oregon Country." *Oregon Educational Journal* (November 1933).

McDonald, Archibald. *Peace River. A Canoe Voyage from Hudson's Bay to Pacific by the Late Sir George Simpson, (Governor, Hon. Hudson's Bay Company.) in 1828. Journal of the Late Chief Factor, Archibald McDonald, (Hon. Hudson's Bay Company), Who Accompanied Him.* Ottawa: J. Durie and Son, 1872. [Reprinted 1971]

Montgomery, Richard G. *The White-Headed Eagle: John McLoughlin, Builder of an Empire.* New York: MacMillan, 1934. [Reprinted 1971]

Norcross, E. Blanche, ed. *The Company on the Coast.* Nanaimo, B.C.: Nanaimo Historical Society, 1983.

Ormsby, Margaret A. *British Columbia, a History.* Toronto: MacMillan, 1958.

Pethick, Derek. *James Douglas: Servant of Two Empires.* Vancouver, B.C.: Mitchell, 1969.

Simpson, George. *Fur Trade and Empire: George Simpson's Journal . . . 1824-1825,* ed. by Frederick Merk. Cambridge, MA: Harvard University Press, 1931. [Revised edition, 1968]

Chapter III. "Exciting Travels for Ranald," pp. 15-18.

Brooks, Charles W. *Japanese Wrecks Stranded and Picked up Adrift in the North Pacific Ocean.* Fairfield, WA: Ye Galleon, 1964. [Originally published 1876]

Carr, Mary Jane. *Young Mac of Fort Vancouver.* New York: Thomas Y. Crowell, 1940. [Fiction]

Gibbs, James A. *Pacific Graveyard: A Narrative of Shipwrecks where the Columbia Meets the Pacific Ocean.* Portland: Binfords and Mort, 1964.

Plummer, Katherine. *The Shogun's Reluctant Ambassadors: Sea Drifters.* Tokyo: Lotus, 1984.

Chapter IV. "Red River Settlement," pp. 19-24.

Ballantyne, Robert Michael. *Hudson Bay . . .* London, Edinburgh and New York: Thomas Nelson and Sons, 1879. [Reprinted 1971]

Bredin, Thomas F. "The Red River Academy." *The Beaver* (Winter 1974).

Bryce, George. *Hudson's Bay Company.* New York: Burt Franklin, 1968. [Originally published in Toronto, 1904]

Campbell, Robert. *Two Journals of Robert Campbell, Chief Factor Hudson's Bay Company, 1808-1853 . . .* Seattle: Shorey, 1958.

Hill, Douglas A. *The Opening of the Canadian West: Where Strong Men Gathered.* New York: John Day, 1967.

Lang, S.E. "Education in Manitoba." *Canada and Its Provinces . . . ,* vol. 20, ed. by A. Shortt and A.G. Doughty. Toronto: Glasgow, Brook, 1914.

Manitoba Essays, 1877-1937. Winnipeg: University of Manitoba, 1937.

Pritchett, John Perry. *The Red River Valley, 1811-1849: A Regional Study.* New York: Russell and Russell, 1970. [Originally published 1941]

Rich, E. E., ed. *Eden Colvile's Letters, 1849-52.* London: Hudson's Bay Record Society, 1956.

Ross, Alexander. *The Red River Settlement . . .* London: Smith, Elder, 1856. [Reprinted 1957]

Wallace, W.S., ed. *John McLean's Notes . . .* New York: Greenwood, 1968. [Originally published 1849]

West, John. *Journal* . . . Vancouver, B.C.: Alcuin Society, 1967.
Wilson, K. "Life at Red River, 1830-1860." Ginn Studies in Canadian History, Ginn and Company, 1970.

Chapter V. "Rebellion," pp. 25-30.
[See also references for Chapter VI, following]
Armstrong, F.H.; H.A. Stevenson; and J.D. Wilson, eds. *Aspects of Nineteenth-Century Ontario* . . . Toronto: University of Toronto Press and University of Western Ontario, 1974.
Curry, Jane. *The River's in My Blood.* Lincoln: University of Nebraska Press, 1983.
de T. Glazebrook, G.P. *Life in Ontario: A Social History.* Toronto: University of Toronto Press, 1968.
Ermatinger, Edward. "Hudson's Bay Territories [Letters written in 1857] . . ." Toronto: MacLean, Thomas . . . , Printers, King Street, 1858. [Baker Library, Dartmouth College]
_____. *Life of Colonel Talbot and the Talbot Settlement.* Belleville, Ontario: Mika, 1972. [Reprint]
Guillet, Edwin C. *Early Life in Upper Canada.* Toronto: University of Toronto Press, 1963.
Havighurst, Walter. *Voices on the River: The Story of the Mississippi Waterways.* New York: MacMillan, 1964.
McDonald, Lois Halliday. *Fur Trade Letters of Edward Ermatinger* . . . Glendale, CA: Arthur H. Clark, 1980.
Miller, W.C. *Vignettes of Early St. Thomas.* St. Thomas, Ontario, 1967.
"The Pioneers of Elgin, Life and Times of Edward Ermatinger." *St. Thomas Times* (Ontario), October 23, 1891.
Prospectus for the Bank of the County of Elgin, September 19, 1854. [Elgin County Museum, St. Thomas, Ontario]

Chapter VI. "MacDonald Sails the Seven Seas," pp. 31-39.
Blond, Georges. *The Great Story of Whales.* Garden City, NY: Hanover House, Doubleday, 1955.
Eitel, E.J. *Europe in China.* London: Luzac; and Hong Kong: Kelly and Walsh, 1895.
Grant, David W. "Macau." *Islands* (September/October 1987).
Hsu, Immanuel C.Y. *The Rise of Modern China.* New York: Oxford University Press, 1975.
Kelly, Marion; Barry Nakamura; and Dorothy B. Barriere. "Hilo Bay, A Chronological History." Prepared for U.S. Army Engineer District, Honolulu, March 1981.
Latourette, Kenneth Scott. *China.* Englewood Cliffs, NJ: Prentice-Hall, 1964.
Munger, James F. *Two Years in the Pacific and Arctic Oceans and China* . . . Fairfield, WA: Ye Galleon, 1967. [Munger's 1850-52 diary originally was published in 1852.]
(The) Seaman's Friend (Honolulu), various issues 1848-1849. [Bishop Museum, Honolulu]
Simpson, MacKinnon, and Robert B. Goodman. *Whale Song.* Honolulu: Beyond Words, 1986.
Stackpole, Edouard A. *The Sea-Hunters: The New England Whalemen during Two Centuries, 1635-1835.* Philadelphia and New York: J.B. Lippincott, 1953.

Chapter VII. "Whaling on Japan," pp. 40-52.
Chang, Richard T. *From Prejudice to Tolerance.* Tokyo: Sophia University, 1970.
Gowen, Herbert H. *An Outline History of Japan.* New York: D. Appleton, 1930.
Murdoch, James. *A History of Japan,* vol. III, parts 1 and 2. New York: Frederick Ungar, 1964.
Norman, E. Herbert. *Origins of the Modern Japanese State: Selected Writings of E.H. Norman.* New York: Pantheon, Random, 1975.

Totman, Conrad D. *Politics in the Tokugawa Bakufu, 1600-1843*. Cambridge, MA: Harvard University Press, 1967.

Yanaga, Chitoshi. *Japan Since Perry*. New York: McGraw-Hill, 1949.

Chapter VIII. "Ainu Capture MacDonald," pp. 53-61.

Batchelor, John. *Ainu Life and Lore: Echoes of a Departing Race*. New York: Johnson Reprint, 1971. [Originally published by the Japan Advertiser Press, Tokyo, 1927]

Etter, Carl. *Ainu Folklore: Traditions and Culture of the Vanishing Aborigines of Japan*. Chicago: Wilcox and Follett, 1949.

Hilger, M. Inez, et al. *Together with the Ainu: A Vanishing People*. Norman: University of Oklahoma Press, 1971.

Jones, Francis Clifford. *Hokkaido: Its Present State of Development and Future Prospects*. London, New York, Toronto: Oxford University Press, 1958.

Kindaiti, Kyōsuke. *Ainu Life and Legends*. Tokyo: Japanese Government Railways, Board of Tourist Industry, 1941.

Peng, Fred C.C., and Peter Geiser. *The Ainu: The Past in the Present*. Hiroshima: Bunka Hyoron, 1977.

Tomita, Torao. *Story of Adventure of Ranald MacDonald: First Teacher of English in Japan, 1848-1849, Translated by Torao Tomita*. Tokyo: Tōsui Shobō, 1979. [Japanese language translation of Lewis' and Murakami's 1923 *Ranald MacDonald* text]

Trewartha, Glenn Thomas. *Japan: A Physical, Cultural and Regional Geography*. Madison: University of Wisconsin Press, 1960.

Chapter IX. "Ranald Taken South by Junk," pp. 62-68.
Chapter X. "Prisoner at Matsumae," pp. 69-77.
Chapter XI. "Imprisoned at Nagasaki," pp. 78-87.
Chapter XII. "Development of Dutch Learning," pp. 88-94.
Chapter XIII. "Ranald the Teacher," pp. 95-100.

Alcock, Rutherford. *Capital of the Tycoon: A Narrative of Three Years' Residence in Japan*, vol. I. New York: Greenwood, 1959. [Reprint of 1863 edition]

Busch, Noel F. *The Horizon, Concise History of Japan*. New York: American Heritage, 1972.

Chamberlain, Basil Hall, and W.B. Mason. *Japan*. London: John Murray, 1899.

Goodman, Grant Kohn. *The Dutch Impact on Japan (1640-1853)*. Leiden: E.J. Brill, 1967.

Griffis, William Elliot. *Japan in History: Folk Lore and Art*. Boston and New York: Houghton, Mifflin, 1898.

_____. *The Japanese Nation in Evolution: Steps in the Progress of a Great People*. New York: Thomas Y. Crowell, 1907.

Heusken, Henry. *Japan Journal*. New Brunswick, NJ: Rutgers University Press, 1964.

Lederer, Emil, and Amy Lederer-Seidler. *Japan in Transition*. New Haven, CT: Yale University Press, 1938.

Murdoch, James. *Ibid*.

New Official Guide—Japan. Japan Travel Bureau, 1970.

Norman, E. Herbert. *Japan's Emergence as a Modern State: Political and Economic Problems of the Meiji Period*. New York: Institute of Pacific Relations, 1940.

Okuma, Shigēnobu. *Fifty Years of New Japan*, vol. I. London: Smith, Elder, 1910.

Osborn, Sherard. *A Cruise in Japanese Waters*. Edinburgh and London: William Blackwood and Sons, 1859.

Paske-Smith, M. *Western Barbarians in Japan and Formosa in Tokugawa Days, 1603-1868*. New York: Paragon, 1968. [Originally published in Kobe, Japan, 1930]

St. John, H.C. *Wild Coasts of Nipon*. Edinburgh: Thomas and Archibald Constable for David Douglas, 1880.

Sansom, G.B. *The Western World and Japan: A Study in the Interaction of European and Asiatic Cultures*. New York: Alfred A. Knopf, 1950.

Transactions of the Asiatic Society of Japan, second Series, vol. XVIII, 1939. [Some material is from *Beikoku Hyomin no Geisen Nagasaki-ko ni Torai Ikken*, Isahaya Nikki, Koka Zakki, bk. 4.]

Trewartha, Glenn Thomas. *Ibid.*

U.S. Army Map Service, Gazeteer to Maps of Hokkaido, etc., 1945. [Hokkaido and Matsumae Peninsula maps]

Vinacke, Harold M. *A History of the Far East in Modern Times*. New York: Appleton-Century-Crofts, 1964. [Originally published 1928]

Williams, Harold S. *Foreigners in Mikadoland*. Rutland, VT, and Tokyo: Charles E. Tuttle, 1963.

Chapter XIV. "*Preble* to the Rescue," pp. 101-6.

Executive Document 84, 31st Congress, U.S. House of Representatives. ["August 28, 1850"]

(The) Seaman's Friend (Honolulu), December 20, 1849.

Chapter XV. "Sailor and Gold Digger," pp. 108-13.

Barnard, Marjorie. *A History of Australia*. New York: Frederick A. Praeger, 1963.

Coleman, Terry. *Southern Cross*. New York: Viking, 1979. [Fiction]

Ritchie, John. *Australia as Once We Were*. Melbourne: William Heinemann, 1975.

Shaw, A.G.L. *A Short History of Australia*. New York: Frederick A. Praeger, 1967.

Younger, R.M. *Australia and the Australians: A New Concise History*. Adelaide: Rigby, 1970.

Chapter XVI. "Home to Canada," pp. 114-19.

Cole, Jean Murray. *Ibid.*

Lewis, William S. "Archibald McDonald: Biography and Genealogy." *Washington Historical Quarterly* IX (1918).

Chapter XVII. "In Japan, Meanwhile," pp. 120-26.
Chapter XVIII. "Perry Returns," pp. 127-38.

Koga, Jujiro. *History of Western Studies in Nagasaki*. Nagasaki: Nagasaki Bunken Sha, 1966.

Murdoch, James. *Ibid.* [vol. III, part 2]

Perry, Matthew Galbraith, and Francis L. Hawks. *Narrative of the Expedition of an American Squadron to the China Seas and Japan, Performed in the Years 1852, 1853, and 1854, under the Command of Commodore M.G. Perry, United States Navy, by Order of the Government of the United States. Compiled from the Original Notes and Journals of Commodore Perry and His Officers, at His Request, and under His Supervision, by Francis L. Hawks, D.D.L.L.D.* Washington, D.C.: A.O.P. Nicholson, Printer, 1856. ["Published by order of the Congress of the United States."]

Perry, Matthew Galbraith; compiled by Francis L. Hawks; abridged and edited by Sidney Wallach. *Narrative of the Expedition of an American Squadron to the China Seas and Japan, Performed in the Years 1852, 1853, and 1854, under the Command of Commodore M.C. Perry . . .* London: Macdonald, 1952.

Sansom, G.B. *Ibid.*

Williams, S. Wells. "A Journal of the Perry Expedition to Japan." *Transactions of the Asiatic Society of Japan* XXXVII (1909-1910). [Yokohama, Japan]

Chapter XIX. "MacDonald in the Cariboo," pp. 139-48.
Chapter XX. "Barkerville, the Big Strike of the Cariboo," pp. 149-58.
Akrigg, G.P.V. and Helen B. *British Columbia Chronicle, 1847-1871.* Vancouver: Discovery, 1977.
"B.C.'s Pioneer Roadbuilder." *Journal of Commerce* (Vancouver, B.C.), January 21, 1974.
Belton, Brian. *Bittersweet Oasis.* Village of Ashcroft, B.C., 1986.
"(The) Cariboo Cameron Story" and miscellaneous associated materials and clippings, Kamloops Museum and Archives.
Downs, Art. *Wagon Road North.* Quesnel, B.C.: Northwest Digest, 1960.
"Hat Creek House," "Cache Creek," and miscellaneous materials, maps, and documents, British Columbia Provincial Archives, Victoria.
"Historic Hat Creek House Preserves Pioneer Flavor." Sun Country supplement, *Ashcroft-Cache Creek Journal* (Ashcroft, B.C.), July 21, 1987.
"Historic Hat Creek Ranch Preserves the Past." Sun Country supplement, *Ashcroft-Cache Creek Journal* (Ashcroft, B.C.), July 12, 1988.
Hutchison, Bruce. *The Fraser.* New York: Rinehart, 1950.
"MacDonald, Benjamin." Typescript ms. [Various archival repositories]
MacDonald, Ranald. Letter to Benjamin MacDonald, January 14, 1874. [Various archival repositories]
MacDonald, Ranald, and John Barnston. "Prospectus and Report, Bentinck Arm Company, January 1, 1862." [Includes handwritten commentary believed to be written by Malcolm McLeod.]
Macfie, Matthew. *Vancouver Island and British Columbia: Their History, Resources and Prospects.* London: Longman, Green, Longman, Roberts and Green, 1865.
Mayne, Richard Charles. *Four Years in British Columbia and Vancouver Island . . .* London: John Murray, 1862.
Ramsey, Bruce. *Barkerville . . .* Vancouver, B.C.: Mitchell, 1961.
Skelton, Robin. *They Call It the Cariboo.* Victoria: Sono Nis, 1980.
"A Trip from Alexandria to Coast." *Victoria Colonist,* August 16, 1861.
Walkem, W.W. "Robert Stevenson, a Pioneer of 1859." *Pioneer Days in British Columbia,* vol. 4. Surrey, B.C.: Heritage, n.d.

Chapter XXI. "Moriyama Serves at USA-Japan Treaty Negotiations," pp. 159-73.
Harris, Townsend. *The Complete Journal of Townsend Harris . . .* Garden City, NY: Doubleday, Doran, 1930.
Statler, Oliver. *Shimoda Story.* New York: Random House, 1969.

Chapter XXII. "Ranald's Interpreters Continue to Serve," pp. 174-85.
Bishop Museum, Honolulu. Various archival materials.
Bush, Lewis. *77 Samurai: Japan's First Embassy to America.* Tokyo and Palo Alto, CA: Kodansha International, 1968. [Partly based on a book by Itsuro Hattori, great-grandson of Murigaki Norimasu]
Kiyooda, Eiichi. "The Visits in Hawaii of the First Japanese Embassy to the United States and of *Kanrin Maru,* the First Japanese Ship to Cross the Pacific." *Shigaku* (Journal of Historical Science) XVI part 2 (June 1937).
Miyoshi, Masao. *As We Saw Them: The First Japanese Embassy to the United States (1860).* Berkeley: University of California Press, 1979.
Muragaki, Norimasu Awaji-no-Kami. *Diary, 1860.* Tokyo: America-Japan Society, 1920. [Translation published by the America-Japan Society]
Namura relatives, personal conversations, Honolulu, Hawaii.
Taylor, Lois. "Rokusei." *Honolulu Star-Bulletin,* March 6, 1983.

(The) United Japanese Society of Hawaii. *A History of Japanese in Hawaii,* ed. by Publication Committee, Dr. James H. Okahata, Chairman. Honolulu, 1971.

Watanabe, Shinichi. "Diplomatic Relations between the Hawaiian Kingdom and the Empire of Japan." Master's thesis, June 1944. [Bishop Museum, Honolulu]

Chapter XXIII. "Ranald Continues His Explorations," pp. 186-99.

Bowen, Lynne. *Boss Whistle.* Lantzville, B.C.: Oolichan, 1982. [An entertaining look at coal mining on Vancouver Island.]

Brown, Robert. *Vancouver Island, Exploration.* Printed by Authority of the Government, 1864. [British Columbia Provincial Archives, Victoria]

Hayman, John. *Robert Brown and the Vancouver Island Exploring Expedition.* Vancouver: University of British Columbia Press, 1989.

MacDonald, Ranald. Handwritten journal, titled "Ranald McDonald's Journal, V.I., Exploring Expedition, Victoria, V.I., 1864" [the title is in Brown's handwriting]. Brown, 2, folder 7, British Columbia Provincial Archives, Victoria.

Mayne, Richard Charles. *Ibid.*

Paterson, T.W. *Vancouver Island.* Langley, B.C.: Sunfire, 1983.

Pethick, Derek. *Victoria: The Fort.* Vancouver, B.C.: Mitchell, 1968.

Chapter XXIV. "MacDonald and the 'Mile Houses,'" pp. 200-04.
[See also references for chapters XIX, XX, and XXVI]

"Calumet Journal, June, 1860." [Kamloops Museum and Archives]

"Hudson Bay Company Journals, December 16, 1860, to November 30, 1862, edited by William Manson." [Kamloops Museum and Archives]

"Kamloops Journal, January 1, 1859, to December 15, 1860." [Kamloops Museum and Archives]

West, Willis J. "Staging and Stage Hold-ups in the Cariboo." *British Columbia Historical Quarterly* XII, no. 3 (1948). [Abridged edition titled "The B. X. Line," date and publisher unknown, in Kamloops Museum and Archives]

Chapter XXV. "Ranald's Adventures and the Canadian Pacific Railroad," 205-15.

Berton, Pierre. *The National Dream: The Last Spike.* Toronto: McClelland and Stewart, 1983.

Dempsey, Hugh A. *The CPR West: The Iron Road and the Making of a Nation.* Vancouver, B.C.: Douglas and McIntyre, 1984.

Innis, Harold A. *A History of the Canadian Pacific Railway.* Toronto: University of Toronto Press, 1923.

McDonald, Archibald. *Ibid.*

McDougall, J. Lorne. *Canadian Pacific: A Brief History.* Montreal: McGill University Press, 1968.

McLeod, Malcolm. Collection, 1249, Box 1-10, British Columbia Provincial Archives, Victoria. Memorials, pamphlets, and letters, including "Pacific Railway, Canada," and "Britannicus Letters and C. [correspondence] Thereon," printed by A.S. Woodburn, Elgin Street, Ottawa, 1869-75.

Chapter XXVI. "Ranching at Fort Colvile," pp. 216-24.
Chapter XXVII. "Ranald MacDonald's Last Days," pp. 225-37.

Brown, William Compto,. Collection. Manuscripts, Archives and Special Collections, Washington State University Libraries, Pullman. Letters and papers; miscellaneous pertaining to Ranald MacDonald, Angus McDonald, Archibald McDonald, and others.

Chance, David H. "The Structure of a Hudson's Bay Post." [Monograph for the National Park Service]

"Coulee Dam National Recreation Area, Washington," Historic Resource Study, September 1980, Denver Service Center, Branch of Historic Preservation, Pacific Northwest/Western Team, National Park Service, U.S. Department of the Interior, Denver, CO.

Graham, Clara. *Fur and Gold in the Kootenays.* Vancouver, B.C., 1945.

Holstine, Craig E. *Forgotten Corner: A History of the Colville National Forest, Washington.* Colville, WA: Statesman-Examiner, 1987.

Howay, F.W.; William S. Lewis; and Jacob A. Meyers, eds. "Angus McDonald: A Few Items of the West." *Washington Historical Quarterly* VIII (July 1917).

(An) Illustrated History of Stevens, Ferry, Okanogan and Chelan Counties, State of Washington. Spokane: Western Historical Publishing, 1904.

Lakin, Ruth. *Kettle River Country: Early Days along the Kettle River.* Orient, WA, 1976.

Lewis, William S. "Reminiscences of Benjamin MacDonald." Eastern Washington State Historical Society Library, Cheney Cowles Museum, Spokane.

McLeod, Malcolm. Collection, 1249 Box 1-10, British Columbia Provincial Archives, Victoria. Letters to and from MacDonald, and papers, memoirs, miscellaneous, etc.

_____. MacDonald to Dye, MacLeod to MacDonald, and diverse other material. Malcolm McLeod Collection, 1249, Box 9, Folder 11, British Columbia Provincial Archives, Victoria.

Oakshott, Thomas I. *Colville: City of Proud Heritage.* Colville, WA: Chamber of Commerce, 1960.

Oliphant, J. Orin. "Old Fort Colville." *Washington Historical Quarterly* XVI and XVII (1920).

Told by the Pioneers, Reminiscences 1936-37. Stevens County Historical Society, Colville, WA. [Various accounts, especially by Nancy Winecoop, Stevens County, pp. 114-9]

Williams, Christina MacDonald McKenzie. Statement to William S. Lewis, May 28, 1921, Eastern Washington State Historical Society Library, Cheney Cowles Museum, Spokane.

Index